FOREWORD

When Life is Indistinguishable from Art

In this book, Robin Shaye affects a miracle: she brings the musty, polysyllabic scholarship of pathological narcissism to life. Ostensibly, her tome is mere fiction and the protagonists, characters on a stage. But the veneer of fiction can't camouflage the intimate, firsthand, and anguished experiences that underlie it. Through the unfolding saga of one doomed relationship, Robin touches savvily upon all the salient features of living with and loving a psychopathic narcissist.

By his nature, the narcissist misleads his nearest into believing they are also his dearest. Devoid of any depth of commitment and emotion, robbed of the ability to love and empathize, besieged by overwhelming sensations of fantastic grandiosity, and consumed by a pernicious sense of entitlement, the narcissist preys upon the vulnerable and then devours them.

The narcissist's "relationships" consist of take-and take. He is an exploiter of the most nefarious kind, giving in return only the bare-bones minimum needed to sustain his victims alive and functioning. Replete with uncontrollable rages and impulses, reckless conduct, indifference to the emotions, needs, and wishes of others, and a predatory mindset, the narcissist is an alien intelligence, vampire-like, and blood-curdling.

However, this reality is efficaciously hidden beneath a well-practiced hypnotic charm, ersatz erudition, displays of virtue, might and money, and the expert simulation of deep and moving feelings for his would be "sources". The narcissist is a master manipulator and an innate conman.

Robin seamlessly embeds in her novel her research into this incredible disorder. By witnessing the harrowing misadventures of Skylar, the reader almost surreptitiously, gets introduced into the core concepts of malignant narcissism and selfishness run amok.

At the end, this tome is both a warning and a plea to learn from other victim's tumultuous lives and to refrain from the malignant optimism that characterized most partners of consummate narcissists.

~ Sam Vaknin author of *Malignant Self-Love: Narcissism Revisited* ~

"…Until You Die":

The Narcissist's Promise

Robin Shaye

Lioness Publications, Massachusetts

Lioness Publications
P.O. Box 3711
Natick, Massachusetts 01760 USA

Design & Text: Lynne Foy
Photo: Narcissus 'Grand Soliel D'Or' (mycornerofkaty.com)

This book is based on true events, however it has been fictionalized and all persons appearing in this work are fictitious. Any resemblance to real people, living or dead, is entirely coincidental.

Library of Congress Number: 2011962845

ISBN 978-0-9848607-0-8

PRINTED IN THE UNITED STATES OF AMERICA

Dedications

To Eliza – who is my reason for everything

To Seth, Adam and Arielle -
with the hope and a prayer for a future of peace, truth and maternal love

To Nick - my rock throughout the process

To all victims and survivors -
with encouragement to stay strong, support along your journey
and the promise of light at the end of the tunnel

Note from the author

The word *narcissist* has flooded the media; in true crime in politics, in celebrities, and in entertainment. But narcissists walk among us, undetected, in everyday society. Narcissists are men or women who feed on how others see them. Being married to a narcissist or being the child of a narcissistic parent creates the same feeling: loving someone who cannot love you as much as they love themselves. Their charismatic personality can run the gamut from fascinating to frightening, often merging with destructive personality disorders. Many are unaware of their deadly charm until it's too late.

"…Until You Die": The Narcissist's Promise is a narrative of Skylar, an idealistic young woman who only wanted a happy family. She held onto the belief her husband, John Bauers would change his heartless ways. But his narcissistic personality disorder, manifested in early childhood, intensified and metamorphosed during his teenage years, combining with sociopathalogical tendencies and creating a cruel monster as he reached adulthood. A narcissistic abuser and sociopath, John presented as a charmer, hiding his true identity as a dangerous and vengeful man without a conscience.

Skylar's frightening journey is written to promote public awareness by providing more insight and recognition, and with the hopes to end the destruction of families torn apart by a captivating narcissist.

Prologue

In Greek mythology, **Narcissus**, or **Narkissos**, and **Self-Admirer** was renowned for his beauty.

Narcissus was the son of the river God Cephisus and the nymph Liriope. When Narcissus was born, Tiresias, a seer, was asked if the child would live a long life. Tiresias replied: "If he never knows himself."

So may he himself love and not gain the thing he loves.

Narcissus, upon finding his likeness in a pool, fell in love with his reflection. He subsequently died of thirst, for if Narcissus had reached to take a drink, he would have shattered his own image into thousands of pieces.

It is said that Narcissus still keeps gazing on his image in the waters of the river Styx. The flower that Narcissus turned into later was used when Hades, God of the Dead, abducted Persephone by attracting her to the sweet scent of the flower.

❧

How many narcissists does it take to change a light bulb?

Just one. The narcissist holds the bulb, and the world turns beneath them.

"…Until You Die":
The Narcissist's Promise

Preface

Skylar Bauers pulled her car into her driveway. The glare of the bright sun bounced off the windows. The weather was still warm for September. Abundant sounds of chirping birds and the blueness of the sky made it seem like a beautiful spring day except for the red and gold leaves on the trees and the smell of autumn in the air. Skylar took no notice of the beauty of the day. She couldn't see anything. She didn't notice the contrasting hot sun and crispness in the air. She impassively got out of her car. The incessant chirping of the birds was silent to Skylar. She moved woodenly toward the door of the house. Her hand was shaking so badly she could barely get the key in the lock. The tears began to blur her sight. Skylar knew if she didn't get inside the house, she would lose control on the front lawn.

The helplessness, the despair, the sadness, and the overwhelming feeling of how unfair life was had been building and was ready to erupt. Skylar slid the key into the lock and opened the door. Once inside, she closed the door and collapsed onto the carpet. Great sobs of rage and frustration burst out of her in waves. Daggers of pain riddled her body. Her stomach knotted tightly. Her sobs became screams of anger and frustration.

"Oh God, why? How could you do this to my children?" Skylar cried out. "Why did you let this happen? What have I done to deserve this?"

Skylar cried until there was nothing left. Still collapsed on the rug, she lay there curled in a fetal position, breathing deeply in an attempt to regain her composure. The sound of the telephone interrupted her thoughts.

Skylar reached for the receiver. "Hello." Her voice was a dead whisper.

It was her mother, Sable. "Skylar? How come you didn't call me?"

Skylar whispered, "They're gone."

"What?"

"He got them! He got my children!" Skylar screamed, bursting into tears.

"Oh, no! How did this happen?" Sable's voice echoed in disbelief. Her voice broke into sobs. "How could a judge give custody of those precious children to that monster?"

It made no sense. Those who knew Skylar found her to be a warm and loving woman who lived for her children. Her children, in turn, adored her. Although married, Skylar had raised her children alone, as her husband was usually absent, ignoring constant requests to join them in family activities. It was unfathomable to think a judge took Skylar's three beautiful children away.

All Skylar ever wanted was a family. Her vision of a mom and dad strolling with their children had faded. The image of a dinner table surrounded by chattering children, a smiling father, and a fulfilled mother serving dinner to her family had disappeared. The beautiful life she had envisioned had gruesomely warped into a nightmarish parody far beyond her imagination. Skylar was awake and aware in her pain as the clocked ticked agonizingly.

As the brightness of the day faded and the sky turned dark, Skylar moved to a chair on her back porch, oblivious to the chill in the air. She looked up at the stars twinkling above her and remembered another night sky, seven years earlier.

Chapter 1

The sky was as dark as ebony ink, a contrasting background to the luminescent celestial display. Skylar was chilled, frozen to where she lay on the gravel-covered ground. Numb and unable to move, she was only aware of the cold evening sky above her sprinkled with an unusual cornucopia of stars. And yelling. No, not yelling – swearing, vile and spewing anger directed at her.

"You fuckin' bitch! Do that again, and you'll see what I do to you!" Suddenly, everything was quiet. Black and bitter and hard and silent. What was she doing on the ground? Her neck was throbbing, tender and bruised by the hands of... her husband? This made no sense. How had her life become a distortion of the comfort and love she thought was her destiny? This wasn't how she was raised. An arctic gust of air took her breath away as she remembered...

Ice. Smooth ice beneath her feet. Skylar was breathing in the frosty air as she skated around the indoor rink at a local college. She turned, whipped her foot, and began spinning, feeling her skating skirt twirl about her. The blast of the horn announced the end of the session. Skylar began skating rapidly around the rink or a few final laps. As the Zamboni slowly drove onto the ice, Skylar exited the rink to where her father was waiting.

"Nice job, Sky!" he commented enthusiastically. "Ready for your hot chocolate?"

This was a Saturday morning ritual they both enjoyed, ice skating and then hot chocolate with a large dollop of marshmallow cream.

Skylar removed her skates and slipped her feet into warm boots. As the Zamboni circled the rink, the skaters were beginning to leave the building as the hockey players were lacing up their skates, preparing for practice. As Skylar walked past the hockey players, the whistles began. Twelve year old Skylar blushed as she shyly averted her eyes.

"Just ignore it." her father whispered as he caught up with her. As they got into the car, he continued, "You are a beautiful girl, Skylar. Someday you'll meet a nice man who will treat you like a princess. He will take care of you and you'll have a beautiful life."

Lying on the cold ground, oblivious to her tears now cooled by the wind, she recalled her father's words. This wasn't the life she was supposed to have. This wasn't the life her father had promised her when she was twelve. If only she were able to ask him what went wrong. She searched her memory for an answer.

Skylar was thirteen when her father's life was tragically cut short by a fatal heart attack. At the funeral, Skylar reflected on her parents' time together. Every evening, the family would gather for dinner, prepared by her mother, Sable. They would enjoy a home-cooked meal and talk about the day's events. Her parents maintained a warm and traditional family lifestyle. The importance of family was stressed and Skylar enjoyed their activities: the beach, the zoo, picnics, and a variety of outings.

Their comfortable home portrayed a picture of love and family. Skylar lived on the south side of Newton, Massachusetts, in a comfortable Jewish community. Skylar's friends were raised with warm family values as well. In her teenage years, Skylar spent most of her leisure time with her friends: shopping, going to the movies, gathering in each others homes, or driving to the beach in the summer. Skylar and her friends would sit and talk about college plans and boys, anticipating their futures would be quite similar to their parents'.

Skylar was a pretty girl with a heart-shaped face, soft brown hair, and huge amber eyes. She was a little taller than average but small boned, so she appeared delicate. Skylar was a fitness fanatic and moved gracefully after years of exercise and dance. She spoke in a quiet voice and giggled like a little girl but she could laugh with gusto. Polite to a fault, her friends would burst into gales of laughter if a burp ever snuck out, as it was so unlike Skylar. She often appeared shy and demure, until you got to know her and learned that she was sharp and witty.

Robin Shaye

Her mother Sable, kept a tight rein on Skylar. She noticed Skylar attracted the attention of many boys, but she seemed to favor the ones who were popular or ran with a faster crowd. The one word she instilled in Skylar was respect. She saw that the bad boys held a certain intrigue for Skylar.

"Don't waste your time," admonished Sable. "After college, you'll find a nice, respectable man, and you'll have a good life. Good girls don't go off and run wild. Men don't respect those girls. I didn't leave the house until I got married. If you want to meet a nice man, it will be easier if you live at home."

At eighteen, Skylar attended a local college, living at home in order to minimize expenses. Although she craved the campus life, she spent enough time on college grounds to feel like a part of the campus community. She excelled at school and graduated with Bachelor of Arts degree in therapeutic services and music.

After college, Skylar worked as a recreation therapist at a local hospital and lived at home. Sable continued her campaign that Skylar should meet a nice man who respected her. Although Skylar tried to comply with her mother, it was the 1980s and the city beckoned her with its electrifying nightlife. The exhilaration of the city was compelling causing Skylar to sometimes balk at the reins and sneak off to meet one of these bad boys. It was frustrating to her and she longed for the freedom to make her own choices.

At twenty-five, Skylar began dating a man from a respectable Jewish family who was tall, handsome, and rode a motorcycle. Sable objected. "He's too wild! And it's too dangerous for you to be riding around on the back of a motorcycle!"

But when his job transferred him to Los Angeles, he cajoled Skylar. "Come with me! You're an adult. You're mother can't stop you."

It seemed to be the perfect time. Skylar had been thinking about a career change. What better place to begin a new career than Los Angeles?

Skylar loved scenic California with its opulence and palm trees lining the streets. She relished her first venture of independence and she learned a lot about herself. She gained inner strength and autonomy. She figured out what she wanted and what she did not want.

When the glow of newness in her relationship began to fade, Skylar discovered that instead of a partner, she was merely a provider. Her presence and paycheck were complimenting someone else's lifestyle. She finally found the courage to end the relationship as she no longer felt a bond or camaraderie. The union had staled into endless and unfounded interrogations and insults. When she announced she was leaving, he cried. Skylar felt a twinge of guilt at leaving so abruptly but she needed to move on.

As the airplane began its descent to Logan International Airport, the illumination of the stars faded into the night sky, replaced by the neon brilliance of the city below welcoming Skylar. The bustling city of Boston - with its complicated puzzle of streets, the high-rise buildings and the views of Boston Harbor - felt like a homecoming to Skylar. She had lost her self esteem in Los Angeles and hoped to regain her bearings in Boston.

Skylar wanted to resume her plans for a career change. She had outgrown the shyness of her earlier years and was now outgoing, bubbly and adventurous. Skylar thought a career as a flight attendant would be the perfect fit. She researched the airlines and obtained applications from the airlines that were hiring. Because the hiring process could take months, Skylar accepted a temporary receptionist position for a real estate development company. She planned on working there until she was hired as a flight attendant.

Skylar's job was located in an office building which was situated along-side the Charles River in Newton. On the other side of the river was the neighboring town of Needham. Skylar sat at a desk in the plush front office, answering the phones and greeting everyone who walked through the door. She enjoyed the busy atmosphere with the constant flow of interesting people and friendly staff. She may have been very comfortable remaining in the position, but she focused on a new career goal, traveling the world, free of any ties and making her own rules. Skylar was ready for a life of adventure and independence.

Chapter 2

Bordering the Charles River on the south side was the town of Needham, the home to Security Safe, a vendor who supplied locks and security services to many real estate companies in the area of Needham, Newton, and the surrounding towns. The company was owned by a man named John Bauers, who was the son of George and Nora Bauers, longtime Needham residents

Shortly after George and Nora married in the 1950s, they purchased a home in Needham, where George owned a hardware store. Like most young couples, George and Nora wanted to start a family. But after seven barren years, they decided to adopt a child. Their Jewish faith was important to them, so they were pleased when they learned of an adoption agency in Maine which specialized in adoptions of babies born to Jewish mothers. In May of 1958, the agency had an infant boy for the Bauers to adopt. George and Nora named their new son John.

Little Johnny was an active baby. He was crawling before the other babies in the neighborhood. When Johnny was seven months old, Nora and George were happily surprised when they learned Nora was pregnant.

Johnny was fourteen months old when Nora gave birth to a baby girl, who she named Audra. This was everything Nora wanted her own daughter, after years of waiting for a child. She lavished her affection on Audra. Although Johnny was barely toddling around the house, his mother's abrupt indifference to him was apparent. No longer did she rock him at night. No longer did she hold him and cuddle with him. Two years later, Nora gave birth to another daughter, who she named

Cara. She showered her daughters with affection and praise. Johnny was three years old and felt abandoned in preschool while his mother was at home with her daughters. Nora cared for her children, but she bestowed most of her love on Audra and Cara. She wasn't there for Johnny.

George and Nora did not reveal to John he was adopted until he was thirteen years old. Although this was a crushing blow, John now understood why he had always felt a sense of detachment within the family. He felt inferior to his sisters and unwanted upon learning his biological mother gave him up for adoption. He felt discarded and unimportant. His need for acceptance grew, and his exterior hardened.

In 1914, Sigmund Freud coined the term *narcissism* to describe self-love, which was taken directly from the Greek myth of Narcissus, a youth who fell in love with his own reflection. According to Freud, healthy narcissism is a trait in most people. They like themselves simply for the sake of survival or self-preservation. When an individual gives their love to someone else and they get love in return, there is a sense of balance. This begins in childhood. A child gives love to his mother, and she returns the affection. As a toddler, John gave love to Nora, but most of her love was given to her biological daughters. The love John offered as a little boy was never replenished, leaving a feeling of emptiness. Narcissistic Personality Disorder (NPD) is a serious, often undiagnosed condition, frequently related to abuse or abandonment in childhood. Confused when his mother's affection was not returned to him, this planted the seedlings of John's Narcissistic Personality Disorder. Freud described Narcissistic Personality Disorder as someone who shows a pervasive pattern of grandiosity, need for admiration, and a lack of empathy.

Like an actor onstage being applauded, the narcissist seeks the same accolade. Offstage, the actor can turn off the act and go home to those who love him as a person without the stage make-up. But the narcissist only lives for the applause and will use whatever he needs to impress, to shock, to awe, to attract, to subjugate, and even to manipulate – as long as the end result is veneration.

John looked outside the family for approval. He possessed high intelligence. Ironically, narcissists are well-liked due to their extroverted nature and John was no exception. He found it easy to charm people. He found validation and approval within his circle of friends, chosen from the class troublemakers. They came from lower income families who considered academics too challenging and not very interesting. John learned he could befriend them easily as well as manipulate them. They looked up to him, and he became a leader. John reveled in having devotees, and was consumed with self-admiration. He finally felt important and held himself in high regard. He created a particular way of laughing and would force this laugh often. He feigned excessive enthusiasm when he talked. He treated each personal encounter as a sales call, with manic determination to win over everyone he met. Each admirer increased John's self worth.

In his teenage years, John began to pursue the girls in school. He would look at them with his big blue eyes and smile, showing his dimples. He would date the girls in his class with the hopes of seducing them. He would call the girl of his desire relentlessly. To the girl, it appeared as if he were totally smitten. But John wasn't love-struck. He just wanted to speed up the process of his seduction and an intimate encounter and then move on to the next girl. As with any hormonally driven high school boy, sex was first and foremost on his mind. But part of the quest for John was simply that the more women who would succumb to him, the better his reputation. Each conquest signified a victory, an affirmation of his charm. Each success fed and fueled the Narcissistic Personality Disorder burning and building within him. It was growing to such a degree that it manifested into severe self-absorbsion, selfishness and disregard for the feelings of others. An extreme narcissist shares the characteristics found in antisocial personality disorders. These individuals, often called sociopaths, lack empathy and/or violate the rights of others.

For John, it was the natural path to follow. He became defiant to his teachers and parents. At night, he would sneak out of the house to meet his friends. They stole from the local convenience stores. They smoked cigarettes and marijuana. They would capture frogs or small animals and insert firecrackers in whatever orifice they could find, light the wick, toss the creature in the air, and laugh when they exploded.

In psychiatry/psychology, the presence of more than one personality disorder in one individual is called *comorbidity*. Personality disorders, in particular, are found to have excessively high comorbidity rates. Particularly frightening is when the components of the antisocial personality disorder (sociopath) and the narcissistic personality disorder join. The clinical diagnosis of the antisocial personality disorder, according to the American Psychiatric Association's Diagnostic and Statistical Manual is: *An individual with a pervasive pattern of disregard for, and violation of, the rights of others that begins in childhood or early adolescence and continues into adulthood.* When these personality disorders merge, the result is someone who may be referred to as a *malignant narcissist*, an individual who has a sadistic, jealous, and vindictive dark side and could be considered a danger

Martha Stout, Ph.D. is a clinical psychologist who served on the faculty in the Department of Psychiatry at Harvard Medical School for twenty-five years. She lends insight in her book, *The Sociopath Next Door: The Ruthless Versus the Rest of Us.* The book is a compilation of individuals she met throughout her twenty-five years of practicing psychology. She refers to sociopaths as *ice people.* In her book, Dr. Stout relates a story of a former patient whose behavior paralleled John Bauers. At a young age, this patient also, would catch frogs, insert firecrackers in their mouths, and watch them explode. As an adult, he would easily charm people with his lies. He had no emotional attachments to other people. A sociopath views women as sexual plunder, according to Dr. Stout. Like the narcissist, the sociopath is undeniably charismatic. When they begin charming people at a very young age, by the time the sociopath is a man, he has perfected his act.

When he was eighteen years old, John was over six feet of lean muscle. He had dark, wavy hair, full lips, and large blue eyes which contrasted against his olive skin. He'd strut down the corridors of his high school, smiling at the girls, showing his dimples. He exuded overt sexuality, and the girls would swoon, hoping he'd favor them with a look or smile. John reveled in their attention, undaunted that many of the girls would be leaving for college and he didn't have enough credits to graduate from high school. Shunning summer school as a way to graduate, John began working full-time at George's hardware store. During the day, as he waited on customers, John received many inquiries from people needing new door locks. Always mechanically inclined, John figured out how to do the installation. Soon, he was servicing all the inquiries that came into the store. He earned money from those jobs in addition to his hourly pay. He also profited from a side business of selling marijuana. He told his parents he was saving his money to buy a motorcycle.

George flatly stated, "You're not having a motorcycle here." Impervious to his father, John simply moved into his own apartment in Needham and bought a motorcycle.

The following month, John informed George, "I'm not working for you anymore. I want to be my own boss." He left the hardware store and began his own locksmith business, using a tiny room in his apartment as his workshop. To supplement his income, John found cocaine to be a more lucrative sale than marijuana.

Business within John's social group thrived. People would ring his doorbell at all hours to purchase cocaine. His girlfriend, Jennifer, moved into his apartment. John introduced her to cocaine. The young couple hosted many parties, where John was able to entice and grow his list of customers. Cocaine was always plentiful, and it was easy for Jennifer to indulge. Her habit spiraled out of control and she stole cocaine from John. When he discovered some of his cocaine missing, Jennifer denied it. She lied to John and accused his best friend, Tom Parsons, as the thief. John viewed her lie as a personal affront and was deeply hurt at her betrayal. But unable to feel empathy to the girl who became a hard-core addict after he had introduced her to cocaine, John violently and heartlessly threw her out of his home and life.

Eventually, the abundance of drug use and sales were discovered by the Needham police department, and John was arrested for possession of cocaine. George hired his close friend, attorney Herb Lewin, to represent John in court.

Herb was a shrewd attorney. He convinced the judge, pleading, "It's his first offense and it wasn't even his cocaine." John avoided jail, and Herb was able to have his record sealed.

John discontinued his cocaine business, as the legal risks were too high. The consequences of selling marijuana were much less, and the appeal was just as great for John's friends. His business was extremely lucrative and his customer list was impressive in its length.

John maintained the admiration, or narcissistic supply, from the positive cues received from his friends, who were in awe of his bravado to continue an illegal business despite his close brush with the law. But the narcissist can never receive too much appreciation. Like an addict, they crave mass love and adulation. They need constant refueling of their narcissistic supply and are insatiable in their quest.

Although John was surrounded by friends, he did not have a steady girlfriend. He needed a woman in order to prove he was unaffected by Jennifer's betrayal and did not miss her in his life. This time, he was determined to find someone who could enhance his image both socially and professionally.

Dr. Linda Martinez-Lewi, author of the book *Freeing Yourself from the Narcissist in Your Life*, has extensive clinical training in narcissism and borderline personality disorders. She describes the narcissist's ability to fixate on who he wants and psychologically seduce them by pouring on every ounce of charm, making the person feel as if they are the only person on the face of the earth. Most people can't resist their magnetism. Sadly, narcissists are deceptive and manipulative in all of their relationships.

And now, John was looking for his next conquest.

Robin Shaye

Chapter 3

In March of 1985, a man walked through the glass doors into the real estate office where Skylar worked. He quickly bypassed Skylar's desk and headed toward the back offices.

Since her job was to screen all vendors or clients, she called to him. "Excuse me. Can I help you?" The man turned around. He appeared to be about her age. He was tall, with thick, wavy black hair and blue eyes against olive skin. He grinned and didn't answer.

Skylar, slightly annoyed at his arrogant posture, again asked, "Can I help you?"

He said, "I'm John Bauers, from Security Safe. I'm just dropping off some keys for the maintenance guys."

"I can take those for you" she offered.

He held out his hand as Skylar reached for the keys. As her fingers touched the keys, John did not release them. She looked up into his glacial blue eyes and felt his hand shift to tighten around hers. At that moment, the head of maintenance walked through the door. She blushed and withdrew her hand as John shot her a dimpled smile, said, "See ya," and left.

Two days later he telephoned the office and formally reintroduced himself to her. He began a manic conversation. His speech was very dramatic, peppered with nervous laughter. He asked her if she would like to go out for dinner and dancing. Skylar didn't want a distraction from her career plans, but she accepted his invitation. After all, it was only a date.

When the doorbell rang on Saturday night, John was at the door wearing a pair of faded corduroy pants, a pink checkered shirt, and a shabby, white leather jacket. He greeted Skylar bizarrely, laughing. At close range, she noticed his head was unusually large. He had a gummy smile with a broken tooth. He had very large nostrils. However, taking a step back, the combination of black hair, blue eyes against olive skin, with full lips and dimples was attractive.

As they drove to the restaurant, John talked non-stop. He laughed frequently as if he found everything he said hilarious. Skylar couldn't follow his humor, but she found him boyishly charming, and his blue-eyed gaze was sincere. Mentally, she compared him to the man she had left in California. Instead of the fast food favored by her ex-boyfriend, she was treated to a sumptuous dinner. After a leisurely dessert, they drove to a nightclub in Boston. John left his truck with the valet. Skylar compared the luxury of valet parking versus the frugal lifestyle in Los Angeles. Inside the nightclub, John took her arm and didn't leave her side. He walked her to the restroom and waited for her. He seemed very protective. His thoughtful manner was a sharp contrast to the indifference she had experienced in California. Skylar liked the feeling.

John announced, "I usually don't drink, but I need a drink because you make me nervous." He quickly finished his drink and invited Skylar to dance. After a few songs, they took a break from dancing when he noticed the club photographer. "Let's get a souvenir of our first date." John suggested. After the camera flashed, the photographer handed them the developing photograph. They looked at the photo and John kissed Skylar, very awkwardly. She found him to be sweet, and weirdly endearing, and agreed to go back to his apartment for coffee.

John lived on the top two floors of a duplex in Needham. They climbed the steep set of stairs on the outside of the building to the entrance of the apartment. In the small kitchen, he prepared the coffee. As it was brewing, he gave Skylar a tour of the two bedrooms and small workshop used for his business. John stopped to show her the bath-room. He pulled back the curtain on the tub and pointed out the dual showerheads, one on either end. He proudly described to her how he had installed it himself so two people could shower together. Skylar had never seen anything like that and was somewhat surprised at his candid explanation.

When the coffee was ready, John poured two cups. They carried the steaming cups up one flight of stairs to the den. It was a cozy carpeted room with a large rust colored sectional couch against the wall. He selected the music and turned on the stereo. They talked over their coffee. They shared their likes and dislikes, their goals and their dreams. He told Skylar he wanted to get married and have children. They talked for a long time, and then he began to kiss her aggressively, pushing her back on the couch.

"Wait." she stopped him.

He became apologetic. Gently, he said, "It's okay - I'm very patient." After their date, John began calling her often. He would take her out for lunch or dinner. He sent flowers to her office. He seemed almost too good to be true. A disturbing deliberation kept nagging at Skylar; she wasn't sure if John was trying to impress her or if he was more impressed with himself. In passing consideration, she realized he never complimented her. He never told her he found her attractive. He never laughed at her jokes. But he was keeping her so busy that she let the thoughts slip away.

After they had been dating for a month, John invited her to go skiing in Vermont for the weekend. She wasn't sure she was ready to go away with him but nervously agreed. His reaction to her consent was bland. She hoped he would show enthusiastic anticipation of a romantic weekend, but he didn't mention anything during the week. On Friday, he picked her up at her office. She had brought her suitcase with her that morning, but John still needed to pack so they drove to his apartment.

Because he hadn't expressed any feelings regarding their first weekend together as well as the probability of their first intimate moments, Skylar tried to warm up to John, hoping to prompt an eager response. Standing beside him as he loaded the luggage into the truck, she nuzzled close and candidly told him, "I can't wait to get up there and be alone with you."

John didn't even look at her. He coldly responded, "Well, you never wanted to before."

It was as if she was talking to a stranger and was embarrassed by his response. She thought her openness would prompt a similar reply expressing warm anticipation instead of his chilling retort. She felt too humiliated to share her thoughts. *Oh God, what did I do? This was too soon. How can I tell him I changed my mind?* Tears blurred her eyes and she turned away so he wouldn't see. She felt a physical pain deep in her gut, a forewarning that her decision to continue in the relationship with John Bauers was very wrong. Something within her seemed to be screaming, *Get out! Run!* But she couldn't get the words out so she ignored the feelings and climbed into his truck.

After driving for a short while, John surprised Skylar when he took a neatly rolled joint out of his jacket pocket.

"Hey, do you ever get high?" He glanced at her. "It may make you talk more. You've been so quiet." He chuckled and lit the joint, drawing deeply. "Here." He passed the joint to her.

"I really don't like pot." she replied, holding the joint tentatively. "Here, take it." She handed back the burning cylinder.

He inhaled again and then carefully extinguished the flame in the ashtray. "Maybe you'll change your mind. We can save it for later."

The ride to Vermont took four hours, and he proceeded to relight the joint at different intervals along their journey. He encouraged Skylar, "Here, take a hit. It will relax you."

She finally put the perfectly rolled cylinder between her lips and inhaled. As the smoke entered her lungs with an acrid burning, she began choking violently. She gagged and coughed, as she reached for a soda, certain she would vomit before she could take a drink. John just laughed as he took back the joint. "Lightweight."

It was dark by the time they finally arrived at the house in Vermont. The house was large and welcoming, made of wood and stone. They entered into a spacious kitchen and rustic living room with a cathedral ceiling displaying wood beams. There was a large stone fireplace in the middle of the room. The bedrooms were on the second and third floor. John and Skylar were staying in an attic room on the third floor. They walked up two flights of a narrow wooden staircase to the attic. Two smaller rooms were on either side of the converted attic. They were identical with sloped ceilings and no door. There was a barren mattress on the floor. Instead of sheets and blankets, John told Skylar to select one of the sleeping bags from the random pile in the corner. It was extremely distasteful to her. After the lengthy ride, the marijuana fumes, and resorting to sleeping bags used by other people, she regretted her decision about the trip.

As she was trying to think of how to handle the situation, John turned off the lights and pulled her down beneath one of the sleeping bags. He kissed her passionately, ignoring her lukewarm response. He roughly pushed her clothing aside. It was over before it began.

"Well, I needed that." John declared. He stood up and began putting on his jeans. There had been no cuddling or intimate conversation. "I've got the munchies. I'm gonna go see what there is to eat downstairs." He left Skylar alone.

Woodenly, she dressed and followed him downstairs.

The kitchen was dimly lit. John found a plate of fruit and cheese in the refrigerator. As he ate, he read a newspaper left on the table, ignoring Skylar. They ate in silence then climbed the stairs to the attic room. John undressed and immediately fell asleep. Skylar felt very uneasy lying beside him. She dozed briefly. Unable to sleep, she opened her eyes. She looked at John sleeping, and saw a stranger. She realized she didn't even know this person. It was an eerie feeling.

Skylar finally fell into a deep sleep but woke up to feel John's hands on her. It wasn't intimate; it was a quick, impersonal act. Afterward, he insisted they shower together, sustaining his confidence in the familiarity of crossing the boundaries of intimacy. Skylar just felt very embarrassed and awkward. After the shower, she donned her ski pants, sweater, and jacket. She accepted a cup of coffee from John, who was waiting in the kitchen.

She was quiet as they drove up the mountain road. At the base lodge, John rented ski equipment for her and bought two lift tickets.

"Here you go" he said. He helped fasten the lift ticket to Skylar's jacket. "We're all set. Would you like another cup of coffee before we start?" She shook her head. "Okay, let me help you out there." He took her arm and carried her skis. He carefully guided her toward the ski lift. Morning had brought back the man that Skylar knew, generous and caring. She was a novice skier, yet John brought her to the top of the mountain and patiently coaxed her down the trails. All day, he skied with her, always gently reassuring her as she cautiously skied down the mountain. Later that evening, he caressed her cheek as they sat in front of the fireplace.

"Skylar, you did great." he said, gathering her close. The strangeness of the previous night faded as she rested her head on John's shoulder and they watched the flames.

After that weekend, their relationship took a positive turn. John introduced her to his friends. They traveled almost every weekend. He took her out for lunch and bought her thoughtful presents. She began to warm up to John and his quirky ways. Everything in the relationship improved. She told him about her plans to become a flight attendant. He confided in her and told her he was adopted and revealed his past as a cocaine dealer.

"After I was arrested, I finally decided to stop snorting or selling. Too many of my friends were getting into trouble due to all the coke and partying we did. I kind of miss it though, because when we did cocaine, we felt like we were part of the Hollywood crowd." John told her, his eyes shining as he remembered how special he felt before the cocaine use became unmanageable.

Skylar was intrigued. There was always something forbidden and deliciously dangerous about the bad boy. He was exciting, adventurous, and unlike anyone she had ever known. His charm was intoxicating. She was besotted and easily dismissed John's disreputable past.

Psychologists believe the narcissist's partner could have a deficient or a distorted grasp of himself/herself to remain with the narcissist. Skylar had recently come out of a relationship with someone who belittled her and diminished her self-esteem. While she felt proud of her strength to leave that relationship, she did not consider the lingering effects, which made her a prime victim for a narcissist's allure. When John utilized every bit of charm to woo her, she was under his spell. He had relished the chase and, like a wolf on the hunt, had captured his prey, savoured his conquest, and waited for the right moment to devour.

As winter melted into a lovely spring, John invited Skylar to accompany him to his friend's wedding. "My parents are going to be there. I want you to meet them" he told her.

Skylar selected a tailored silk dress of cream and peach to wear to the wedding. She wore delicate cream-colored sandals adorned with a little coral fastener on the side. She wanted to make a good impression when she met John's parents.

When they arrived at the wedding reception, John immediately took Skylar by the hand and looked for his parents. He found them standing near the bar.

"Mom, Dad, this is Skylar." John slipped his arm around her waist. Skylar smiled and said, "Hello." She offered her hand.

"Oh! Nice to meet you!" George Bauers smiled as he firmly shook her hand. He was short, fat, and appeared jolly. He noticed the way John tightly held Skylar and joked, "If you let go of her, will she fall down?" John laughed with his father.

Nora Bauers stood there studying Skylar. She was a very short woman. Skylar seemed to tower over her in heels. Nora's hair, once auburn, was now white and cut short. She had watery green eyes behind glasses. Her teeth were yellow and crookedly protruded.

She spoke in a squeaky voice and said, "Hello," to Skylar. She didn't offer her hand. "Do you work?" she bluntly inquired.

"I work as a receptionist right now, but I'm hoping to get a job as a flight attendant" Skylar replied.

"Oh." Nora exchanged glances with her husband. "That's interesting." There was an awkward pause in the conversation.

"I'm gonna introduce Skylar to my friends" John interjected enthusiastically.

"It was nice to meet you." Skylar said politely as he pulled her away.

"Don't worry. My mother's always like that. She's a little odd" John whispered as he led her to a large group of people who were friendly and boisterous. They invited John and Skylar to join their table for lunch. After they ate, the music began. John paraded her through the room and proudly introduced her to everyone. The music began and he led her to the dance floor. The song was slow and romantic. John pulled Skylar close.

The warmth of the weekend was still with her when she received her first invitation to interview for a flight attendant position in Dallas. John's reaction was unexpected, as he was not supportive or encouraging.

"You know, I thought about it and I decided I don't want you traveling when I have to sit at home."

"But John, I'll be working. It's not as if I am on vacation. And a flight attendant's schedule actually allows more time at home than a traditional nine-to-five job. I'd get at least twelve days off every month! Most jobs only allow eight days off." She excitedly explained.

"Well, I guess we'll just wait and see." he begrudgingly wished her luck.

The interview in Dallas went exceedingly well. Within days of her return, Skylar received a certified envelope inviting her to a training class in Dallas that summer. If she wanted to accept a place in the class, she would need to call the airline by the following Friday.

John took Skylar out for dinner that evening. Once they were seated and had ordered dinner, she breathlessly showed him the papers.

"I got in! I can't believe it! The interviews are very competitive. Oh my God! This is so great! Out of all those people, they chose me!"

John answered her smoothly. "That's great, hon! But I wish you'd think it over. I had other plans for us." He took her hands. "We could have such a great summer. We can go to my parents Cape Cod house and travel a bit. And after the summer, who knows? I would like to settle down. I'm not getting any younger, you know." He smiled at her and kissed her hands.

Skylar was confused. "But what about my offer letter? I've worked really hard trying to get a position as a flight attendant."

John, acknowledging her ambivalence just smiled and said, "Honey, you can think about it. I know you'll make the right decision." He had never told Skylar he loved her, yet he was hinting at marriage. He never told her how his close friends believed he would never settle down with one woman, yet he was suggesting permanence.

Skylar was torn. She didn't want to abandon a career she had worked so hard to attain, yet she couldn't imagine not being with John. It was unclear to her whether he didn't want her to leave because he felt intense love or because he felt fierce possession. The line was indistinguishable.

Caught up in John's charisma, the novelty of the relationship, the boundless activities and a whirlwind of social events was exhilarating for Skylar. He was an adrenalin rush. She was concerned that his manic lifestyle would not translate into the stability needed for a traditional family. However, she had also experienced the sweet side of John when she saw that his interactions with the children of his friends were tender and caring. It seemed that he was offering marriage if she did not accept the airline's offer. Although she had worked diligently on her new career goal, she was in a quandary. When she tried further discussion with him, to clarify what he had been proposing, he only focused on discouraging her choice of a profession. Unable to get a definitive answer from him, Skylar kept putting off the phone call to the training director until it was too late. The airline had filled the class, and they withdrew their offer.

Chapter 4

Skylar partially blamed herself for losing the opportunity with the airline. She had been waiting for an answer from John instead of focusing on her goal. But what puzzled her was his reaction. When she told him she wasn't going to training in Dallas, he simultaneously became cool and unresponsive.

As they sat in his apartment watching television in early June of 1985, Skylar tentatively asked, "John, is something wrong?" He had been distant for days.

"Yeah. We've been together for three months, and I'm not in love with you. I fell in love with Jennifer after three weeks. I don't think I'll ever be in love with you," he flatly stated.

Skylar's head began throbbing. She couldn't believe what she just heard. She didn't know what had suddenly changed. She couldn't believe she had given up a chance to become a flight attendant at John's veiled promise. She got up from her place on the couch and began putting on her sneakers. All she could think about was how she had allowed him to persuade her to discard a potential career she had worked so hard to attain. She had permitted him to convince her to simply throw it all away.

"Skylar, wait," John said.

But she didn't wait. She got up and left. Her emotions vacillated from anger and hurt toward John to berating herself for being so stupid and allowing him to influence her. As she drove home, she wondered why he had been so adamant she refuse the opportunity for a career she had worked so hard to achieve and then suddenly dropped this bomb.

There was no way she could have equated John's behavior with a psychiatric illness or a personality disorders.

Steve Becker, MSW, LCSW, is a licensed clinical social worker who was among a group of men known as the *10 Men of Union County*, New Jersey, who were recognized and honored for their work to confront domestic violence in the community. He has written, presented, and published work on sociopathology, narcissistic phenomena, and the abusive mentality. According to Dr. Becker:

> The "malignant narcissist" is driven by the sociopath's (or psychopath's) pursuit of omnipotent control over those he seeks to exploit. He is a power-hungry, often charismatic, ruthless, and exploitative personality whose grandiosity serves more psychopathic than classically narcissistic purposes. The malignant narcissist is someone whose most toxic narcissistic qualities have attained malignant status (hence the concept). In the end, however, he is as cold-blooded, callous, exploitative, and deviant a creature as the most dangerous sociopath.

When Skylar arrived home, she went into her room, prepared to sob into her pillow. Instead, she noticed the notebook on her desk where she tracked the airlines that were hiring and where she had sent other applications. She still had a chance! She wiped away tears as her anger and sadness turned to excitement at the realization that she could still get hired as a flight attendant.

As the new week began, she attended a group interview with an airline in Boston and was waiting to hear whether she would be invited to the second phase of interviewing. She tried to focus on her career and not on John, but he called the office constantly for weeks. She didn't know whether it was work-related or merely an excuse to talk.

She was cordial but aloof.

One afternoon, as she left the office, she found John in the parking lot, waiting by her car. He told her how much he missed her and wanted give the relationship another try. It was timely as she had just been asked to attend the final flight attendant interview in Miami. She admitted she missed him but stood firm as she told him she was still pursuing a career as a flight attendant.

Taking her hand, he said, "You know, I've had a lot of time to think about it. And if that's what you want to do, I feel I can be supportive."

Skylar believed the sincerity she heard in his voice and she agreed to go out for dinner.

The time apart seemed to change him. He told her he had stopped smoking pot, and it made a difference in his personality. He appeared happy and was very loving and attentive. They discussed her upcoming interview. She reminded him she was going to accept the position, if offered, with the airline. John reiterated his support and told her they'd make it work.

Final interviews for flight attendant positions were challenging, lasting several hours. Skylar interviewed well in Florida, and was confident of the outcome. Two days after her return home, she received a telephone call from the airline offering her a place in the July 1985 training class. She was thrilled to learn all new flight attendant trainees would be based at Logan International Airport in Boston, Massachusetts.

The evening before Skylar left for training, John took her out for a romantic dinner. He insisted she stay with him all night. In the morning, he passionately kissed her at the gate before she boarded her flight to Florida. Upon her arrival in Miami, she spent the day unpacking and meeting the other women in her training class. After dinner, she was pleasantly surprised when John called.

He declared, "I got home today and I missed you so much I had to call you. I love you, little girl." John truly meant this. Without Skylar physically present, John did miss her and realized he loved her. He hated to be alone, which is a typical trait of a narcissist. He was almost never without a girlfriend. Now that Skylar was away, he felt lost and tightly held on to the small amount of time when he could hear her voice, sweet, loving and reassuring him of his desirability.

He began calling her on a daily basis. He would tell her how much he loved her and missed her. When he hung up, he would grab the keys to his car, and go out for the evening. When he returned home, he would write long amorous letters to her. He sent her all sorts of funny, loving and sexy cards. Although he was conveying very deep love for Skylar, he needed constant female companionship. He initiated contact with a former girlfriend. He felt spending time with an old friend didn't mean anything. He met a girl from Canada who was staying in Boston for the summer and he began taking her to dinner and out dancing. He felt he was being kind by showing someone the city. It meant nothing. He met a girl who was from the Midwest, and working as a nanny. She needed someone to help her get her driver's license. John offered to assist. It meant nothing; he was just being a nice guy. Although he would insist it meant nothing, he was out practically every night Skylar was gone. But he told her he was keeping busy with work and not doing much of anything else.

When he met Skylar at the airport, five weeks later, he ran to her, grabbed her, and picked her up in a tight hug. For Skylar, it was a warm and loving welcome. It felt so nice to be back in Boston where the air was cool and breathable and with John again by her side.

In the morning, he drove her to pick up the car she arranged to purchase when she returned to Boston. She had been using her mother's car, but now she needed her own. This was the first car she ever purchased. Upon their arrival at the dealership, a white Pontiac Firebird with pinstripes and a decal of a big bird on the hood was in the front of the building.

"That's it!" Skylar squealed. "What do you think? Isn't it gorgeous?" she excitedly asked him.

"It's nice…for you" he blandly responded. He felt the car was below his standards. When he saw her bewilderment at his unenthusiastic response, he added, "Hey, let's go out for dinner to celebrate your first new car!"

At dinner, he surprised her when he announced, "I want you to be my wife." Most of John's friends were married, and several of them had already started families. They were both twenty-seven years old, and it seemed to be the right time to settle down. John loved Skylar. She was adventurous and active. She didn't try to take center stage with him. She was warm and loving. She didn't have drug problems. He knew she wouldn't cheat. He also found her to be far more refined than anyone he had ever dated, which would be a boon if he ever had to take her someplace with some of his higher-end clients from work. He felt she was a good choice for a wife. It was September 1985 and they had known each other for five months.

That weekend he took her to look for an engagement ring. He didn't know any jewelers, so Skylar suggested a jeweler her family had been doing business with for years. Upon their arrival to the store, they were shown a selection of engagement rings. Skylar admired a modest gold setting adorned with six tiny stones on either side. The jeweler placed a round diamond, weighing 1.3 carats, in the center. As she admired it, John said, "Well, I am not going to buy the ring with you here. I want to surprise you."

Skylar was elated, thinking of the ring they had chosen.

A few days later, John told her, "I went back to that jewelry store. I went with this friend of mine who knows about diamonds. He told me that diamond we were shown was not a good quality stone. He said we shouldn't get it."

Her face fell. "But, my family has known him for years. He wouldn't show me a diamond that was not a good quality."

"Well, I'm tellin' ya, he did." When John was challenged, he changed his way of speaking. "You shouldn't believe everyone, Skylar." When she didn't say anything, he said, "But guess what I did get." He pulled a small box out of his pocket and handed her the box.

With a huge smile, she eagerly opened the box to find the gold setting she loved, but there was no center stone. She looked up at John quizzically.

"I'm gonna look for another diamond for the ring. I just can't afford to buy one right now." He acknowledged the disappointment in Skylar's face. "Hey, it might be sooner than ya think!" He smiled and took the box Skylar held. "I'm gonna put this in my safe for now."

After his promise, John went on a spending spree. He bought a state-of-the-art color television. He installed a new motor in the old car he owned, which he had purchased in high school. He took Skylar to the sporting goods store and selected skis, boots and poles for her. The clerk rang up the order, and John wrote a check for the items. Once he got his receipt, he picked up all the ski equipment leaning by the counter - including a second, seemingly random pair of skis and followed Skylar outside. In the truck, he began to laugh and laugh.

Skylar smiled and asked, "What's so funny?"

John excitedly replied, "I just got a free pair of skis! It was so easy! I just put the Dynastar skis near the ones I bought for you, and the cashier didn't even notice." The smile faded from Skylar's face, and she looked shocked. John told her, "They mark their merchandise up anyway. They won't even notice the loss. It's no big deal." He boldly returned to the store the following week and bought new bindings which were fitted to the skis he had stolen.

It was late fall, and the weather was turning colder. Skylar was enjoying her job as a flight attendant. She flew domestic routes all over the United States. It was a varied and hectic schedule made more difficult by John's insistence that she telephone him every time she landed.

He would relentlessly grill her, "Who's in the crew? Are there any men flying with you? Are you going out with them? I don't want you going out to dinner if there are men going too! I can't stand much more of you flying around! You better start thinking about quitting this job, or I am going to start dating."

Once, a pilot took her picture and left it in her mailbox inside the airport office. When she showed the picture to John as they drove home, he threw it out the window of the car and screamed, "Why was a pilot taking your picture?!"

Skylar remained silent when John interrogated, threatened, or screamed. She attributed his strong reactions to stress from her erratic schedule. She was sure he would eventually adjust.

She was on a layover when he called to tell her the lease on his apartment wasn't being renewed. He called a real estate broker, who showed him an apartment on the other side of town which was available immediately. The apartment was half a duplex on a quiet, dead-end street. It was a sunny unit with two bedrooms and one bath. There were hardwood floors throughout the apartment, laundry hook-ups, a tiny deck, and a garage. John had some friends help him move and was settled in the new apartment when Skylar returned home.

As she admired the new apartment, John announced, "Since you're always away, I should have a vacation too. I'm gonna go skiing in Utah with my friend."

She reminded him she was working when she was away, not taking a vacation. And although she had five days off, John left for his trip.

When he returned at the end of December, he hugged Skylar tightly and whispered, "I couldn't wait to get home. I didn't want to miss giving you a kiss at midnight on New Year's Eve." They hosted an impromptu yet festive New Year's Eve party. The merriment continued past midnight as John kissed Skylar to welcome in 1986.

Two days later, she returned to work. She was on a particularly arduous trip with grueling, twelve hour days consisting of fifteen airports.

After three demanding days working, an exhausted Skylar arrived at John's apartment. She craved a long, hot shower. As she relaxed in the steam, the curtain suddenly flew open and John jumped into the shower.

He began dancing around, saying "Soon, Honey, soon!"

"Soon for what?" Skylar asked him.

"To give you your ring." He hugged her in the wet spray. Skylar suddenly felt energetic and optimistic. John had *finally* accepted her career. Everything was going to work out.

But, in the morning, he told Skylar her engagement ring was contingent on her quitting her job. As the weeks went by, he continued to complain that she was never home. He disliked her working environment, being surrounded by traveling men, male flight attendants, and pilots.

Finally, he exploded, "I can't marry someone with such an erratic schedule!"

Skylar couldn't stand the pressure and she reluctantly resigned her position as a flight attendant.

A calmer John began taking her skiing every weekend. He presented her with the engagement ring in Vermont on Valentine's Day weekend by thrusting the ring in Skylar's face as she searched for her ski socks. Although there was no declaration of love on one knee, she was pleased and surprised to see the ring, now complete with a large diamond in the center. She *had* made the right decision leaving the airline. They were officially engaged! She kept looking at the diamond on her left hand. Even going up on the chairlift, she would take off her ski glove and look at her engagement ring. She was filled with joy.

When they returned from Vermont, Skylar and her mother Sable began making wedding plans. They found a synagogue and a caterer. Sable gave deposits as she secured the different vendors. Skylar tried to share the information with John, but he didn't appear very interested. In fact, he withdrew. He would ignore her while remaining cheerful to everyone else.

When Skylar asked him what was wrong, he flatly replied, "I don't want to get married and I don't want to marry you." As if a switch was flipped, John suddenly changed his mind.

Skylar had enough. She didn't need the constant ups and downs. She couldn't turn her feelings on and off like John. She was heartbroken, yet a little relieved at the same time, knowing the drama was over. The wedding plans were terminated, and all the deposits were forfeited.

One weekend, Skylar drove to John's apartment knowing he was in Vermont skiing. Using her key, she went inside and found her skis, boots, and poles. She collected her equipment and left the apartment, locking the door behind her. Then she slipped the keys through the mail slot so he would find them on the floor when he returned home.

Sable had never been a fan of John since he tried to dissuade her from becoming a flight attendant. She easily saw how he tried to control and manipulate her daughter. She had little faith in anything he said or did. She knew her gut instinct about John Bauers was accurate after she received a call from her friend, Rose, who lived in Needham.

Rose had conveyed to Sable how she would like her son Mark, to meet Skylar. She would tell Mark countless times, "You should meet

Sable's daughter. Skylar is so sweet and lovely. She's such a nice girl."

Mark never met Skylar. However, growing up in Needham, he knew John well. He was shocked when he learned John was engaged to Skylar. He remembered how Rose wanted him to meet "a refined girl, like Sable's daughter, Skylar."

He immediately called Rose. "Mom, tell Sable NOT to let her daughter marry John Bauers. We used to be friends years ago after high school. There is something *really* wrong with him."

Sable felt sorry for her daughter but she sensed it was a reprieve from making a big mistake. She suggested, "Why don't you go to Florida and visit your grandmother for a while? And you may want to think about selling that ring so you won't be holding on to a bad memory." Skylar agreed and made her airline reservations. Before she left, she decided to take the ring to a local jeweler for an appraisal. After cleaning the stone, it was carefully examined by the jeweler.

With a sigh, he asked, "Do you know what this is? This diamond is what's called a *clarity enhanced* diamond." He explained, "This stone is a very low quality, cheap diamond, filled with inclusions. Some jeweler was able to bleach out the inclusions with a laser. You see, after you put it in the cleaner, these kinds of stones start to give off pink rays and you can see all the inclusions. I also found a large crack along the side."

Skylar felt betrayed. She couldn't wait to get out of Boston. She called the airline and changed her flight to leave that evening.

Sable wasn't surprised when John began calling the house, looking for Skylar.

"Just tell me where she is," he would insist.

But Sable refused to tell him anything.

This angered John, who was accustomed to getting what he wanted. So, he began spreading rumors about Skylar, telling people she was crazy and had broken into his apartment.

When Skylar returned home, she was well-rested and relaxed, looking tanned and beautiful. She heard about the rumors John had been spreading, but he no longer bothered her. She was ready to move on. She contemplated returning to the airlines and requesting one of the bases in another state. She needed changes in her life and didn't want any reminders of John Bauers. As she was reviewing her options, she was also spending times with her friends. They would go out to eat and go dancing. She was having fun, and any thoughts of John Bauers were fading fast.

But John hadn't stopped thinking about her. He called Skylar. "Please, honey. I am sorry I said things about you. I want to see you and explain." He was incessant.

Against Sable's wishes, Skylar met John at a local restaurant. He was waiting for her and turned up the full wattage of his charm.

"Skylar, I've been doing a lot of thinking. It really bothered me, because I felt as if I had no control with the wedding plans. I guess I needed to put the brakes on. But I missed you so much. I just want to be able to see you. Let's start over. Please think about it."

As proof of his sincerity, he promised to pay Sable for all the deposits she had lost when he cancelled the wedding. He visited Sable, and apologized profusely. He convinced everyone of his desire to turn over a new leaf. Skylar felt as if he was making a huge effort. When they went out, he was charismatic and accommodating. She enjoyed her time with John, for the most part. But there was something bothersome; a premonition, a gut feeling, a little voice telling her to get out of the relationship. She felt it was lingering jitters from his prior break-ups, and she didn't follow her instincts. One night, John asked her if she would consider wearing her engagement ring again and move in with him. He promised her that once she moved in, they would set a wedding date.

He cajoled her, "I'll pay all the household expenses, and someday, I promise I'll replace the diamond in your ring." Suddenly, after John's pattern of indecisiveness, he wanted to commit himself to Skylar legally.

In December 1986, Skylar moved into the Needham apartment and he took her out for an elegant dinner where they toasted their reunion and engagement.

As a narcissist, his indecision had little to do with Skylar. She was soft and sweet and lovely but she was also bright and determined, with her own ideas and goals. John was used to women who were far more compliant but far less interesting. Most of the women he had dated were content to be at his side and in his bed. His opinions were their opinions. John had tried and tried to break Skylar's feistiness without luck. He loved everything else about her, which made him constantly return to her. But John had concerns what others would think of him if he got married. Would they think he was weak? What would happen to his reputation if he took a wife? Most of his friends had married. John felt he had success as a single man. Could he receive the same admiration as a married man? He had never been faithful to anyone. Could he be committed to one woman? Everything about him and every decision he made was critical to what others were ultimately going to think about him.

A leading expert on narcissism, Sam Vaknin is the author of *Malignant Self Love - Narcissism Revisited*, which is a work of reference about the Narcissistic Personality Disorder. He describes the narcissist as one who *"needs approval, admiration, adoration and attention − in other words, externalized ego boundary functions. The narcissist casts his parents, siblings, children and friends as his audience in the theater of his inflated grandiosity."*

Skylar loved John and the energetic spirit he awakened in her with each new experience. She loved the new level of physical activity of his lifestyle, but she refused to put her own desires or goals on a shelf. It was easy to fall back into the familiarity of a relationship with him each time he promised he had overcome his fears of commitment and was ready to move forward, Skylar felt perhaps this was the road, albeit rocky, they needed to take which would lead them to matrimony.

Chapter 5

John enjoyed living with Skylar. She was happy as well. The wedding plans were coming together. It was lovely and peaceful, for a short time. The first argument ensued when Skylar found difficulty with John's desire to "smush the wedding cake in your face at the wedding. It will be funny!" She was mortified, yet he kept insisting.

Finally, Skylar tearfully said, "If you disrespect me like that, I will divorce you!"

"Okay, if you don't wanna have fun, then I won't do it," he grumbled, disappointed.

There was another argument when they were shopping for wedding bands. The jeweler asked John, "Can I measure your finger for your ring size?" John held out his right hand. The jeweler smiled and said, "I need your left hand."

John stated, "I want to wear the ring on my right hand."

The jeweler explained the tradition of wearing the wedding band on the third finger of the left hand, as it was believed there was a vein, artery, or nerve there running directly to the heart. Worn on the left hand, the ring stands for marriage, as once believed because it is on the same side of the body as the heart.

Despite the jeweler's lovely explanation, John refused, saying, "Doing things different than the norm makes me unique and interesting."

According to the *Diagnostic Criteria for Narcissistic Personality Disorder*, from the *Diagnostic and Statistical Manual of Mental Disorders, Fourth Edition (DSM-IV)*, the third criteria listed in diagnosing narcissism is,

<u>Believes that he or she is special and unique</u>. According to Sigmund Freud:

> *Healthy narcissism is found in most individuals as an honest recognition of self-image and self-esteem. It forms a constant yet realistic reflection of one's self, mature goals, and an ability to form deep relationships. However, pathological narcissism, which possibly develops as a way to fill a void in childhood, produces megalomania and the need to be seen as the most special and the most unique."*

Because John needed to be seen as the most extraordinary, he had his wedding band fitted to his right hand.

Two weeks prior to the wedding, John's friend called to tell him she didn't feel comfortable attending the wedding as she had a feeling Skylar disliked her. When he ended the call, he screamed at Skylar. "My friend said she won't come to my wedding because of you! You better lose this attitude and be nicer to my friends!"

Skylar, who was always nice, had finally reached her limit. She called Sable and told her she wasn't getting married. Sable begged her not to cancel the wedding. In her heart, Sable did not want her marrying John Bauers. She felt he was everything bad. But she also knew he would, again, charm her back if the wedding was cancelled. Against her true feelings, Sable assured Skylar they were both having pre-wedding jitters and everything would work out.

Paradoxically, there was a series of events, ranging from tragic to horrific, which could have been viewed as an omen to cancel the wedding.

- On June 23rd, John's black cat was hit by a car. The veterinarian was unable to save his life, and the cat had to be euthanized.
- On the evening of June 24th, two of John's friends were brutally murdered in their home.
- John's best man was mugged and he was hospitalized for several days.
- The organist for the wedding ceremony died suddenly.

Trying to move on from the tragedies and get into the spirit of the wedding, a group of friends took Skylar out for dinner in Boston three days before the wedding. John had protested. He didn't want her going to a restaurant that had a bar area, but his sisters, Audra and Cara, told him he was being silly. He begrudgingly relented after warning Skylar not to go into the bar. During dinner, Audra and Cara eagerly shared information about their brother.

Cara told Skylar, "Johnny is very selfish. He can be very charming, but he comes first."

Audra shared her views as well. "When Johnny was in high school, he would only date girls who were easy and would have sex with him."

"Are you trying to warn me about your brother?" Skylar asked with a smile.

"No, he was just a typical guy in high school," stated Audra.

"No man is perfect – even though they may think they are" Cara said, laughing.

After dinner, Skylar drove to Sable's house. She was staying there for a few days prior to the wedding to relax and go for her final gown fitting. The following morning, John called her.

"I just got back from the doctor. I'm sick with strep throat or mono. He gave me an antibiotic. I don't know how I can get married on Sunday if I feel like this."

At that point, the myriad of accidents and deaths came flooding back to Skylar. She felt all were a forewarning to cancel the wedding. She repeated John's conversation to Sable, ending with her stating matter-of-factly, "That's it. The wedding's off."

"Listen to me, Skylar. He's on antibiotics. It's Friday. By Sunday night, he should be feeling much better." When Skylar's face remained impassive, Sable encouraged her. "Come on. You have a gown fitting today. Let's go."

They drove to the bridal boutique. Skylar's gown was gorgeous. It was elegant in its simplicity with a dramatic ruffle off her shoulder. It fit perfectly. Skylar looked at the dress in the mirror and began to feel optimistic about the wedding. After making arrangements to pick up the gown after pressing, they drove back to the house.

"I'm going to call John to see how he's feeling." Skylar said as she dialed his number.

"Hello?"

"Hi! How are you feeling, honey?" Skylar asked sympathetically.

"I can't talk now. Tom Parsons just drove in from Maine. I'll talk to you later." John hung up the phone, abruptly.

"How is he feeling?" Sable called out from her room.

"Okay, I guess. Tom is there." Skylar walked into Sable's room.

"Well, then he must be feeling better, if he has company. He probably felt worse this morning when he woke up."

Skylar thought that sounded sensible. She spent the remainder of the day relaxing in the sun and packing for her honeymoon. John didn't call her.

She woke up feeling nervous the day before the wedding. The only appointment on her schedule was her manicure at noon. John called her just as she was leaving the house.

When she answered the phone, she heard John's voice threatening, "If you don't come here right now and do my laundry, I am not getting married tomorrow."

"What?"

"You heard me. What are you doing? Relaxing with your mother while I'm here sick? You should be helping me!" his voice rose.

"John, I am on my way to get my nails done."

"Why are you getting your nails done?" he demanded.

"Because we are getting married tomorrow," Skylar explained. "I will help you with the laundry after my manicure."

"Okay." His voice sounded a little softer. "I'll be here."

Skylar hung up the phone. She attributed John's anger to his illness. She put it out of her mind and drove to the manicurist. Once completed and ensuring her nails were dry, Skylar drove to the apartment in Needham. John was sitting on the couch watching television.

"Hi." He greeted her. "Look at these pictures. Tom took them yesterday. His wife, Heidie was here, too." He handed her the Polaroid pictures which were in a pile on the couch.

"How are you feeling?" Skylar asked, taking the pictures.

"Pretty awful," John replied.

Skylar looked at the pictures. There was a picture of John sitting on the couch looking wan but smoking a joint. There was a picture of John and Tom, laughing. There was a picture of John blowing smoke rings, the burning joint in his hand.

"If you feel sick, why were you smoking pot?" Skylar asked.

"Because it made me feel better," John retorted.

"Fine. What laundry needs to be done?"

"I already did it," he said. "I'm goin' out for dinner with Tom tonight, so I guess I'll see ya tomorrow." He dismissed her with the wave of his hand.

Skylar had trouble sleeping that night. She woke early and nibbled on half a bagel as the hairstylist curled her hair. She was a bundle of nerves.

The synagogue was a short distance from the house. Skylar carried her gown into the bridal chamber and slipped the dress on. It was perfect. The crisp white silk complimented her tanned skin. Her headpiece and veil were simple with delicate seed pearls and beads, framing one side of her face. She felt beautiful. The formal portraits were being done prior to the ceremony, so Skylar walked out of the bridal suite to present herself to John. She waited for his reaction.

He looked at his bride, in her beautiful gown on their wedding day and flatly commented, "Kind of low isn't it?" He pointed to the neckline of the gown then he abruptly turned to boisterously greet a friend as Skylar stood stunned that his reaction wasn't complementary or loving. Tears threatened, and she blinked rapidly, trying to prepare a happy face for the photographer, who had begun posing the wedding party.

Pictures completed, everyone lined up for the ceremony.

Skylar stood at the back of the line. She watched the bridesmaids and groomsmen begin to enter the synagogue. As the line got shorter, she began having trouble catching her breath. She stood at the back of the line, gasping for air. She began to get dizzy. She couldn't speak, and she was unable to ask for help. *Oh, my God! I am going to pass out right here on the floor, she thought.* Her heart was palpitating. The room was spinning. Everyone else had disappeared into the synagogue, and Skylar stood alone, breathless and perspiring. As the door opened for her, a blast of icy air from the air conditioning hit her face and revived her. She regained her composure and began to walk down the aisle.

Years later, thinking about those few heart pounding moments before walking down the aisle, Skylar believed it was God's last attempt to save her from marrying John Bauers.

Immediately after the wedding ceremony, Skylar and John were whisked away by a limousine for a leisurely ride to the reception site. Upon arrival, they entered the garden terrace, where the guests were waiting. They stood together as everyone offered their congratulations to the newlyweds. Afterwards, Skylar went into the facility's bridal chamber to enjoy the hors d'oeuvres with her new husband. She carefully ate a few tidbits as the train on her gown was pinned up by the facility coordinator. When she completed pinning the train, she left the room. As soon as the door shut, John grabbed Skylar, pulling down the top of her gown and lifting up the skirt. He ripped down his tuxedo pants and positioned her on top of him.

"John, stop! I don't want to do this!" she pleaded with him, as she struggled to get away.

"You were away all week! I don't want to wait! You better stop struggling, or you'll rip your dress. Now be a good girl and take care of me." They were now husband and wife.

John showed no sign of illness the next morning as they boarded the airplane for their honeymoon. The location had been a long arduous battle. John viewed the honeymoon solely as his opportunity to either reconnect with old friends and girlfriends, indulge in his hobby of searching for interesting bottles of wine to add to his collection, or buy himself the boat he always wanted and cruise the New England coastline. Skylar wanted a honeymoon where they could spend time alone and bond as a couple. She had little interest in wine unless it was being served with dinner. She had no desire to cruise the coastline, especially since she was prone to seasickness. They eventually settled on Aruba and Puerto Rico.

In Aruba, they stayed in a small hotel, on the beach. The beds were double-sized, and John refused to share a bed with Skylar, as he hated to be touched when he slept. The second day of their honeymoon, John introduced himself to a couple he had noticed on their flight from Boston. He suggested they join them on the beach. Seated on the sand, the man accepted John's proffered joint. They sat there and smoked pot. Afterward, John and the man went snorkeling, leaving Skylar to make small talk with the woman. The honeymoon had turned into time for John to make a new friend he could hang out with instead of his wife. If the other couple was busy, John went into the town to look for a diamond ring. He had decided he should buy a diamond ring for himself, since he had purchased a diamond ring for Skylar.

Skylar couldn't wait to leave Aruba. She prayed their time in Puerto Rico would be more enjoyable. Their accommodations in Puerto Rico were beautiful and she was pleased to see the king-sized bed and balcony that overlooked the ocean. Although the location was nicer, the quest was still the same. John searched the stores looking for his diamond ring during the day.

Walking down the moonlit path toward the restaurant one evening, John suddenly looked at Skylar and said, "Go back to the room and put on a bra." She was wearing a pretty, gauzy white sundress with little straps. The dress was anything but immodest.

Skylar laughed. "You're kidding."

His eyes narrowed. "If you don't change, I am not taking you out for dinner." He turned around and walked defiantly back to the room.

She followed him, resolute that she was not changing her dress. John sat on the bed, opened a magazine and waited for her to change. Instead, she went out on the balcony and sat down. She knew if she gave in, he would continue to dictate what she wore. Determined, she marched back into the room, called room service, and ordered dinner in the room. Before she replaced the phone, he took the phone and placed an order as well. When the food arrived, he was pleasant and behaved as if nothing had transpired. They flew home at the end of the week.

Skylar was excited to be home, as she was starting a new job selling fashion photography packages. On her first day, she was introduced to Lori Donnaccia, the woman who was going to teach her about the company and her position. Lori was tall and lanky with glossy black hair, pretty brown eyes, a crooked nose, and a wide mouth with big red lips. She was friendly and bubbly. It was an instant connection. They felt as if they had known each other for years and became good friends.

Each day, as Skylar would dress for work, John began his morning ritual of checking her attire to make certain she was wearing a bra. He never left the house before she was dressed. She found his behavior insane: she was slim and small boned with small hips and breasts and she didn't need a bra. One morning, she dressed in a beautiful dress from an upscale store. The dress was black cotton with a loose, tailored top. The skirt fell in generous folds, almost to her ankles. John ran his hand down her back.

"Take that off. You're not wearing a bra!" he commanded.

"This dress is not inappropriate. Look at the front. You can't even tell," she pleaded.

"I said take that off!" he said loudly.

"No!" she yelled.

"Fine, then I will." He grabbed Skylar by the front of the dress and pulled hard. The buttons came popping off.

"John! Stop it! This is an expensive dress!"

He kept pulling at the dress until it began to tear. "I don't care. I told you not to go out without a bra!" He pulled the dress off her, and tore it to shreds. "Here you go." He tossed the ripped dress in her lap. "I gotta get to work." He pointed to the clock on the wall and added, "You're gonna be late." Then he turned and left the apartment.

John began dictating what she wore in the privacy of their home as well. He didn't want her walking around wearing just a nightgown.

She protested, "But its summer. It's too hot to wear a robe."

"If my friends come by, I want you covered," he demanded.

"If someone wanted to come by, they should call first," she replied.

"My friends have always come by whenever they feel like it!" he raised his voice.

"Well, we're married now, so they need to call," she insisted. Seeing the rage in his face, she softened her voice. "Why don't I keep a robe in the closet downstairs, just in case we have a visitor?" she suggested. Much calmer, John agreed.

As Skylar was getting ready for bed on evening, he came upstairs and saw her changing.

"You're getting undressed in front of the window!" he accused.

She looked at the window which was located near the foot of the bed and partly covered by the bureau. It was literally impossible to see inside the second floor window. "Oh, John," she laughed, "No one can see inside." She continued changing, oblivious to his demeanor.

"I guess you need a lesson." He grabbed her, lifting her up over his shoulder.

She began screaming and struggling. "Stop, John! Put me down!"

He dragged her down the stairs, opened the front door and placed her on the front stoop. "Maybe this will teach you to close the shades at night," he said as he slammed the door.

Skylar was barefoot, wearing only a pair of slacks and a bra. She rang the bell. "John! Let me in!" She huddled in a ball, trying to cover herself.

Ten minutes later, he opened the door. "Get in! Everyone can see you!"

After that, if she forgot to close the shades or if John saw she had already changed and the shades were not drawn, he would pick her up and drag her outside, regardless of what she was wearing, telling her he was teaching her a lesson. It became his routine to deposit her outside to teach her a lesson for anything that displeased him. If she talked back, he threatened to wash her mouth out with soap.

One afternoon, Skylar returned from work to find two decorative hair combs in her top dresser drawer. She never wore hair combs. She approached John, holding hair combs.

"Who was in the apartment?"

"No one was here." He didn't look up from his magazine. When she didn't respond, he glanced at her, "Ya think I had someone here who put those in your drawer for you to find? They're yours," he insisted, meeting her gaze with defiance until she turned and walked away.

John, a true narcissist, was a chronic philanderer. It wasn't a case of temptation or dissatisfaction at home. A study published on October 4, 2006, by psychologist Ilan Shrira found that narcissists are more likely to philander and dump their partners than people who value fidelity and closeness in their relationship.

"Narcissists tend to view sex very differently than other people do," said Shrira, whose study appeared in the *Journal of Social and Personal Relationships.*

> *"They see sexuality more in terms of power and influence*
> *contrasting to those who associated sex with caring and love.*
> *As a result, narcissists tend to go through relationships that*
> *are usually devoid of much intimacy. Even when they are in*
> *a relationship, they always seem to be on the lookout for*
> *other partners and searching for a better deal. Possibly*
> *because they think multiple partners enhance their self-image."*

By Christmas of 1987, Skylar began feeling nauseated. When her period didn't come, she suggested they purchase a pregnancy test at the drugstore. She followed the directions on the box. When she saw a positive result, she was filled with awe at the realization she was carrying life. She approached John. "It's positive!" she beamed, happily.

"I don't think you should have it," John said, and walked away.

Skylar was devastated by John's reaction to her joyful announcement. He remained isolated for the day. But that evening, he approached Skylar, "I've thought about it. All my friends are having kids, so I guess we may as well start."

John never became excited about the pregnancy. He was uninvolved, distant, and disinterested in the pregnancy. He didn't behave as an excited prospective father. He refused to go to the obstetrician appointment. He did not want to hear the baby's heartbeat. He declined to go to the ultrasound appointment to see the first pictures of the baby. He reluctantly allowed Skylar to place his hand on her stomach only one time to feel the baby kick. He did not want to buy a crib or a changing table for the baby.

But Skylar was very excited and wanted to remember every moment of her pregnancy. She bought a journal to record every thought and feeling. She wrote her first entry:

Saturday, January 2, 1988 - Today I went to the bookmobile to buy a few books about pregnancy and to begin a "pregnancy journal" so I will remember my pregnancy and birthing experience and years down the road, give this to my first-born.

She intended the book to be a written documentation of the details of her progressing pregnancy. However, once she had their first baby, she continued writing, documenting milestones and cute anecdotes. She intended the journals to serve as wonderful memories for her children. Her earlier journals were sugarcoated; she omitted details of her marriage and hid the abuse. She didn't feel those precious keepsakes for her children should contain the horrible truths about their father. Instead, she conveyed love and attraction for John. She tried to portray him as a loving father and husband. She tried to convince herself. She wanted the children to think their mom and dad had a very special relationship. However, in September of 1990, an episode of abuse so loathsome occurred that Skylar had to start admitting the unpleasant truths in her journals and to herself.

Chapter 6

In March 1988, the advertising agency where Skylar worked filed Chapter 11 and closed its doors. Skylar registered with a temporary employment agency that serviced the Needham area. After work, as she drove down her street, she saw John's new friend, Bill, parked in front of their duplex. He visited John daily. When Bill was there, John would give Skylar a perfunctory greeting then sit in the backyard with Bill and smoke a joint. On weekends, Bill would call in the morning to ask John if he wanted to go fishing and skiing with him.

Irked by his constant intrusions, Skylar asked John, "Doesn't he know you have a wife that you should spend time with on the weekends? He's so annoying."

He replied, "He likes to do guy stuff with me. I work all week so why should I have to sit home because you're pregnant? You'd like him if you got to know him. I think I'll invite him to dinner next weekend." He ran for the phone to invite Bill for dinner.

The following Saturday night, when the doorbell rang, he warned her, "You better be nice!" before she opened the door.

Skylar graciously welcomed Bill, who acknowledged her with a nod. She went into the kitchen and began bringing food to the table. During dinner, she sat quietly as Bill and John proceeded to get drunk.

At one point during the meal Bill announced, "I have to fart!"

Skylar looked toward John, hoping he would say something, but he was sitting there chuckling. An explosive sound emanated from Bill. "Yeah, baby!" yelled John. He and Bill began guffawing while Skylar sat mortified.

When dinner was over, Bill got up and started flinging the flatware into the sink from the dining area. John and Bill kept pouring drinks. They screeched and giggled like teenage girls. Skylar was disgusted by the evening's events, so she excused herself, feigning exhaustion from her pregnancy. She marched upstairs and shut the bedroom door. She curled up on her side and fell asleep immediately. She slept soundly through the night.

In the morning, John said, "Didja hear me last night? I was so sick. I had to get up and puke about three times."

She was unsympathetic. "That serves you right for drinking so much. And that Bill is obnoxious."

John replied, "Well, at least he's not boring like your friends."

Skylar walked out of the room. She vowed never to have Bill for dinner again.

The weather began to turn balmy, an early promise of a steaming summer. Skylar was about six months pregnant and she felt good.

One evening, as she was getting ready for bed, John announced, "I'll be back soon. I have to go pick up some pot." His marijuana supplier lived about twenty minutes away.

Skylar finished washing up and walked into the bedroom. In his haste to leave, John had left the door to his floor safe opened. It had always been off limits to Skylar and the door was wide open. So she looked inside. She saw a few handguns. She saw the poem she had written for him when they were dating. She smiled as she reread it. She placed it back in the safe.

In the back of the safe she noticed a pile of envelopes. In disbelief, she saw there were several letters from his ex-girlfriend Jennifer, and some unclothed pictures of her. There were tearful letters from a former girlfriend, written after their breakup and letters from a third ex-girlfriend, written when Skylar was planning their wedding. The Canadian girl John met when Skylar was in flight attendant training sent several intimate letters and a photograph of herself wearing only John's favorite t-shirt. There were even a few sexually explicit notes from a man.

She scooped up all the correspondence and photographs. She

ripped the letters to shreds and buried them in the waste basket in the kitchen. She started to tear up the pictures when she heard John come home so she quickly threw them in a kitchen drawer. John went upstairs, noticed his safe opened, and realized Skylar had been in the safe. He raced down the stairs.

"What did you do with my letters?!" he screamed. "You took my letters, you bitch!"

"What are you doing with love letters from your ex-girlfriends?" she asked.

"Those were MY letters!" John shouted.

"Oh yes, they were interesting. Especially the ones from that guy," Skylar stated sarcastically.

"Give me his letters! Hey – I don't even know the guy. He was someone who had a crush on me. I need those letters because I'm trying to discover who the guy is."

"Well, I guess you'll never know," Skylar answered flippantly.

"Where are my pictures? Where are Jennifer's pictures? You fuckin' well better give those back to me!" His eyes blazed and he took a step forward.

Skylar was scared at his reaction and was afraid for the baby. She grabbed the photos in the kitchen drawer and threw them at him. They fell to the floor and John knelt to pick them up. He gathered them in a pile and stood up, glaring at Skylar as he spat angrily, "Don't come near me, you fuckin' bitch!" He walked upstairs and Skylar heard the bedroom door slam.

She sat on the couch, in shock at her discovery. She felt betrayed. The altercation had drained her, and she wanted to go to sleep. When she tried to open the bedroom door, she found it locked. She got the key and gingerly opened the door, her hand on the door jamb. Suddenly, John threw his heavy work boots at her hand. She jumped back, startled. He leaped out of bed and slammed the door shut. He stuck a match in the lock so the key wouldn't work. Skylar was exhausted, so she went downstairs and drifted off to sleep on the old couch.

The sound of a toilet flushing woke her very early in the morning.

She painfully stretched, her body stiff from sleeping on the couch. The shower began running, so Skylar tiptoed upstairs and into the bedroom. She noticed the poem she had written for John ripped in half and left on the dresser. She crawled into bed and immediately fell into a sound sleep. When she awoke, John was already gone. Her poem was still on the dresser, but it was now in unsalvageable shreds.

When John returned home later he didn't comment on the previous evening, as if it never happened. Skylar was already in the habit of not reigniting the flames of a fight if it appeared to be over. She found it less stressful to ignore it and try to move on.

A week later, as they were talking about making room for the baby, Skylar suggested looking for a house.

John agreeably said, "Call a real estate broker and start looking. But don't look in Newton. I'm not gonna live where you grew up," he warned. "I wanna be in the country."

Although she had hoped to live in her hometown, she was excited at the prospect of a house and was willing to explore other towns.

"Skylar, I want you to sign a prenuptial agreement in case we get a divorce, so you can't have the house," he looked at her, waiting for her reaction.

She was flabbergasted. She was thinking about the baby they created, and John was thinking about a divorce. "Too late, we're already married, so I cannot sign a prenuptial agreement," she flippantly informed him.

John smugly retorted, "If you don't sign a prenuptial, then don't bother looking for a house. We'll stay here." He assumed she would then agree to sign a prenuptial.

She surprised him when she replied, "Fine. Then the baby can sleep with us, since you're using the other bedroom for your office."

He was at a loss for words. Skylar left the room. She could make due with the cramped quarters. She was sure John would eventually realize his request was ludicrous. But until he did, the search for a house was put on hold.

In July 1988, when Skylar was eight months pregnant, she registered for a weekly class at the hospital which prepared expectant parents for labor and delivery. John complained about attending. He proclaimed the classes as boring. Each week, on the evening of class, he would come home late or was unable to tear himself away from Bill, still ever present. They were late for class every week.

John would admonish, "Skylar, these classes are so corny and silly. You just go in and have a baby. What's the big deal? Only weird people go to these stupid classes."

He took on a pompous attitude about everything. When Skylar tried to discuss names for the baby, he mocked every name she suggested. "Those names are hideous! How can you think of such horrible names? If it's a boy, I think we should name him little Johnny Junior, after me. If it's a girl, I think Jennifer is a good name."

"The baby is not going to be a junior, and I am not naming my baby after your ex-girlfriend. You better think of something else," she told him.

But he didn't offer any other suggestions. He had already decided. "I am just gonna fill out the birth certificate after the baby is born, so you better get used to it!" he threatened.

Skylar was scared but boldly snapped back, "You know what? Don't even bother coming to the hospital. In fact, I will tell them when I get there that I don't want you near me."

Because it appeared as a real warning, he began working with her on selecting a name. They finally decided on Joshua or Jillian. He liked the fact that both names began with the letter "J," the same as John.

That summer was brutally hot. One steamy Sunday, John told Skylar he was going to New Hampshire with his friend, Phil Lewin. Phil was three years older than John but lived with his parents so his father could help him make decisions and monitor his drinking and drugging. Although he had been married twice and had a son, Phil was very much like a child, even prone to temper tantrums when things didn't go his way. In many ways, he was John's puppet.

They were going to look at the ski boats. Skylar had been home all week and wanted to go as well.

John said, "You can't go. You're too pregnant."

"I'm not too pregnant, John. I haven't been out all week." Suspiciously, she stated. "I think you are planning on buying a boat." She remembered a day at the lake when John sat on the beach and stared at the boats enviously and refused to talk until they left the beach.

"Skylar, I am not buying a boat. But you really can't come. It's too risky. What if you go into labor up there?" He kissed her on the cheek.

"I'll see you later."

Skylar had no choice but stay in her air conditioned bedroom while John spent the day with his friend in New Hampshire. It was evening when he returned. He ran upstairs to Skylar.

"Honey, I had to do it." John excitedly told her he had purchased a new competition ski boat with a top-of-the-line stereo system, as well as the equipment needed for waterskiing.

"You lied to me," Skylar stated. "You had already made the decision to buy a boat long before you went to New Hampshire. We should be buying a house, not a boat."

"I can find some office space and move my equipment in there. We can clean up the other bedroom for the baby." He was excited about his boat and tried to pacify Skylar.

"Well, that will be great. Where is the baby going to sleep?" Skylar asked sarcastically. John had steadfastly refused to buy baby furniture, complaining it was too expensive. "I know!" Skylar exclaimed. "Maybe the baby can sleep in the boat!"

John laughed. "All right. I get it. Tomorrow, when I come home from work, we will go to the store and pick out baby furniture." He was merely placating her, but it worked.

Skylar was thrilled. She threw her arms around John's neck. "Thank you!" She was so excited by the prospect of choosing baby furniture, yet instinctively knew if she questioned him further about his extravagant spending, he would not let her select baby furniture.

On Monday, John began looking at available office space. He found a tremendous space in a high-end industrial park, so he began to move everything from the apartment, including his wine collection, to the new office. He set up his wine and surrounded it with glass walls, happily boasting, "Now I can sit at my desk, smoke a cigar, and look at my wine collection."

He arranged an area of the office with a couch, a glass coffee table atop an Oriental rug, and a stereo system. He bought a refrigerator, microwave, and a set of crystal wineglasses.

When the second bedroom was empty, Skylar could see all the dirt clinging to the floors and walls. She washed as much as she could and left the rest for John to finish. When the room was cleaned, she was allowed to design the room. She selected a crib, changing table, carpet, and curtains for the room. This was the first time she didn't have to ask him for permission or approval, and she reveled in her creativity. Even though she was eight months pregnant, she worked night and day to make a beautiful room, decorated in a palette of shades of white and cream with pastel colored balloons. Pleased with her efforts, Skylar closed the door to keep the room clean. Excitedly she thought, *The next time I come in here, I'll be holding my baby!*

She was two days past her due date, in early September 1988, when intermittent contractions began on a Sunday evening. After three hours, they subsided. On Monday, she experienced random contractions in a variety of intensities throughout the day. Tuesday was the same and she hoped her doctor's appointment that morning would provide more information.

"John, maybe you should drive me," Skylar suggested, breathless after one of her stronger contractions.

"I can't miss work. Just do that panting thing, and you'll be fine" said John, leaving the apartment without a backward glance.

As she dressed for her appointment, the telephone rang. It was Sable.

"Are you still having contractions? John is driving you to your appointment today, isn't he?" her mother asked.

"Actually, he had to work. I'm going myself." Skylar told her.

"You shouldn't be driving there yourself. I'll drive you," Sable insisted. She drove Skylar to her obstetrician's office and helped her walk in as she was in extreme discomfort.

After the examination, the doctor said, "Well, there's been some progress. You could go into hard labor at any moment. You'll have your baby before the weekend."

That night, contractions began again with increased intensity and regularity. It was barely Wednesday morning when John drove Skylar into the hospital. Her contractions had become stronger and she moaned from the pain.

John started shouting enthusiastically, "Yeah, yeah! Go, go, go!!!" as if he were cheering his favorite sports team. He didn't offer a word of comfort or soothing encouragement.

Once settled in a labor room, the nurse reviewed the Lamaze breathing with Skylar so she would be more comfortable. John put on the headphones he had brought and fell asleep in the chair. She breathed through each contraction on her own as John slept soundly, only waking when the anesthesiologist came in to administer the epidural anesthetic. She couldn't feel her contractions. She also couldn't move her legs, and after a while, they began to painfully cramp. "John, can you please rub my legs? They really hurt." she requested.

"No, I'm too tired. I am going out to get breakfast." He rose from his chair.

"Why don't you get something here to eat?" Skylar suggested.

"I hate hospital food," John declared

"Well, what happens if the baby comes?"

Reassuringly, John said, "You'll be fine." He left the room and returned four hours later.

"Where were you?" Skylar asked frantically when he walked into the room.

Casually, he answered, "I went home and I ate. Then I smoked a big fat doobie."

She shook her head. "Great..so you're stoned. I'm in labor, and you're smoking pot."

Wryly, he replied, "I can handle it. What's goin' on?"

"The doctor came in and broke my water. They had to give me

pitocin because my contractions slowed down. I am finally at seven centimeters," she reported.

"Wow! That's good!" John was overly animated.

Suddenly, the nurses came running into the room. "We're losing the baby's heartbeat!"

They started flipping Skylar from her left side to her right side. The doctor came in to examine her and felt the umbilical cord near the baby's head. Every time she had a contraction, the baby's head was compressing the cord and affecting the heart. Skylar was prepared and rushed into an operating room for an emergency Cesarean section.

John was so high he couldn't move. He put his head in his hands and thought he may faint. The nurses could smell the odor of marijuana and didn't let John go in with his wife.

One nurse put her hand on his shoulder. "Why don't you wait here? Someone will come and get you once the baby is stabilized." She handed him a sterile garment. "Put this on when you are ready."

The nurse waited until the birth was eminent and then allowed John to enter the operating room. The doctor had just grasped the baby. Skylar felt some pulling and suddenly the baby was out.

"It's a boy!" the doctor announced. And then she heard the first cry of her new son, who was healthy and beautiful.

The nurses washed Joshua and wrapped him up snugly in a blanket and placed a little cap on his head. The doctor finished the surgery, and Skylar was wheeled into the recovery room, where John was waiting. The nurse helped her sit up and handed Skylar her son. Joshua was a beautiful baby weighing almost nine pounds. He had dark hair and dark eyes. He had dimples and a tiny cleft in his chin. Skylar looked at Joshua in wonder and amazement. Her medication was beginning to wear off, and the pain was intense. She squirmed uncomfortably.

"Well, it's a good thing you had a C-section. Now you won't be all stretched out." John told her.

Skylar was disgusted by his words and thought, *You're never touching me again.*

She was in the hospital for several days. When John visited, he made her get out of the bed so he could lie there with Joshua on his chest. He seemed so excited about having a son.

When she returned home, she was disappointed when John left her alone all day. Because she was recovering from her surgery, she was not allowed to walk up and down stairs. John brought a cooler into the bedroom filled with ice. He put several cans of soda and sliced turkey in the cooler with a loaf of bread and a knife on the dresser.

"You're all set," he said, "Now I won't have to interrupt my day." He turned to leave.

Skylar stopped him. "John, why can't you spend more time with us?"

"I have to work. Enjoy him now, because when he gets older, he's mine." His voice was tinged with annoyance.

Sensibly, she suggested, "Why can't we both enjoy him?"

Matter-of-factly, he answered, "Because a boy wants to be with his dad. I'm gonna teach him to fish and ski and get lots of pussy."

She couldn't believe what she heard. "That's disgusting! You are not going to tell him anything like that!"

"How else is he going to learn how to get pussy? From his friends?"

She felt sick. "You are his father, and you should teach him how to have respect for women and nothing more."

John could not teach Joshua respect for women because *he* had no respect for women. The narcissist, according to Sam Vaknin, believes firmly that women are out to "hunt" men by genetic predisposition. Narcissists are misogynists. They hold women in contempt and abhor the thought of being really intimate with them. Usually, they choose submissive women for partners whom they disdain for being well below their intellectual level. John selected women who were willing to sit quietly at his side. They would smoke his pot, snort his coke, and go to bed when he was ready. They didn't challenge him or argue. Skylar was having problems with John because she was not typical of the women he had relationships with in the past. She was not below his intellectual level. She had an opinion and a voice. She wanted a husband who was a partner and she continued to fight for that equality.

As Skylar began to recover from her C-section, she would take Joshua for long walks in his carriage daily. She joined an exercise class for babies and new moms. She enrolled in a baby massage class and a class with other moms to discuss first-time mother issues. Later on, the new moms formed a playgroup which met weekly at each mother's home.

When Joshua began eating food, Skylar made the foods herself most of the time. She would buy the meat, fruit, and vegetables, cook everything, and grind it into a fine paste. Skylar had to go to the market every day as John seldom gave her enough money for more than a few items at a time. When she couldn't afford all the ingredients for natural food, she would count her change and buy Joshua a jar of commercial food. Occasionally, John would hand a bag of marijuana to a customer for a wad of cash. He would hand it to Skylar for grocery shopping. It made her feel uncomfortable, as if she were part of an illicit transaction. Sometimes, she would take Joshua in his stroller to her father-in-law's hardware store and ask him for money for food until John told George not to give her any money.

Skylar began to regain her strength after her C-section and increased the lengths of Joshua's walks. He loved it, and it was a good way for Skylar to lose the weight had she gained during her pregnancy. In addition, she went to the gym and exercised in the house.

One evening, John watched Skylar as she was getting undressed for bed. "You're too fat. I think you should stop nursing Joshua so you can lose some weight."

"That won't help. And I am working on it. I work out all the time," she explained.

Arrogantly, he replied, "You need to work harder. I have a reputation, you know.

People are used to seeing me with thin, good looking women."

Several components of narcissism are clearly evident from John's comment. John had an exaggerated sense of self-importance, believing he had a reputation according to the caliber of women he dated. John was preoccupied with fantasies about success, power, or beauty. He believed people would judge him according to the women he dated, the car he drove, and the success of his business. He worked hard to get the admiration that was vital to feed his narcissistic ego.

The months sped by. Skylar loved taking care of Joshua. She recorded every milestone in her journal. Joshua was starting to sit up and move about. He would chortle and laugh when she played with him or when he noticed the springtime flowers erupting during walks in his carriage. Skylar had hoped John would begin spending more time with the family, however he viewed the warm weather as the chance to go out on his boat as much as possible, leaving Skylar and Joshua alone. John went water skiing every night after work and never returned home until nine o'clock or later if he went out for dinner with one of his friends. On the rare nights he came home earlier, he would linger outside for hours, meticulously cleaning his boat.

When she would express her desire to have John home at night with the family, he would scream, "I work hard and I deserve to have some time with my friends."

She asked, "Can't you come home a little early from skiing and be with us?"

He answered snidely, "I didn't buy this boat to sit in the driveway." One night, when he was waxing his boat, Skylar went outside. She was fed up.

"John, leave the boat alone. Come inside."

He refused, "I didn't finish polishing the boat. I need to make sure it's perfect. I can't be seen in a boat that is all spotted with water. It doesn't look make me look good."

She was tired of being ignored. "You care more about this boat than you care about Joshua and me!" The seat of the boat was on the grass as he cleaned the interior. Skylar gave the seat a little kick with her bare foot.

John went ballistic. He screamed, "That's it!" and leaped out of the boat.

She panicked when she heard his voice and saw him heading in her direction. His pale blue eyes were bulging in anger. She had never seen anyone with such fury on their face. Frightened, she turned and began running. She was terrified as she tried to escape his wrath. John ran after her and he was much faster. She had only reached the driveway when he grabbed her and flung her to the ground. She landed on her back, her head hitting the concrete. Before she could move, John was on top of her with his hands around her neck.

He was screaming into her face, "Keep your fuckin' hands off my boat, you goddamn cunt!"

She had been struggling to escape, but when he began choking her, she felt her body go numb. All she could feel was the cold cement and gravel beneath her. He was screaming, and everything else was black and cold and hard. Suddenly, he released his grip and stood up. He climbed back into the boat and calmly began polishing as if the altercation had never happened.

She gingerly stood up and slowly walked into the house. The back of her head hurt. She put her hand under her hair and felt the little pieces of gravel embedded in her scalp. She climbed the staircase and went into the bathroom. She put on the light and looked in the mirror. Her hair was disheveled. Her neck bore the bruises from John's attack. Her face was red and blotchy, presumably from crying, but she was so traumatized from the attack that she didn't remember crying. Her reflection in the mirror jolted her into reality, and she got her camera. She vaguely knew she should photograph her injuries, so she woodenly took a few self-portraits. She was suffering from mild shock and didn't remember the rest of the night.

Skylar later reflected on the incident and asked herself, *Why didn't I call the police that night? Why didn't I leave him?* She couldn't answer because she simply didn't know.

But she wasn't the only victim who remained silent. Eleven years following the evening when Skylar was brutally attacked by her husband,

Dr. Susan Weitzman identified the problem of spousal abuse in her book, *Not To People Like Us*, which documented abuse cases which cut across all economic lines. She referred to this abuse as upscale violence. From an article in *People Magazine* (July 2, 2001), Dr. Weitzman explained upscale violence as abuse that occurs against women who hold at least a bachelor's degree and live in a household where the combined income provides a comfortable lifestyle.

She stated, "There are reputations at stake, both hers and his. Besides, everyone tells her what a great life she has, so she thinks the problem is with her."

Dr. Wietzman believes the major characteristics of the upscale abuser differ from the lower-income abuser. In the lower-income abuser, the causes are often due to unemployment, alcohol, and drugs. In upscale abuse, the men tend to have a sense of entitlement and believe they are above the law. When their insatiable and outrageous demands aren't met, rage erupts. The upscale abuse victim rarely reports her husband to the police, as they believe contacting the police is something only the lower class victims do. If the upscale victims report their husband to the police, oftentimes, the women are not believed.

Dr. Weitzman explains, "The men have the power and leverage to make good on their threats of loss of custody, income and lifestyle. These men have the ability to wage a legal battle with endless and frivolous lawsuits."

The onset of an act of physical abuse seemed to set off a decision for John. He wasn't remorseful; he was angry. *That goddamned Skylar! he thought. Fuck her for makin' me lose control like that! I gotta get her in line. I gotta control that bitch.* So, he began to make rules. The first rule he enforced was controlling her time with her friends. It was easy to do because she had to rely on him to take care of Joshua if she went out.

"Why should I come home after workin' all day and then have to baby-sit? I work hard, and I don't do half the things I wanna do," he tersely responded when Skylar would ask him to watch Joshua. "After work, I wanna go skiin' or fishin' with my friends." he would purposely change his way of speaking when she confronted him, as he knew it annoyed her.

"It's not baby sitting, it's spending time with your son." she explained.

He protested, "I do spend time with him on the weekends."

"We go to the lake. You are with your friends while I watch Joshie. Why can't we take him to the zoo or playground? It would be just the three of us." She pleaded for family time.

"That's borin'," he rebuffed.

Skylar craved a traditional family. When John announced his decision to set up his old fish tank, she happily thought it would be something they could all enjoy. She looked forward to showing Joshua the pretty tropical fish swimming in the tank and pointing out the colors.

John disagreed. "I want aggressive fish! Not stupid tropical fish that do nothin'."

He set up his tank, keeping it sparse of any pretty rocks or plantings. The tank was barren and ugly. Every few days, there would be a dead fish in the tank, partially eaten from an attack by a more aggressive fish. One by one, fish were being killed. Skylar didn't even bring Joshua near the tank because she didn't want him to see parts of a dead fish floating at the top of the tank.

When most of the fish were dead, John announced, "These fish ain't doin' it for me. I need something' more aggressive."

He went into a pet store and asked if they had any piranhas. He was shown to a dark, unlabeled tank.

"Not too many people ask for piranhas," the clerk told him.

"Yeah, this is more like it!" John exclaimed. He bought two fish. To Skylar, they looked like ordinary looking fish, about the size of a silver dollar. He put them in the tank with the remaining fish, which were no match for the piranhas. Within a very short time, the piranhas dominated the tank. All the other fish were dead.

Unlike the former fish, which ate powdered fish food, the piranhas ate live goldfish. John was thoroughly fascinated with the whole feeding process. He loved the chase, and he loved the attack on the goldfish. But in order to enhance the sport, he would starve the piranhas for weeks at a time. When he thought they were ravenous, he would buy a plastic bag filled with goldfish swimming in a small amount of water. He would then assemble some of his friends to witness the slaughter. He would lower the plastic bag of goldfish into the tank with the piranhas. The piranhas had grown and were now about the size of Skylar's palm. The hungry piranhas would start biting through the plastic bag. One could almost see the panic in the little eyes of the goldfish. When the piranhas ripped the plastic bag, the goldfish would scatter throughout the tank. The piranhas would stalk them slowly until they finally drew in for the kill. Then, they would tear the goldfish apart.

John and his gathering of friends would sit in front of the tank and loudly cheer on the piranhas as if they were at a sporting event. Skylar's friend Lori witnessed it, and yelled at John, telling him he was cruel and sick. But he continued to indulge in this activity, whether or not he had his friends there. Eventually, the piranhas died.

Since the fish didn't work out, Skylar thought about getting a dog. She had grown up having a dog and knew Joshua would love it.

John scoffed, "I'm not getting some little dog or a stupid terrier! If we get a dog, I think we should get an aggressive breed."

"I think we should get a breed that is gentle and good with children." Skylar answered.

"Well, I guess we'll never get a dog," he retorted smugly. "Why don't we go visit Tom? Then you can see his dog and all the other animals on the farm."

In the summer, John would take Skylar and Joshua to Maine to visit Tom and Heidie Parsons at their farm. He would leave the house with Tom to play golf or fish. Skylar would take Joshua to the barn to see the dog, kittens, and cows. Heidie would stay inside and continue with her chores as if Skylar wasn't there. Although she tried to befriend Heidie, her friendly overtures were never reciprocated. Heidie would cook and clean while Skylar played with Joshua and Heidie's children.

When Tom's mother was there, she demanded, "Skylar, don't just sit there. The kids can play by themselves. Help Heidie dust the house!"

It didn't make sense to Skylar to drive four hours to Maine to help Heidie clean her house while John was playing golf or fishing with his friend. But she quietly complied and helped Heidie fold the laundry, do the dishes and peel potatoes.

However, time on the farm wasn't all bad. There were times when John would ask Heidie to watch Joshua, put his arm around Skylar, and announce they were going on a romantic ride. This was one of the few times he made her feel special. She had fallen in love with the exciting image he portrayed, and when he turned on the charm, she was again smitten, forgetting everything else – the control, the neglect, and the abuse – just for the opportunity to spend time with the glimmer of the man she thought she had married. She would happily climb on the back of the all-terrain, her arms tightly around John's waist as he drove through the paths in the woods until they reached a wide open field. He would undress and tell her that he wanted to make love there. It seemed as if they were the only people for miles. He was tender, sweet and loving in the tall grass. The sun was high in the sky and the only sounds were the birds and the buzzing bees.

Chapter 7

It was September of 1989, and Skylar planned a party for Joshua's first birthday. The food was plentiful, the cake was beautifully decorated, and the mood was festive. She had decorated the yard with colorful balloons and streamers, and placed the stereo speakers outside, so the music resonated through the backyard.

After the guests left, Skylar was bringing the leftovers inside. John began picking up the crickets, chirping in the grass. He slowly put each cricket into the electric insect repellent light hanging in the yard. The bug zapper was for mosquitoes and other flying insects, yet John found it amusing to put crickets in the unit. He laughed as each cricket touched the electrical current and sizzled. Skylar looked at him in shocked disgust. She quickly picked up Joshua and took him inside the apartment, puzzled at John's cruel behavior that seemed unchangeable.

Skylar focused all her attention on her son whom she loved with an intensity she had never felt before. Every moment was a gift with her cherubic son. It seemed as if the year had flown by since she had Joshua. It was time for his one-year check-up with the pediatrician so she took Joshua for his appointment.

As Dr. Kemble listened to his heart, he frowned. He told Skylar, "I hear a little heart murmur. It's probably nothing, but I'd like you to go to Children's Hospital and have it checked out." He wrote the telephone number for her on a slip of paper.

Skylar felt sick with fear and began to hyperventilate. Dr. Kemble suggested, "Why don't you call your husband on my phone?" He handed her the telephone.

"Joshie may have a heart murmur." sobbed Skylar when John

answered, as she tried to calm her breathing. "Dr. Kemble wants him examined in the hospital. Will you go with us?"

John snapped, "I'm too busy. Calm down and call your mother. She can go with you."

Aware that she needed to handle it on her own, Skylar composed herself enough to drive home. She called Sable, who insisted on accompanying her daughter.

"I can't believe John won't go! What kind of father is he? I'll go with you so you won't be alone. Make the appointment." Sable told her.

Two weeks later, Skylar and Sable took Joshua to Children's Hospital. His examination was quick and non-invasive. The diagnosis was that Joshua had a musical murmur which was not unusual in small children due to the thinness of their chest cavity. As it was benign, Joshua would not need follow-up care. Skylar held her baby close and whispered a prayer of thanks.

As the weather began to get colder it signified the end of water skiing, so season. Skylar assumed she would have her husband home again. But John anticipated the change in weather by setting up a dartboard in his office.

He boasted to Skylar, "It'll be a great place for my friends to hang out, smoke cigars, and play darts." John stayed late at his office several nights each week.

One chilly October evening, Skylar had made spaghetti and meatballs for dinner. She sat in the living room as she waited for the pasta to cook. Joshua toddled to her with his arms raised and she picked him up. He put his head on her shoulder and Skylar noticed his head felt very hot. She took his temperature, and was shocked to see 104 degrees on the thermometer. She gave him some baby Tylenol and put a cool cloth on his forehead. She turned off the stove as she waited to take his temperature again. When there was no change, she called Dr. Kemble, who recommended putting Joshua in a tepid bath. She sat Joshua in the tub with a few inches of water and poured the water on his body. Joshua cried. His skin was still burning. Frightened, Skylar called Dr. Kemble again and he told her to take him to Children's Hospital.

Robin Shaye

She frantically called John at his office. "Joshie is sick! He has a temperature of 104 degrees and I can't get it down! Doctor Kemble told me to take him to Children's Hospital."

"So take him," John said, sounding unconcerned.

"Are you coming with me?" she asked.

"I'm busy. Maybe you can get your mother to go with you."

"Busy playing darts?" Skylar slammed down the phone, disgusted.

She called Sable, who predictably said, "I'll get ready. Pick me up on the way."

When she got to her mother's house, Sable opened the back door of the car, so she could sit with Joshua. "Poor little baby," she cooed as she stroked his hot cheek.

After Joshua was registered in the hospital's emergency area, a doctor examined him thoroughly and ordered several tests. During that time, his temperature began to diminish. The doctor determined that he had a virus and told Skylar she could take him home advising she carefully monitor his temperature and fluid intake. It was almost midnight when Skylar got home. She quietly walked into the bedroom and saw John lying in bed, fast asleep.

When Joshua recovered, Skylar began taking him for walks in the neighborhood. He found a fascination with the vehicles and would point out each one with his tiny finger. He'd play in the falling leaves and screech in delight as he jumped into the large piles on the lawn.

In late October, John informed Skylar he was hired for a job installing locks for one of his more prestigious accounts. "It's their new office building in Miami. The company president is flying me down to Florida and getting me a hotel room. It'll take about three days, but I need extra time to prepare everything. It's a lot of money!"

"What's the name of your hotel?" asked Skylar.

"You don't need the name. I don't want you callin' there and botherin' me. You can page me if you need me," he answered.

He left on a Tuesday morning. That afternoon, he called Skylar and his voice was filled with enthusiasm. "I ran into my friend Paul Redmond on the plane! He's here to pick up his new cigarette boat. He's meeting some friends down here and invited me to come out on the boat! Unbelievable!"

Skylar was doubtful. Yes, it was unbelievable. When she had worked as a flight attendant, she had never run into anyone she remotely knew, either on the plane or at the airport. She suspected meeting his friend, who just happened to be picking up a new boat, was a calculated coincidence.

Later that evening, John called her. "Honey, it was great! His boat is mint!" He lowered his voice. "Everyone here is drinking and picking up women except me. Did I tell you that I love you and if I had to marry you again I would?"

Although still skeptical, she melted at his sweet words and eagerly anticipated his return home. On Sunday, John came home with a check for $25,000.00.

He exclaimed, "I should use this toward a boat like Paul's!"

"What about a house?" Skylar suggested, tentatively.

"Or a house," he said. This time, he didn't mention *prenuptial agreement*.

Skylar knew it would be a race to find the right house before he found the right boat.

She began looking for a house in Sharon, a lovely town southwest of Boston. Many new families originally from Newton moved to Sharon, as it was more affordable.

By November, she had found a newer, brick contemporary colonial. The interior was modern yet cozy. There was plenty of room to grow. She was elated, as the house felt so right. She made another appointment for that Saturday so John could see the house.

On Saturday, they drove to Sharon. John stayed silent as he walked through the house. Skylar was sitting on pins and needles as she waited for his comments. By Sunday morning, John still hadn't shared his opinion on the house. As she made a pot of coffee, she nervously tried to gauge the right moment to ask him about the house. She poured his coffee and handed him the cup, then warily asked, "Do you think you want to put an offer on the house in Sharon?" She held her breath.

John answered, "Maybe."

It was exactly at that minute that the phone rang. It was their real estate broker calling with the news about a house which just came on the market in Medfield. They could see it that day. Medfield was a quaint and quiet town, adjacent to Dover, one of the most affluent towns in Massachusetts.

John and Skylar met the broker in Medfield at noon. The exterior of the house was ordinary, but the interior boasted an unusual floor plan. Beautiful hardwood graced the entrance of the house, which was actually the second floor of the four levels. There was a lovely dining room and cozy kitchen on that level. Off the kitchen were steps leading to the lower level, which consisted of a narrow den, half bathroom, laundry/utility area, and a screened-in porch, which was level to the backyard. The windows looked out over a half acre of land sprinkled with mature trees. The living room spanned the entire third level with a cathedral ceiling, bay window, and fireplace. The fourth floor was where the three bedrooms were located as well as the full bath.

"Yeah, this could work." John commented. Skylar thought the house was pretty, but she was unsure how she would feel about going up and down the steps repeatedly.

On the ride back to Needham, John and Skylar sat quietly immersed in their own thoughts. The decision on which house to choose was the silent question. Skylar was analytical. She liked to think through big decisions and weigh the options. She needed to feel comfortable with her decisions. She was ambivalent about living in Medfield. Although it was closer to Sable, there was no synagogue there. She preferred Sharon as a community, as it was similar to where she was raised.

Logistics were insignificant to John regarding his workday, as his accounts were located in many towns and his larger accounts were neighboring Sharon. His concern was being close to the lake in Natick, where his friends water skied. He had no patience for analyzing or contemplating the best move for the family. He was impulsive.

John broke the silence first. He wanted to make an offer on the Medfield house right away. He warned, "If we move to Sharon, you'll never see me. I need to be able to water ski after work. If we live in Sharon, I'll have to find a place to park my boat in Natick, so I can pick it up after work. Sharon is too far away from the lake."

With that threat, the decision was made. There were little negotiations on the purchase and sale agreement. Everything moved quickly, and they prepared to close on the house in early 1990.

Prior to the moving day, John took Skylar to a furniture store. He had agreed to purchase a new bedroom set when they bought a house. "I want a set with a king-sized bed." He announced to the salesman.

Although it may have appeared to be a romantic purchase, his request was specifically so he could sleep without being touched. The contemporary set was as cold and impersonal as John was when in bed with his wife. Skylar never fell asleep in her husband's arms.

Psychologists would label John as a *somatic narcissist*. According to Sam Vaknin:

> *The somatic narcissist flaunts his sexual conquests, parades his possessions, exhibits his muscles, brags about his physical aesthetics or sexual prowess or exploits. The somatic narcissist uses other people's bodies to masturbate. Sex with him is likely to be impersonal and emotionally alienating. The partner is often treated as an object or sex toy. As he invests as much affection and emotions in inanimate objects as healthier people do in human beings, cuddling or being affectionate to a person is unnatural.*

They began packing in December. By New Year's Eve 1990, Skylar was feeling very tired and nauseated. When she was late for her period, she took a pregnancy test. She was excited when she saw the positive results. She was pregnant. Happily, she went out and bought a card with a picture of a sleeping baby. In the middle of the card, she wrote, *"Guess what??"*

When John returned that evening, she gave him the card. He opened the card and read it. His expression was bland.

Robin Shaye

"You're pregnant? How did that happen?" He paced the room.

"The usual way, I guess." Skylar had been hoping for an enthusiastic response.

"Another baby," he sighed. "Well, I guess it's as good a time as any to have one. But how are you going to help with the move if you're pregnant?"

One evening, a few weeks prior to the move, John wanted to make love and Skylar complied. Suddenly, he became very aggressive and violent. He held her wrists, pinning them down to the bed. He began to brutally move and fiercely pounded into her. Animal noises and grunts emitted from him. It felt like an attack as if he was trying to pummel the baby out of her. She began screaming and struggling.

"John, you're hurting me! Stop!" She couldn't escape and began to shriek and sob. "Get off! Stop!" She twisted her body so she was able to release one hand. She pushed at him and was able to wiggle away, crying. "You're trying to make me lose the baby." he said nothing.

She curled up in a ball, holding her stomach and softly crying. She heard him walk out of the room and down the stairs. A few minutes later, the front door slammed. Alone, she drifted off to sleep.

Skylar was awakened by bright sunlight and the smell of roses.

"Wake up, darling," John crooned.

She opened her eyes and saw four vases, each holding a dozen roses. "Four dozen roses, because we are going to be a family of four." He snuggled close to her. "I love you, honey. I just got carried away. I thought you might like something a little different."

"I don't think this is the time to be experimenting," she whispered, with tears in her eyes. "You hurt me, John."

"I'm sorry. I won't do that again. Unless you want me to." He grinned, but she didn't find it funny. "You wait right there. I bought some muffins and made coffee. I'll give Joshua his bottle this morning, and you can have breakfast in bed."

Sipping the creamy coffee as she ate a warm blueberry muffin provided some comfort. The roses smelled amazing. John sat on the bed and rubbed her neck.

"Please forgive me, honey."

She relaxed and closed her eyes. The thought of her husband violently battering her internally to possibly cause a miscarriage was too horrifying to accept. It was easier for her to erase the appalling episode.

An hour later, he left for work. Skylar began to clean up the kitchen as Joshua was watching television. Suddenly, she felt a sharp pain in her pelvic area. When she caught her breath, she felt a dull, aching cramp in her stomach.

"Mommy will be right back," she told Joshua. She went in the bathroom and saw streaks of blood. Frightened, she called the doctor. He asked, "Did it just start on its own? You weren't doing something strenuous?"

The terrifying vision of the previous night would not easily fade from Skylar's memory. She shook the disturbing thought away.

"No, nothing." she answered. She was scared and embarrassed to tell the doctor what she thought may have precipitated the bleeding.

"Well, sometimes women bleed for no real reason, and sometimes it's the start of a miscarriage. There's really nothing you can do if it is a miscarriage. Just monitor the bleeding and don't do anything strenuous," the doctor answered.

She tried to rest until John came home. She told him about the spotting and what her doctor had advised. "Well, I guess that gets you out of moving." he flatly responded.

The move was scheduled for the beginning February. At Skylar's urging, John asked his mother if they could take her piano to the new house. Nora agreed as Skylar was the only one who played, and unused, the piano had been relegated to their basement. John rented a truck and enlisted the help of a few friends who would move everything into the house. Skylar had carefully packed and labeled everything according to room so his friends would know where to put each box.

Upon arrival at the house, John told his friends, "You don't have to bring the boxes in the house. Just put them in the garage. Skylar is home doing nothing all day. She can move everything in." Then, he took everyone out for Chinese food.

Robin Shaye

After dinner, they returned to their new house and looked at the garage filled with boxes. "You better start on this right away," he told her, "I need to get my boat in here."

During the week, as she was unpacking boxes, the doorbell rang. Standing there was a blond woman, about her age, with a friendly smile.

"Hi, I'm Sally Beaux. Welcome to the neighborhood. I live across the street." She noticed Joshua peeking around the corner. "Oh! What a cutie."

"This is Joshua," Skylar said, picking him up.

"I'm having my first in October," stated Sally.

"Congratulations!" Skylar exclaimed. "I'm having my second in September."

"That's so exciting. Listen, would you like to come over for lunch today?"

She accepted. She took Joshua's hand and crossed the street with Sally. She learned that Sally was a hairstylist with a tiny salon in her basement. "We'll have to do this again." Sally declared as Skylar and Joshua left. It had been a fun visit and the start of a friendship.

Shortly after Skylar met Sally, she got a call from her obstetrician. One of her prenatal tests showed a possibility the baby had Down's syndrome. The nurse asked her if she wanted to have an amniocentesis, and Skylar said, "Yes."

She hung up the phone and immediately called John, crying hysterically, "There may be something wrong with the baby!"

He said, "Skylar, calm down. Tell me what happened."

"One of my tests came back," she sobbed. "There's a possibility the baby has Down's syndrome. The doctor asked me if I wanted to have an amniocentesis."

"A mongoloid? No fuckin' way. You *better* get that test. And if the kid's a retard, I want you to have an abortion," he demanded.

At Skylar's insistence, John accompanied her to the hospital for the amniocentesis. He allowed her to hold his hand during the procedure. Afterward, he drove her home and helped get her settled on the couch with Joshua.

"I'll be home late since I had to waste my time all morning," he said before he turned and left.

Two weeks later, Skylar received a call from the doctor's office. They wanted her to meet with the genetics team at the hospital that afternoon. Due to expediting the meeting, she was frightened and she called John.

"They have the results. They want us there right away."

"No! I had to go to your amnio. I can't waste my time with this shit too! Maybe your mother can go – she's got nothing better to do!"

"My mother is coming here to baby sit Joshie. I told her it was a routine visit so she wouldn't worry. This is your baby too, John. You should be here!"

"Skylar, I am fuckin' warnin' you!" He paused and his voice softened. "This is just routine bullshit. If something was really wrong, they'd tell you over the phone. You can handle this without me. I'll see you tonight." He hung up the phone.

Skylar took a few deep breaths as she prepared to greet Sable. She presented a calm she did not feel when her mother arrived.

"It's just a check-up and I'll be home right afterward." She kissed Joshua and got into her car.

Driving into town, she felt her heart was palpitating and her palms sweating. *It's just routine…just routine…*she repeated to herself. She repeated it like a mantra until she pulled into the garage at the hospital.

Skylar had almost convinced herself the appointment was going to be a quick routine review of her amnio. She was visibly startled when she opened the door of the genetics department and was greeted by a large group of doctors. As she listened to the doctor's voices with escalating fear, she tried to remember all the alarming information. Although the baby didn't have Down's syndrome, there were other concerns. The doctors explained their findings with intricate sheets of genetic results.

"The baby is not going to be mentally or physically handicapped. There could be issues pertaining to growth. We would recommend further testing in order to determine the severity of this baby's diagnosis."

That evening, she cried in fear as she told John everything that the doctors had explained and the myriad of tests recommended.

He merely said, "Well, check it out."

Skylar had to tell Sable, who immediately insisted she would take care of Joshua during the time Skylar went to the hospital for additional testing. After numerous tests were completed, the wait seemed never-ending. She felt as if she were sleepwalking as the days passed agonizingly slowly as she waited for the telephone to ring.

In mid April 1990, the doctor called with the findings. She happily reported that the outcome of the tests administered showed a health baby boy who had a possible problem with his growth. Time would tell with constant follow-up care after birth. The problem was correctable, should his growth be compromised. Skylar wept with happiness.

The fog she had been living in since scheduling the amnio had lifted. She spoke to Sally every day. Sometimes they would go shopping. When she would take Joshua for a walk, Sally would join them. Skylar enjoyed having a friend who lived right across the street. As the weather was getting warmer, Sally introduced her to the other women and their children from the neighborhood. In the afternoon, Joshua and the neighbors' children played in the yard as the group of women would sit and watch the children frolic. It became routine for the mothers to take turns bringing out snacks for the children, usually grapes, cherries, or Popsicles as the warmth of summer permeated the days.

But in the evening, John would yell at Skylar, "What did you do today? Hang out with your friends? I'm slaving away, and you're sitting around! Let's see how long it takes you to blow it with these women." He reminded her of their neighbor in Needham who was her friend. As abruptly as a flick of a switch, the woman broke off all contact with Skylar. She didn't answer the phone, come to the door, or acknowledge Skylar in the street.

John walked away, irritated at the thought of Skylar chatting with her friends while he was at work. His irritation faded as he recalled his spontaneous visit the previous year to Skylar's friend, a German woman, living across the street in Needham. John was determined to stop the visits, the giggling, and company.

"I need to warn you about Skylar, because I like you." he told her. "When you had your miscarriage, Skylar told me she was glad another Nazi wouldn't be coming into this world."

When the woman's face paled, John felt smug he had delivered an effective lie. He smirked as he left the woman's house, and as he relived the satisfying memory. Now, he had three women in Medfield to convince, but he was certain he could handle the task.

John needed to ensure Skylar was isolated from others. It angered him at the unfairness of working while Skylar was having fun with friends. She was cultivating relationships and creating a strong circle of protection with people who lived close. That made him vulnerable to anything she might say, which was an excruciating lack of control. *Maybe she would ruin my image*, he thought. No, he had to break these bonds so she would depend only on him.

The summer days were cooling to tepid nights in August. One evening when John wasn't home, Skylar thought it would be fun for Joshua to visit his father's office and surprise him with his favorite ice cream. They drove to John's office and saw his parked truck.

Skylar told Joshua, "Let's go surprise Daddy."

Happily, Joshua skipped alongside Skylar. He was a month shy of his second birthday, so this was very exciting. They walked inside the brick building and to his office door. Skylar knocked on the door. She waited and then knocked again. Finally, she heard him unlocking the door. He opened it a crack and peeked out.

Joshua yelled, "Sapize, Daddy!" He was dancing around in glee.

John's eyes narrowed. "What are you doing here?" he bluntly asked.

"We came for a visit," Skylar explained cheerily.

"Well, you can't come in now."

Skylar was confused. "Why not?"

"You need to call first before coming to my office." He raised his voice. Joshua started whimpering.

"We brought dessert." Skylar lifted the paper bag which bore the name of the ice cream store. She tried to open the door, but he held the door tightly and wouldn't let her in.

Joshua's whimpers turned to tears. "Sapize, Daddy," he whispered through his tears.

But Joshua's tears had no effect on him. He held the door firmly and glared at Skylar.

Suspiciously, Skylar asked, "John, who is in there with you?"

"No one." John opened his eyes wide.

Skylar recognized his look. He always tried to affect honesty by opening his eyes wide.

"Just let me put the ice cream in your freezer," she said.

John opened the door and stepped into the hall. He grabbed Skylar's shoulders and shoved her away from the door.

"Mommy!" Joshua shrieked. Frightened, he ran to Skylar.

John had already returned to the office door. He went back inside and slammed the door, yelling, "I'm busy working, and I don't want any fuckin' ice cream! Just go home!"

Skylar knelt down to comfort Joshua. "It's okay. Daddy's just really busy. Let's go home. We'll have the ice cream." She took his hand, and they walked out to the car.

Later on, lying in bed and listening to John's snores, Skylar asked herself, *Why didn't I just wait in the car and see who came out of his office?* It was the first time she let a twinge of doubt about John's fidelity creep into her thoughts.

There was little time to ponder as the arrival of the new addition was eminent. From Skylar's journal on Wednesday, August 29, 1990: *Cary Bauers has arrived! He's gorgeous! He weighed seven pounds, one and a half ounces at birth.*

Skylar opted for a scheduled C-section. Although the surgery went very smoothly, Cary was taken to the NICU (Neonatal Intensive Care Unit) because the doctor thought he aspirated some amniotic fluid. John took a Polaroid picture in the NICU and brought it to Skylar's hospital room. He dropped it on her bed and said, "I gotta run."

Skylar stayed in her room alone, waiting for the nurse to bring Cary to her room. She was only offered a glance when he was born, as he was quickly whisked away. She stared at his picture, eagerly anticipating the chance to hold her new little boy. She called the NICU each hour to learn Cary's status. Each time she called, a nurse would tell her, "A little later."

After dinner, she placed another call to Cary's nurse. As she held the phone she saw her friend Lori walking down the hall toward her room. In her ear, she heard the nurse's voice.

"Mrs. Bauers? Unfortunately, Cary is not doing as well as we expected. He's having a lot of trouble breathing right now." Skylar started crying hysterically.

Lori rushed to her. "What's wrong?" She took the phone. "Hello? I'm Skylar's friend. Is something wrong with the baby?"

Skylar calmed herself and motioned for the phone. Lori handed it to her. The nurse explained that Cary's lungs weren't developed, and the doctor was going to put a tube in his lungs, or intubate him, in order to help him breathe.

The nurse said, "The doctor is doing it now. We'll see how he does with that and call you in the morning."

Lori took the phone. "Where's John?" she demanded.

"I don't know. I haven't heard from him all day." Skylar wiped her tears.

She was shaking so hard in fear, that she couldn't hold the phone, so Lori called the house looking for John. There was no answer. Lori tried George and Nora's phone number. There was no answer so Skylar suggested she page him. Thirty minutes later, the phone in Skylar's room rang.

"Yeah, what's going on?" John demanded.

She reported, "Cary is having breathing problems. They are putting a tube in his lungs to help him breathe. Why aren't you here? You knew he was having problems!"

"Skylar, I had to work. I don't know if this tube thing is such a good idea."

"Well, maybe you should have been here so you could discuss that with the doctor. You knew I was having the baby today! You should have arranged your schedule!"

Robin Shaye

"Skylar, calm down. This isn't good for you." His voice became gentle. "What else did they say? When are they putting the tube in?"

"They just did it. They told me they'd call me in the morning and let me know how he's doing," she answered tearfully.

"I can't come in now with Joshua, and my parents can't watch him. I'll come in the morning. Call me later at home if anything happens."

In the morning, the NICU nurse called Skylar. "Since Cary has been intubated, he doesn't have to work as hard to breathe. I'll be monitoring his oxygen levels. Even though he'll sleep most of the time, I would encourage visits."

John had just arrived, and they walked to the NICU to see Cary. He looked peaceful, despite the breathing tube. John stayed briefly, but Skylar watched Cary for an hour. When she got back to her room, she asked the nurse if she could order a breast pump to help get her milk flowing. She wanted to be able to nurse Cary when his tube was removed.

Her days became a routine of pumping her milk, walking to the NICU, watching Cary, and praying. By the third day, Cary's lungs were developed and functioning. He was breathing on his own.

From Skylar's journal on Saturday, September 1, 1990: *Thank you, God. My sweet Cary seems to be out of the woods and on the road to recovery from premature lung development. Yesterday morning, Cary's oxygen was lessened and he was doing better. He was still attached to tubes and monitors, but he looked so cute and was peacefully asleep. I watched him for a few hours during the day. Tonight they are removing the tube! I am waiting to go see him.*

The NICU nurse told Skylar she could nurse Cary when he woke up that evening. She replied, "Call me at any time. I will stay up all night and wait."

The phone rang at one o'clock in the morning. The nurse said, "Hi, Mrs. Bauers. Do you want to nurse Cary?"

Skylar went right to the NICU. She finally got to hold her baby. Cary was small and beautiful. He had no problem nursing. Afterward, she sat in the rocking chair and held him close, giving a thankful silent prayer that her son would be fine.

Skylar was released from the hospital two days later, but Cary needed to remain for observation. She rented a breast pump so she could bring her milk to the hospital.

She wasn't allowed to drive after her C-section surgery, but John said, "Can't you get a friend to drive you to the hospital? I can't take all this time off."

Skylar's friend Marci volunteered to drive her to the hospital and play with Joshua as Skylar nursed Cary. The day before he was discharged, she was able to give Cary his first bath, and Joshua was allowed into the NICU to watch. He was thrilled with his new brother and kept saying, "Cary, Cary." Skylar was overwhelmed with love she as introduced her boys.

Cary was twelve days old when John drove Skylar back to the hospital. He strutted quickly to the nurse's station in the NICU and presented the nurse with an elaborate basket of candy he had purchased.

"How nice!" exclaimed the nurse. "Thank you, Mr…" the nurse hesitated, unsure of who John was until she noticed Skylar tentatively walking behind John, holding Joshua's hand. "Mr. Bauers," finished the nurse, now aware of his identity.

"I just want to thank you for taking care of my son," John exclaimed dramatically. "I was so worried, but you guys did a great job." He chuckled.

Although John had visited Cary in the NICU one time during the entire week he had been there, he was determined to be remembered and receive admiration for rewarding the NICU staff with a generously flamboyant gift and not for his absence.

Chapter 8

Cary was ten days old when he first slept in his own bedroom. Skylar had lovingly decorated the room in shades of blue with little white and blue bunnies. There was a soft blue carpet on the floor and a rocking chair. Cary was a good baby, always happy and alert. He had a beautiful smile that lit up his face. Joshua adored him.

Skylar took the boys for walks through Medfield in their double stroller on the warm early autumn days. She scheduled weekly play dates with a group of Joshua's toddler friends. By later September, it became apparent Skylar's small, two-door car no longer accommodated two growing boys. She felt a sturdier car with four-doors would be safer.

Gauging John's mood, she approached him one evening and suggested, "The boys are too big for my car. I think we would get a good deal if I traded in my Firebird. We could get a new station wagon."

"Skylar, *I* don't have a new car, so I'm not getting you a new car. I have three more years of payments on my boat. You can get a used car, maybe an old Cadillac. We need a luxury car for when we go out with friends. Then I can tell everyone that my wife drives a Cadillac."

Skylar's Firebird was in fabulous condition with very low mileage and she was able to quickly sell her car to a private party. Almost immediately after it was sold, John told her about a Cadillac Sedan de Ville which was for sale in Needham. It was years older than Skylar's car, with triple the miles, but John insisted they see it on Sunday evening.

On Sunday evening, Skylar looked at the worn, silver Cadillac in Needham, and wondered how she would be able to drive a car that large. When she took it on a test drive, she was able to get used to the size of the car and enjoyed its smooth ride.

Skylar asked the owner if the tape deck worked, and John interjected, "Of course it works." He warned her, "You had better take it, or else you won't have a car all week. I can't keep looking for you."

Although it was the only car they saw, John knew he had backed Skylar into a corner. Apprehensively, she agreed, and John made arrangements to purchase the car. The first time she drove the car, she popped a cassette into the tape deck. It didn't work.

There were things at home that did not work either. Periodically, the utilities would get shut off for non-payment of the monthly bill. Because John did not want Skylar to see his business or personal correspondence, including the household bills, he had all his mail sent to a private post office box. But he was lax in remembering to pay the monthly utilities.

It was very frustrating, so Skylar suggested, "Why can't you have the bills sent to the house? If you open a joint checking account, I can take care of those bills."

John refused. "No! I make the money here, and I need to handle it."

She had to ask him for money anytime she needed something. She had no access to cash, a checking account, or a credit card. John had to approve every purchase. When she attended a Tupperware party, as all the women were writing checks for their order, Skylar, embarrassed, had to tell the hostess, "I have to ask my husband."

John had his own credit cards, but he had taken all of Skylar's credit cards and cut them up with a pair of scissors. He told her, "Call the companies and have them send the final bill to my office. I'll pay them." She only had charged maternity clothing and baby items on her cards. However, when the bills were sent to John, he never paid them.

As the cool October weather set in, they renovated their bedroom. They hung new marble-patterned wallpaper in beige with accents in soft pink and green, in their bedroom. John bought a statue of a nude embracing couple and placed it on the bureau. "This is the theme of our room," he declared.

Robin Shaye

Suddenly he began staying home and spending time in the newly decorated bedroom with Skylar. He wanted to make love every night and in the morning before he went to work. On the weekends, when the boys napped, he would grab Skylar and take her into the bedroom.

He would tell her, "Most women would be so jealous if they knew how much I always want you. Their husbands probably barely ever touch them."

This became his mantra…even when he had a girlfriend, a fact of which Skylar was unaware.

But John's loving ways never lasted very long, to either Skylar or his sons.

From Skylar's journal on Wednesday, November 21, 1990: *Cary has bronchiolitis. I brought him to Children's Hospital on Sunday. We were there for almost eight hours. During that time, Cary was given Ventolin inhalation treatments and X-rays. The team of doctors was trying to decide if he needed to be hospitalized or not. They told me that babies who were intubated (on a respirator) at birth were prone to those kind of infections.*

When she got home, John was awake and so was Joshua. He was excited to see his brother and mother. She asked him why he hadn't put Joshua to bed, since it was ten o'clock.

He snapped, "That's your job."

She was too tired to retort and didn't want to say anything in front of Joshua, so she picked him up, brought him into his room, and sung him a lullaby as she tucked him into bed.

Winter began in earnest. It was too cold to take the boys out in their stroller, so Skylar spent most days with them in the playroom, located on a concrete slab on the first level of the house. There was no radiator for heat, but the furnace was right there, which kept the room toasty warm. There were six steps leading up to the door of the kitchen. As long as the door to the kitchen remained closed, the playroom stayed warm. If the door was open, it allowed the heat to drift up throughout the four-level house. Two-year-old Joshua would climb the stairs, and open the door to the kitchen, causing the playroom to become cold.

Skylar asked John to mount a simple hook and eye lock on the den side of the door, so the door would remain shut. She wanted something easy to flip open, especially if she was carrying a load of laundry upstairs. Instead, he installed a keyed lock and hung the key on a nail in the door jamb. He installed similar locks in the doors of every room. He hung the keys on little nails in the door jambs. If Skylar forgot to replace the key, they would get locked in a room. She would have to call John to come home and let them out.

By mid-December 1990, John was no longer at home very much. He would come home after the boys were asleep. One night, he came home and found Skylar in bed reading a magazine.

She smiled and greeted him pleasantly as he entered the bedroom. "Hi, Honey."

John looked at Skylar, expressionless. Woodenly, he stated, "There's nothin' to eat here."

She answered, "There's meatloaf in the refrigerator. I saved some for you."

He sneered, "I hate your meatloaf. You're supposed to make it in a pan so it can soak up all the juices. Yours is too dry. And I won't eat meatloaf unless there's mashed potatoes and gravy. Did you make that too?"

"We don't like it drenched in fat. It's too greasy and unhealthy. But I can make gravy if you want. I have a mix in the cabinet." Skylar reached for her robe and started to get out of bed.

"No! I am not in the mood for your fuckin' meatloaf!"

Skylar, stunned, sat back and looked down at her magazine. She didn't want to start an argument. For a few moments, there was silence.

John was ramped up for a fight and taunted her. "I suppose you went to the gym today?" Skylar didn't answer and he took her silence as an affirmation. "So, you had your fun. I was workin' all day, and you were here havin' fun."

"John, I go to the gym to work out. It's not as if it's fun. I am trying to stay in shape. It's for you too," she explained.

John looked at her nastily. "Well, you're not workin' hard enough. Maybe you should get a tummy tuck."

Skylar wanted to keep the peace so she disregarded John's insult.

But, his tone became sarcastic, clearly trying to get a rise out of her. "I suppose you talked to your mother today?" He approached Skylar, who was trying to ignore him.

She focused on her magazine and deliberately turned a page. Without looking at him, she suggested, "Maybe *you* should come home for dinner once in a while. I don't understand why you care what I make for dinner when you aren't even here."

She wasn't acquiescent and she wasn't backing down, so her comment infuriated him. He grabbed her magazine and threw it on the floor. Before she could react, he grabbed her by both wrists and pulled her to her feet. He could feel her delicate bones, and felt a small thrill when he saw the terror in her eyes. He was in charge, so he took a step closer, and screamed into her face.

"You are a fuckin' bitch! Don't you tell me what to do and when I should or shouldn't be here! You have no right to go to the gym or be on the phone when I have to work. You're nothin' but a little cunt!"

Suddenly, his pager, which was attached to his belt loop, began beeping. He released her wrists by hurling her back on the bed. As Skylar fell, her head slammed back into the teak headboard with a loud thud. John didn't look at her. He grabbed his pager from his belt, looked at it, and walked out of the room to make a phone call in private.

Stunned, Skylar felt the back of her head. It was tender but not bleeding. She sat up gingerly, gently rubbing her head.

Minutes later, John yelled upstairs, "I need to do an emergency job!" She heard the door slam. She knew there would be no more fighting that night.

She was often numb after enduring a violent argument with John. Still in her robe, she woodenly made her morning coffee and drank it, staring into space. She thought about taking Joshua to the story hour at the library. He enjoyed listening to the stories as Cary slept in his infant seat. She would be able to have some down time and clear her head. Since she was particularly stressed, she thought this excursion was an especially good idea. She dressed the boys and put them in the car. Joshua was bouncing in his seat with excitement. The library was a short drive, and they arrived in plenty of time. She found a seat for Joshua, and the story hour began. As he sat enthralled and listened to the story, Skylar walked through the library with Cary dozing in his little seat.

Two large flyers caught her eye. The words **DOMESTIC ABUSE** in bold letters screamed out to her, on the first flyer. As she read, she learned when most people think of abuse, they have visions of a man slapping or beating his wife. She learned that domestic abuse was also a pattern of controlling behavior. There were twelve questions pertaining to the treatment of a partner. The questions began with, *"Has your partner ever..?"* Criticism, hitting, controlling, jealousy, denying access to finances, humiliation, sexual abuse, and manipulation, were all on the list of components of domestic abusive behaviors. Each component of abuse was arranged on a large pie chart, title Wheel of Power and Control. Skylar shook her head in disbelief when she realized she could answer each question in the affirmative. As she continued to read, she learned that men who abuse liked to feel as if they were in charge of their relationship. They would isolate their partner in order to increase their dependence on their abuser. The most frightening information was how the abuser would threaten their victim: "If you leave me, I will take the children away from you."

The second flyer showed a diagram called the Cycle of Domestic Abuse. Skylar was vaguely aware of experiencing a cycle although she couldn't give it a name. Clearly explained below the diagram were three phases in the Cycle of Domestic Abuse: the Escalation Phase, the Acute Battering Phase, and the Honeymoon Phase. The description was exactly what she was experiencing in her marriage to John. There would be very abusive times with him that would abruptly stop. Following that, their relationship would be warm and loving. And at some point during that stage, Skylar would anticipate some explosion.

She took both flyers as this was an epiphany for her. She finally saw everything so clearly. She realized that she was an abused woman. It wasn't until she saw it on paper that she recognized the problems in her marriage were far more acute than she knew. Now she could comprehend that not only was she a victim, but her children were victims as well.

Chapter 9

The components of domestic abuse that Skylar saw on the flyer in the library comprised an accurate description of what was occurring in her marriage. It was undeniable, yet she was afraid to take an offensive stance with John. Her sons were everything to her. If she challenged him or if she left him, what would become of them? Would he help support them? He barely supported them as it was. It definitely fitted the description of the monetary or financial abuse she had read about at the library. John controlled all the resources, so Skylar was essentially helpless, as she always had to ask for money. Even getting grocery money was problematic.

When Skylar would ask, "Can I have some money for groceries? I really need to go shopping today," John would slink to where she was standing and reply, "Well, maybe if you blow me, I can come up with a few dollars."

One time, he said, "You know, I'd give you grocery money all the time if you'd do one thing for me." He paused.

Skylar anticipated he was going to ask for something like keeping up with the household laundry, her least favorite task. She looked at him and suggested, "You want me to keep a better handle on the laundry, right?"

He chuckled, "Well, yeah – that would be great. But that's not what I want."

"Oh. Well, what do you want?" she timidly asked.

"I would like to invite another girl into our bed," John answered.

"What?!" she was shocked and disgusted. "You want to have sex with some other woman? Here? In our bed?!"

"Well, she'd be having sex with you too." He explained. He felt it was something perfectly logical to ask his wife.

Skylar, trying to keep her voice even, replied disdainfully, "I'm really not into that."

"But it would make me so happy," he wheedled.

"No, John. This is not what married people do. Forget it." She left the room. She found his request grotesque. She made it clear to him that was not an option.

But his request didn't just vanish from her mind. She felt disgusted. She was miserable in her marriage. All she ever wanted was a traditional family lifestyle with a husband who wanted to be home for dinner. She wanted a husband who loved his wife and children more than his friends and possessions. It wasn't merely her opinion, as John would freely admit to her that he came first. He would proclaim, "I am king! There can only be one boss and that's me." Skylar didn't want a boss; she didn't want a dictator. She wanted a partner. And now she wanted a divorce.

She found an attorney in the telephone book and made an appointment. She went to his office with four-month-old Cary, snug in his baby seat. It was a short meeting. Skylar told the attorney she wanted a divorce and he told her he required a retainer of seven thousand dollars. Skylar didn't even have seven dollars, so the meeting was over. She picked up Cary's baby seat, got into her car, and drove home. She was stuck.

John's control had escalated. He wouldn't let her out of the house for anything other than what he felt was necessary. He demanded grocery receipts from her, and he would check the receipts against the purchases. He would insist that she give him the change, even if it was just pennies, jeering, "I make the money here. You do nothin'." He would scrutinize their telephone bills. He would berate her for the amount of time she was on the telephone. If she did an errand, he would time her. He monitored and tried to control every aspect of her life including what she read, how she did her hair, who her friends were, and what she wore.

His insults were constant. He told Skylar she was stupid for reading celebrity gossip magazines, which she found relaxed her after a busy day with the boys. He mocked her for not selecting reading materials that were educational.

He criticized her hairstyle. He had his own personal template for female beauty. Face, brains, personality - none of that mattered to him. He only found beauty in women who were skinny with long, straight hair. When Skylar had her hair styled, John called her ugly.

He had more complaints than compliments. He would complain she wasn't nice to his friends. Although she was cordial, his friends ignored her and didn't try to talk to her. Their conversations focused on times in the past, before Skylar. Conversely, John complained she was too friendly with the neighbors. He called her friends "boring". Even though her friends they were polite and tried to engage John in conversation, he remained distant and superficial.

Since John controlled the finances, he wouldn't give her money for clothes. Skylar had to wear the stretchy polyester outfits she had worn during her pregnancies, adding a belt so they looked less like maternity clothes.

When they were invited to his friend's wedding in February 1991, Skylar declared, "The invitation says black tie. Should I wear my maternity clothes? What would that do for your reputation?" sarcastically reminding him of the time he boasted of his reputation of being seen only with "thin, good-looking women."

Reluctantly, he handed her a credit card and ordered, "Don't spend more than one hundred dollars."

Skylar drove to the store, hoping to find a pretty dress that would hide the last little bit of weight from her last pregnancy. She selected and tried on many dresses with growing frustration. She reached for the last dress, a gorgeous black velvet sheath. Optimistically, she donned the dress, zipped the back and looked in the mirror. The color complimented her fair skin and fit her body in a way that hid her tummy and flattered her figure. Upon looking at the tag, Skylar saw that it cost $175.00. But it was the best one she could find. She purchased the dress and modeled it for John when she got home.

He said, "You did good. That's a nice dress. Yeah, I like it." Skylar smiled at his approval and did a turn on her toes. "But I'm not buying you a dress for $175.00. You better take the tags off, and don't spill food on the dress. After the wedding, you can return it." Skylar slowly lowered her heels. "Don't look at me like that. You heard me. Save those tags!"

The day of the wedding, Skylar polished her nails a deep red. She washed and curled her hair. She carefully applied her make-up, creating smoky, sultry eyes, and glossy lips. She brushed out her curls, and her hair fell in soft waves down her back. She pinned one side back with a jeweled barrette and slipped on sheer black pantyhose and stiletto heels. Then she asked John to help her with the zipper of the dress.

When she turned around, he said, "Wow! Maybe we shouldn't go out, huh?" He approached her. "How about a quickie?"

Skylar replied coyly, "Why don't we wait until we get home? It will give us something to look forward to when we get home." She knew if she complied with his sexual advances, he would ignore her all night. If she didn't, he would be affectionate and attentive.

The wedding was held in an elegant restaurant. On the way to the room, Skylar was stopped by a couple who complimented her and told John, "You have a beautiful wife."

He replied, "Yes, I do." He gave Skylar a little squeeze. He was uncommonly attentive and she was elated. He slipped his arm around her waist as they entered the reception hall, and found their seats. The wedding was beautiful, the food was excellent and the music was energizing. They were caught up in the festivities and as they slowly danced the last dance near the glass windows overlooking the city, John tenderly kissed Skylar.

At home, Skylar was glowing from the evening. John had been so sweet and loving. She quickly went to check on the boys before going into the bedroom. John was already in bed, waiting for her. As she turned to put her shoes in the closet, he said, "Skylar?"

"Yes," she said with a smile.

"Make sure you hang up the dress so it doesn't get wrinkled, and put the tags back on. You can return it tomorrow."

When she got into bed, she woodenly submitted to his embrace. She looked at the ceiling and thought, *He's never going to change.*

Although John had the ability to show affection, it was limited. Once he got what he wanted, he was cold, distant and insulting. He was critical of everything, even Skylar's choice of music. He deemed her musical selections as stupid. He forbade her from playing the genres of music she preferred when he was home.

He would state, "I know so much more about music. I can't believe you actually have a degree in music when I have such better taste."

Ironically, they did agree on one band. When John bought a CD by the Swedish group ABBA, Skylar was thrilled and listened to it often.

After a few weeks, he declared, "I wish I never bought that CD. I hate ABBA!"

Skylar did not play the CD when he was home.

Later that week, she invited Sally and her husband for dinner. After dinner, John said, "I'm gonna put on some music. What do you want to hear?"

Skylar whispered to Sally, who laughed and asked for ABBA.

John said, "I hate that fucking CD. We're not listening to it. In fact..." He walked to the cabinet where the CDs were kept and he removed the ABBA CD from its case.

Skylar yelled, "No, John! I like to listen to that!"

"Too bad!" He snapped the CD in half. "I bought it, I paid for it, and I can break it if I want." he sneered.

Skylar was painfully embarrassed. She thought John would find it funny when Sally asked for ABBA, but instead she was humiliated. Nevertheless, she pasted on a cheerful face.

Days later, John became sweet as the honeymoon phase of the abuse cycle began. He displayed kindness toward Skylar instead of disgracing her. Although every time she remembered him breaking the CD, she felt the blush of shame within her gut but it was so much easier for her to just to let the incident go when he turned on the charm.

He became amorous, spending as much time in bed with her as possible, always reminding her, "Most women would be so jealous if they knew how much I always want you."

The dull skies of winter were brightening as the sun began to shine brightly, welcoming springtime in New England. In May of 1991, Skylar began feeling uncommonly tired. She was late for her period. She asked John to buy a pregnancy test. On Mother's Day morning, she brought the test into the bathroom and watched the little stick turn pink.

John looked in, "Well, what are the results?" She handed him the pink stick and the box. He looked at the stick and read the box. "You're pregnant?" he asked in disbelief. "Three kids," he said. "We can't have three kids. You're gonna have to get an abortion." He walked out of the room.

Skylar lay down on the bed and began to hyperventilate. Her heart raced. He can't make me! she screamed in her head. She forced herself to breathe evenly and calmed herself. She knew there had to be a way to change his mind. She felt this was God's plan. Cary was only nine months old. Having another baby so soon didn't seem strange to her as she had friends with siblings even closer in age. After having two babies, Skylar already had an image in her mind of her baby's sweet face. She was determined not to let John force her into an abortion. She thought about what she was going to do. An idea formed in her mind on how to convince him they were having this baby. She felt certain her plan would work. She got up, went into the bathroom, splashed some cold water on her face, and fixed her hair. Then she walked downstairs, prepared to fight for her baby.

They were meeting Sable to take her for a Mother's Day brunch. They were going to the Sheraton Hotel in Needham. They always served a lovely brunch, and being in Needham, it was a popular place for many people who knew the Bauers, either through work or preschool. As they walked into the restaurant, John greeted a few of his clients who were there enjoying brunch. Skylar put on a pleasant face when she saw her mother. Sable reached for Cary, who was in Skylar's arms and she bent down and gave Joshua a kiss.

"How are my boys?" she asked. Sable did not yet know that she was going to play an important part in changing John's mind.

Throughout the meal, John was sullen and silent. Skylar acted cheerful and cut up little pieces of fruit and omelet for Cary. She kept a smile on her face and waited patiently for the right moment.

"I need to go pee pee, Mommy." exclaimed Joshua. Skylar looked at John.

"I'll take him." he said, not wishing to be alone with Sable, having to make small talk. He got up, taking Joshua by the hand and they walked down the hallway to the bathroom.

Sable asked, "What's wrong with him? He's barely said two words."

Skylar said, "He's speechless because I'm pregnant."

Sable's face lit up. "Another baby! Why didn't you say something earlier?"

Skylar motioned to her to be quiet and glanced back in the direction of the restrooms. No one was there. She lowered her voice and said, "John told me he wants me to have an abortion. When he comes back, give him a big Congratulations. Make sure you say it loud enough for these people to hear. He won't make me do it once other people, especially some of his clients, learn that I'm pregnant."

"What?! He wants you to have an abortion?!" Sable was shocked. "Is he crazy?"

"Mom, just say it. And make sure it's loud. The people sitting over there are his customers." Skylar nodded in the direction of a nearby table.

When John returned with Joshua, Skylar kicked her mother's leg under the table.

Sable loudly declared, "John, I heard about the good news! You must be so happy that Skylar's going to have another baby!"

John's eyes narrowed. Skylar shrugged and surreptitiously glanced around. She saw smiling faces. John noticed it too and his face broke into a grin that Skylar knew he had to force.

"Yep! Another kid! I was surprised myself."

The waitress had returned to clear the plates and had overheard the news.

"Congratulations on the new baby!" she said, smiling at them.

Joshua looked at Skylar and asked, "Where's the new baby, Mommy?"

"It's in Mommy's tummy, sweetheart!" she answered him, broadly smiling back.

John reluctantly resigned himself to another baby. He kept taunting Skylar daily, by telling her, "It's another boy." He would whistle the catchy tune from the theme song of the 1960s television show, "My Three Sons." Although she never said it, John knew Skylar was hoping this time for a baby girl. She ignored his taunts and nasty comments.

Despite his cruelty, he still made overt sexual overtures toward Skylar. Remembering how forceful he was when he learned she was pregnant with Cary, Skylar would make excuses. Finally, he demanded she comply.

He told her, "That's it. If you don't take care of me, I'll find someone else who will! Not only that, you can forget about getting any grocery money!"

"Only if you're very careful. Please don't hurt me." she whispered.

"Skylar, I am not going to hurt you." he answered.

Although he kept his word, she found sex was very painful during her pregnancy. John insisted on compliance and continued the threats, even though he knew she was experiencing a lot of discomfort and would grit her teeth until he was finished. It hadn't been like that in her pregnancies with the boys. In addition, as the pregnancy progressed, she was experiencing severe nausea throughout the entire day.

From Skylar's journal on Wednesday, June 12, 1991: *Felt extraordinarily sick today. Can't remember feeling this sick with Joshie or Cary. Even so, I took the boys to the little playground in Westwood. I put Cary in an infant swing and Joshie beside him in a toddler swing. I gave Cary a push, and he immediately burst into hysterical laughter. He loved it. It was really cute. Joshie wanted a big push, but suddenly I felt really sick and dizzy, so we packed it in a little earlier than I usual. I began to drive away and Joshie said, "I had fun, Mommy."*

Her obstetrician suggested she schedule an amniocentesis as a precaution because her pregnancy with Cary had been problematic. He would have the results in two weeks.

Although Skylar still experienced severe nausea and dizziness, she wanted to make sure she provided Joshua and Cary with special outings. She adored her sons and loved the smiles on their faces as she took them on day trips that summer, their favorite being an excursion into Boston's well-known Public Garden, so they could ride the Swan Boats and see the duckling statues from their favorite book, *Make Way for Ducklings* by Robert McCloskey.

One evening, she told John about how much fun the boys were having on their outings. She described Joshua's face and reaction to watching his very first movie, they had seen earlier that day, as Sable watched Cary.

Instead of enjoying her reviews, John retorted, "Look, that's *your* thing. You take them to the movies and the zoo and the dog shows – whatever stupid activities you do. Enjoy it now, because when they're older, they're mine." He found no joy in hearing her anecdotes, and his comments left Skylar painfully disappointed and confused. She attributed his reaction to stress as they waited for the results from her amniocentesis.

In August, Skylar received a telephone call from a nurse in her obstetrician's office. "Mrs. Bauers, we have the result of your amniocentesis. Everything is fine, and the baby is healthy." The nursed paused. "I also have the sex of the baby, if you want to know."

"Yes," Skylar answered in anticipation.

"You're having a girl. Have a great day!" The nurse said.

Skylar burst into happy tears as she immediately called John. "I just heard from the doctor. He told me everything is fine, and we are having a girl!"

Surprised, he replied, "A girl? Hmmm. Okay. Do you still like the name Jillian?" He was referring to the first girl's name they had selected when Skylar was pregnant with Joshua.

"Yes, I do." she agreed, joyfully. She hung up the phone in blissful happiness.

The summer was ending. Skylar was feeling better and she concentrated on preparing Joshua for preschool. She suggested to John that they both bring him for his first day of school in September 1991 but John said he was too busy. So on the first day of school, Skylar brought him alone. As they walked into the classroom, the teacher was taking pictures of the parents with their child to put on a classroom display of *Mommy, Daddy and Me on My First Day of School*. Skylar smiled brightly as the teacher took a Polaroid picture of Joshua sitting on her lap but she felt heartsick thinking how Joshua's picture would be the only one without a daddy.

As the parents were leaving the class, Joshua hugged her tightly. "See you later, alligator," he said.

From Skylar's journal on Friday, September 27, 1991: *Something strange happened this morning when I brought Joshie to preschool. He began clinging to me, and said, "I want you to stay." He cried and screamed. The teacher was surprised to see him so upset. She said, "It's odd, because he didn't do this for the first three weeks of school. Maybe it's a delayed reaction." I reassured him I would be back later and he calmed down. When I picked him up, he was very happy to see me and told me he had a good time. I think perhaps the reason Joshie was so clingy was because he's getting very attached to me as John is not here very much at all. I'm afraid he's beginning to feel abandoned by one parent and doesn't want to lose the other one.*

Joshua's anxiety also could have been caused by what he was hearing at home. John would have loud altercations with Skylar. Trying to take back control, she would throw out the grocery receipts and the itemized pages of the phone bill. She despised the monthly interrogations.

"Where's the rest of this bill?" he demanded, wanting to inventory Skylar's calls.

"I guess I threw it out," she replied vaguely.

"You fuckin' little cunt! You did it purposely! You don't want me to know how long you are talkin' to your fuckin' mother!" He dumped the garbage on the kitchen floor and began going through the trash, trying to find the itemized portion of the bill. "I told you not to talk to your mother!" He looked at the floor covered in garbage and trash. Then he looked at Skylar in disgust. "Clean this shit up." He took his jacket and left, slamming the door behind him.

He wanted to cut Skylar's ties with her main source of support. He would force her to end her telephone calls. She devised a simple code for her talks to Sable. If John came home during their conversation, Skylar would whisper, "He's home," and immediately hang up. Sable expected the abrupt endings or the quick whispered calls if John was in the house. This rule only applied to Skylar because John kept his own calls on his recently acquired cell phone private.

If Skylar was nearby when he received a call, he would purposely walk away so she couldn't hear his conversation. If she asked who had called, he would retort, "It's none of your business." He was always extremely secretive, but sometimes he would reveal tiny hints about the origins of his private calls. He would tell her detailed stories of the women he would see during the day.

"You should see how many women approach me every day!" he declared. He bragged about how women would invite him into their house or office during the day. He described notes left on his truck with telephone numbers. He boasted about one woman who bluntly told him, "Anytime you want me, you can have me."

The stories of his daily encounters certainly didn't enhance her opinion of John. She felt sick listening to the incessant reminders from John announcing, "I love women." It oddly reminded her of the line, "the lady doth protest too much," from William Shakespeare's *Hamlet*. Skylar didn't believe John loved women. He was losing his credibility with his announcements because he would declare it too often, too strongly, and too dramatically.

Narcissists cannot maintain a stable, long-termed, committed, and healthy relationship. John, as a somatic narcissist, relied on his body and sexuality as sources of narcissistic supply.

In contrast, Sam Vaknin states: *"The cerebral narcissist uses his intelligence and his professional achievements to obtain the same. Narcissists are either predominantly cerebral or overwhelmingly somatic. In other words, they either generate their narcissistic supply by using their bodies or by flaunting their minds."*

John had an attitude of arrogance and a pelvic-thrust swagger. He would smile and undress women with a blue-eyed stare. He was proud of his sexual conquests and liked to brag about his sexual prowess. Vaknin states: *"Both types, somatic and cerebral, are autoerotic; psychosexually in love with themselves, with their bodies, or with their brains."*

Despite his vanity, John was lax in his hygiene. Although he showered every morning, he would wear the same unwashed underwear and jeans for days. He never washed his hands after going to the bathroom, which disgusted Skylar.

When she would admonish him for not washing his hands after a bowel movement, he would say, "Skylar, I use toilet paper to wipe, not my hand."

He never cleaned his ears because he didn't like anything in his ears, so his ear canals were yellow with wax. He never brushed his teeth before going to bed. Even on the nights he would smoke a cigar, he wouldn't brush his teeth because he complained, "I hate the taste and feel of toothpaste in my mouth."

Anytime she would confront him about his personal hygiene, he would have an explanation justifying his actions. It was some manifestation of John's antisocial characteristics as well as some of his need for control. He was the one who needed to make all the decisions.

Because of the narcissist's grandiose self-image, he often thinks of himself as almost "God-like." According to Dr. Maria Hsia Chang, Professor of Political Science at the University of Nevada: *"Gods are not subject to the morality that governs lesser beings: <u>rules don't apply to me</u>." The narcissist refuses to subscribe to society's moral rules and ethical standards. Instead, morality is subjective: 'Nobody can judge me.'"*

On Thanksgiving morning in 1991, John announced he wasn't going to Sable's for dinner because he was sick. He stayed in bed all day, complaining of nausea, until Tom Parsons called, asking if he could visit. John got out of bed, showered, and dressed. When Tom arrived, John led him to the back porch and lit a joint. After Tom left, Skylar asked John if he was joining them for dinner.

He said, "No, I am not well enough to deal with your mother and her fuckin' dogs."

Sickened, Skylar took the boys for Thanksgiving dinner without him. When she got home, she brought the boys upstairs and tucked them in their beds. After kissing them goodnight, she went downstairs to the kitchen to get a glass of water.

John approached her in the kitchen. "Did you bring me anythin'?"

She didn't look at him. "No, you told me you were nauseated."

John, his voice rising ever so slightly said, "Well, I was gonna feel better eventually."

She felt her heart lurch, anticipating where this was heading, but she answered, "I thought you were feeling better when Tom was here."

"No, I wasn't feelin' better." he sneered.

She didn't want to play his game. He feigned his illness to avoid a family obligation. She was hurt and angry, but couldn't help asking, "Then why did you smoke a joint with Tom, if you're so sick?"

He grabbed her by both arms and shoved her up against the wall. He screamed in her face, "You are a selfish bitch!!"

Skylar heard Joshua's voice, "Daddy, you don't do that!"

Neither had heard him patter downstairs into the kitchen. Skylar turned toward her son. Enraged, John shoved Skylar again, this time harder, so her head banged against the wall. Joshua burst into tears causing John to take his focus away from Skylar, who was able to slide out of his grasp. She ran to her son and picked him up and Joshua wrapped his arms tightly around her neck.

Skylar locked eyes with John, who glared at her. With his voice drenched in sarcasm, he announced, "Looks like I'm gonna have to spend our grocery money. I'm goin' out to eat."

Skylar turned away in disgust as John left. She kissed her little boy's head, soothing him tenderly before carrying him upstairs and tucking him into bed. It wasn't until she got back into her room that her heart stopped palpitating. She began to feel a bruise on the back of her head. She breathed deeply and stretched out in her bed. As she closed her eyes, her hands went to her rounded belly. Her daughter would be here in a little over a month. *Maybe that will mellow him,* she thought as she drifted off to sleep.

In the morning, Skylar awoke to find John in the kitchen making breakfast and cutting up fresh strawberries. The fury in his eyes from the previous night was gone. As she put Cary in his high chair, he approached her, "You don't know how lucky you are. Most husbands won't ever make breakfast. Most husbands won't even have sex with their wives. If I was cheating on you, I wouldn't want you all the time. And the only thing I ask is just one time to have another woman join us."

Skylar was repulsed. "Read my lips John. Not interested." she reiterated flippantly.

She remembered the Wheel of Power and Control flyer she took from the library. One piece of the pie chart was called "Sexual Abuse." John had attempted to abuse her sexually by his demands for sex in trade for grocery money, his physical assaults during sex, and his attempt to deny her reproductive freedom. After his request to invite another woman into their bedroom, Skylar was frightened of the man she had married, and she was terrified that this man was also the father of her children.

Chapter 10

Four weeks prior to Skylar's due date, the boys began sharing a bedroom. They enjoyed being together. In the smaller bedroom, a new rose colored carpet was installed in addition to the white furniture Joshua has used, creating a dainty and feminine room, perfect for a baby girl.

From Skylar's journal on January 7, 1992: *Jillian is here! She's beautiful!*

John admired his new daughter from afar and declared, "She's never going out on a date."

From Skylar's journal on February 11, 1992: *John has been working a lot. He's not here very much. Joshie really misses him, and it's hard to explain his absences. One night, John was actually here for dinner, and Joshie got so excited and exclaimed, "We're all here!"*

When Jillian was four weeks old, John began his demands for sex, ignoring the doctor's order to abstain for eight weeks. But, he was relentless, so Skylar submitted to the pain, knowing it would be brief. She still held onto the idealistic hopes of having a loving marriage, so the pain was almost worth holding her husband in her arms and pretending it was special. However, she couldn't pretend away his continuous campaign to bring another woman into their bedroom.

"But honey, you'll like it. We'll both be there making you feel good."

It was ironic he used her enjoyment in his reasoning as he was a selfish lover. He cared only about his pleasure. John didn't look at intimacy as a way of providing pleasure; like everything, it was a competition. If John couldn't win, then there could only be a tie. His logic to

Skylar was, "If I can only have one orgasm, then you should only have one orgasm."

Selfishly, he refused to take any responsibility for birth control. Skylar was unable to take birth control pills. She had allergic reactions to the diaphragm and she was squeamish at the idea of a foreign object, placed in her body. So, she suggested John follow his friends who got a vasectomy.

He balked at her suggestion and said, "I guess we'll just take our chances."

Skylar loved having three children. She found the transition from two children to three fairly easy. It was simple for her; instead of changing one diaper, she was changing two. Her usual routine hadn't changed much. Jillian had the same temperament as Joshua and Cary. She was a good baby, always smiling and always content. Joshua adored her and Cary, still too young to understand how she got there, tolerated her. Skylar was the sole caregiver from morning until evening. When Joshua got home from preschool, she would play games, build blocks or put on music for the boys, keeping Jillian close by. She would eat dinner with the boys, bathe them, and read stories before bedtime. After that, she'd nurse Jillian, and tuck her into her crib. Then she would get into bed and relax. John usually returned home by ten o'clock, but sometimes he wouldn't return until midnight.

1992 was a cold winter. Because Jillian was an infant, Skylar didn't go out much except for daily transporting Joshua to school, a weekly playgroup for Cary, or sporadic trips to the market. She tried to be cautious to avoid exposing the children to illnesses. Ironically, she became ill with strep throat in February. Sable came to the house to take care of the children. The doctor advised Skylar to stay away from Jillian because she was contagious. That meant she had to wean Jillian from breast milk. Reluctantly, she stopped nursing.

When she recovered, John offered to take her to Florida in March. They would stay at Paul's house. His friend Paul Redmond, had just purchased a new cigarette boat, and John was as excited as a little boy in anticipation of a trip to Florida. Skylar was pleasantly surprised at the thought of a trip to Florida but she was apprehensive about going away with John because it almost felt as if she would be going away with a stranger. He was barely home and their conversation was limited to the children. It had been a long time since Skylar felt as if she and John were a couple. She was also hesitant to leave the children but John assured her he had found a competent babysitter named Maree Labarini, who worked as a maintenance secretary for one of his accounts. Maree was a single mother with two daughters. John assured Skylar that she was an excellent sitter with solid credentials, so Skylar arranged a meeting.

Maree Labarini was painfully thin with mousy brown hair and acne scarred skin. She was very withdrawn, never maintained eye contact and sat fiddling with her hair or clothing. She spoke quietly of her experience and love of children. After the meeting, Skylar checked all the references Maree had provided. Skylar spoke to several women who used Maree as a sitter. She was told Maree was a responsible woman who used sound judgment. She just related to children better than to adults. Satisfied, Skylar agreed that she could baby-sit when she and John were in Florida. She made the job easier for Maree by preparing meals for the boys, which she left in the freezer. Jillian just had formula and baby cereal, which was easy for Maree to prepare.

On the day they were leaving, Skylar found it excruciatingly difficult to say goodbye to her children. Tearfully, she kissed them all and left for the airport. Excitement began to set in as they boarded the airplane bound for Florida. When they were seated, she turned to John, but he had put on his headphones, cutting himself off from everything except his music. She sighed and opened a magazine.

But once they arrived at Paul's house, his demeanor changed. He was very affectionate toward her. He was attentive to her needs and so amorous, that Paul commented they behaved like newlyweds. Their relationship was more loving during the entire vacation than it had ever been. The glow of this new-found love was still with her when they returned home.

Robin Shaye

Apparently John felt it as well because, she would hear him talking on the phone to his friends, telling them, "The trip was so good for our marriage. We fell in love again."

A month after their return, John approached Skylar. "Honey, have I told you lately how much I love you, and if I had to do it all over, I'd still marry you?" He snuggled closer. "I have to tell you something. Paul wants me to change the locks in his house. He just broke up with his fiancée, and she still has keys. He's going to fly me down there."

"Why can't he get someone in Florida to change the locks?" she was puzzled.

"Because I need to change his locks up here, too. I can install the same lock down there, and he'll only need one key for both houses. He's gonna pay me double, and I get a trip to Florida too!" He looked earnestly at her, opening his eyes wide. He was going to go anyway and she didn't have the energy to argue.

The simple lock job was merely an excuse to go back to Florida. He wanted to spend time on Paul's boat and go to the waterfront bars. Set right on the dock on the intra-coastal was a bar which was considered the hot spot of Naples. It drew an abundance of women. This time, he was there without his wife and took advantage of that to replenish his narcissist supply. Driving up in Paul's boat was enough to draw the attention of the women at the bar. After that, it was easy for John to charm the woman of his choosing. He didn't hide the fact he was married. It made it easier for him to maintain control. Upon his return from Florida, John was in the throes of a long-distance relationship. He was absent from the home at night in the privacy of his office on the phone with his new paramour.

As the spring brought flocks of tourists into Boston to shop in the upscale stores on Newbury Street, John began to frequent the stores as well. He was spending money exorbitantly and so often, that the sales people would greet him by name. He reasoned his purchases were for Skylar.

"I'm doing it for you so I'll have something to wear when we go out beside my jeans and work shirt."

He bought designer slacks, silk dress shirts and leather jackets, sometimes two at a time. Skylar didn't believe his rationale for his extravagant expenses. She found it odd as well as selfish. She had recently asked him if he would buy a belt for her which cost $28.00. He had refused to buy the belt yet he was purchasing socks for himself at the cost of $35.00 a pair.

Along with his sleek new wardrobe, John began a new hobby of smoking cigars. He made the rounds of the cigar stores and spent money on a sophisticated cigar collection, which he kept in a large, expensive humidor. He voraciously read magazines geared to cigar smokers. When Skylar commented she disliked the smell of cigars, John proclaimed, "All successful men smoke cigars. All the actors in Hollywood smoke them. And I'm just like them."

On rare occasions, he would allow Skylar to go out for dinner with a friend after she would tentatively ask his permission. If he agreed, he wanted all the details of her evening. He would ask her what time was she meeting her friend, what time they were having dinner, and the name of the restaurant. He would make telephone calls to her friend prior to dinner to check on the plans, and ask what time she ate lunch to determine if it made sense they would be eating dinner at a particular time. He would calculate the driving time, add in the time it would take to eat, and gauge the drive home. He would tell her what time he expected her home. Prior to leaving, John would review her outfit. She was able to fit into her pre-pregnancy clothes and John would question why she was so nicely dressed. He would accuse her of wanting to go out and meet men. She would patiently explain she couldn't wear the same clothes she wore when she was taking care of the children. John's interrogation made it almost impossible for Skylar to enjoy the few hours with her friends.

One evening, dressed casually in jeans and a sweater, Skylar was leaving to meet Lori at a nearby restaurant. She got into her car and started it. As she was fastening her seatbelt, John suddenly ran out of the house with a wild look in his eye.

He was screaming, "Get out of the car!" He banged on the hood with his fist. "You're not going anywhere!" He grabbed the door handle, but Skylar quickly locked the doors after seeing the look on his face. He started screaming, "Get out of the fuckin' car!" She was terrified. John looked crazed, with his face flushed and his eyes bulged in blazing anger. He took a step back and then began kicking the back window, his anger unrestrained.

Skylar threw the gear shift into reverse and pushed the gas pedal hard. The car screeched into the street. She slammed on the brakes, shifted to drive, and stepped hard on the gas. The tires squealed as she pulled away from the house. Her heart was pounding as she traveled the winding, unlit, country roads. She kept looking in her rearview mirror, terrified he was going to follow her. Afraid for herself, she was very concerned for her children.

When her heart slowed its frenetic beating, she found the main road. She pulled into a gas station and called John from the pay phone.

When he heard her voice he started screaming, "If you don't get your fuckin' ass home, I'll leave, and the kids will be here all alone."

"I'm afraid you're going to hurt me," her voice trembled in fear.

"Skylar, I am not going to touch you." He sounded a little less angry.

"Okay. I will be home in a few minutes." She wanted to call Lori first. She dialed her number. When Lori answered, Skylar simply said, "John won't let me meet you tonight."

"I know. He just called me. Skylar, he's *crazy*. He started screaming at me. He told me not to meet you," Lori told her.

Skylar described how he had charged outside. "I was so scared he was going to break the glass. I have his sneaker prints on my windows. I've never seen him so out of control. It was even worse than the night he threw me down and choked me. I was petrified he was going to hurt me again. And he threatened to leave the children alone. I have to go home."

She drove home and nervously got out of the car, and entered the house, tentatively.

John was waiting calmly, and said, "Phil just called. He's havin' a problem with his girlfriend. He needs to talk to me." Dressed in his designer clothes, John left.

The days became warmer as summer was upon them. Paul had returned from Florida and called John.

"Hey, I'm up here with my new girlfriend. You and Skylar, come meet us for dinner. Ya gotta see this girl, man. She is so fuckin' hot."

John called Maree to babysit and informed Skylar they were meeting Paul for dinner. She was pleased with a sudden night out. As they walked into the restaurant, they saw Paul waiting with a stunning blonde woman who looked as if she walked off the pages of *Cosmopolitan*. Introductions were made as they were led to a table. As John and Paul talked, Skylar tried to start a conversation with Paul's girlfriend, but she didn't say much. When she excused herself to go to the restroom, every man in the place turned to watch her.

John started telling Paul, "Oh, my word! Look at her! You are a lucky son-of-a bitch! Look at her ass! Oh, she is mint!"

It was humiliating for Skylar to have her husband wildly lust after another woman to his friend in her presence. However, it wasn't the first time he had acted that way. It was reminiscent of the time they went out for brunch before their wedding.

A cute waitress had approached and asked, "What would you like?"

John had grinned at her and answered, "I'll have you!" He had little regard for Skylar and thought nothing of degrading her in public. The pain of that memory hadn't faded much.

The summer days began to cool as Skylar planned birthday party for the boys. Joshua was four and still attending preschool at Temple Beth Shalom in Needham. He would go in the morning, and Skylar would pick him up at noon. Cary was two and stayed home with Jillian, who was eight months. Skylar's days were occupied with her children. John was barely home, but she felt the tradeoff of being the sole caregiver of the children was worth not having to deal with him.

Just before the frost of winter set in, Skylar's great-uncle died. He had left inheritances but it was going to take months to distribute the checks.

John was eagerly anticipating Skylar's money. He asked, "When are you getting your money? Do you know how much? What are you going to do with it?"

She also inherited some of her great-uncle's belongings, mostly household items for use or to display in his memory. John sulked for days, disappointed that he didn't get anything.

The winter of 1993 began with a vengeance, filled with many days of snowstorms New Englanders called Nor'easters, which brought in wet, heavy snow. John hired someone to plow the driveway, because even a Nor'easter couldn't keep him home. But eventually, all the snow had an effect on his business. Everything slowed down. He took advantage of that time and hired a carpenter to renovate the sun porch into a man's room. The roof was raised to a dramatic cathedral ceiling, lined with cedar wood, which continued down the walls. Large glass windows surrounded the room. A niche was created for the television and stereo and a soft carpet was installed over the concrete floor.

John announced, "This is my room. I don't want you in here unless I'm here. I built this room so I can have privacy. You better not let the kids in my room."

He took the old sectional couch that had been in the children's playroom and moved most of it into the new room, leaving only two pieces in the playroom. There was no place in the playroom for Skylar to sit with all the children unless it was on the floor. To match the glass walls of the room, he had placed a glass door between the playroom and his man's room. The children would see John through the glass and cry because he wouldn't allow them in his room.

When the weather calmed, Skylar arranged an evening out with another couple. She was pleased when John agreed to go out for dinner. He usually complained about her friends, so this was a rarity. During dinner, Skylar and her friend chatted with while the men discussed business. Skylar overheard John saying, "We are barely making it financially." She was mortified.

On the way home, she asked, "Why did you tell him that you had no money – especially since it's not true?"

He said, "Because the next time I see them, I'll tell them business is great and I have a lot of money, which will impress them."

In disbelief, she said, "What are you talking about? You just lied."

"A financial comeback is even more impressive," John replied.

As an abuser, humiliating Skylar was routine. From shameful flirting with other women, insulting her, or embarrassing her in front of her friends, his humiliation was constant. His conduct that evening was actually typical behavior toward someone who challenged the narcissist. He disliked all of Skylar's friends, particularly the ones who appeared successful. That evening, he was faced with someone who he felt rivaled his intelligence as well as his success. Ironically, he was facing a man who valued outside appearances as well. The man was a narcissist in his own right, but John couldn't compete with his smoother style and more polished act. So he reverted to a narcissistic tactic of inspiring sympathy as well as admiration for his stoicism.

"When the narcissist defense is operating in an interpersonal (1:1) or group setting, the grandiose part does not show its face in public." wrote Dr. Bruce Gregory, corporate behavioral specialist of California, in *The Impact of Narcissism on Leadership and Sustainability,* a chapter from *Pathways to Sustainability: The Age of* by Andrew Cohill, Ph.D. and Joseph Kruth.

Despite his claim of poverty, John was spending an insane amount of money. He traded in his red Toyota for a cream colored one because he wanted the color of his truck to be the same as his boat. Then, he brought the truck and the boat to a company that specialized in customized auto painting and detailing.

He described the job he wanted, "I want the same color and font with my company name, painted on my truck. It's gotta match perfectly."

Security Safe was painted on the side of John's truck in the same shade of red as the lettering on the boat. It seemed to be an extravagant endeavor for someone who was barely making it financially.

Robin Shaye

There were warm days in 1993 where John would stay home to work on the house. Skylar helped him with the outdoor tasks by mowing the lawn or climbing a ladder to paint the house. She saw Sally and her neighbors sitting in the backyard, but they ignored her when she waved. They no longer sat in their front yards. It seemed as if they were purposely avoiding her.

She expressed her confusion to John. "Suddenly, they won't talk to me."

He was less surprised than Skylar. He did not want her sitting in the yard socializing while he worked. He thought of his visit to Sally that winter.

"Skylar thinks she's better than you and the other neighbors." he told her with his earnest, blue-eyed stare. "She says she wants to move so she can be with people who are worthy of her company."

He sardonically told Skylar, "It's just like our former neighbor. You always say or do something to ruin a friendship with a neighbor."

This wasn't an unusual comment. Periodically he would tell her, "My friend's wife has a problem with you" or "my friends won't go out with us because of you."

John wielded the power and, as an abuser, implemented this as a control factor. He needed to isolate Skylar from anyone who may have become an ally. He isolated her from every neighbor, then systematically started picking off others. Skylar never had a problem maintaining friendships. Suddenly and abruptly, women who she had befriended ignored her. Because John was so convincing, she was too embarrassed to ask any of these women if she had done anything to offend them. He had shattered her confidence for so many years, the thought of asking a simple question to someone who had once been a friend was impossible for her. She couldn't understand what was happening in her life. She almost felt as if John was trying to drive her crazy.

Biderman's Chart of Coercion from an Amnesty International publication, *Report on Torture*, explains the brainwashing of prisoners of war. Those who seek to control their intimate partners use methods similar to those of prison guards. They manipulate the mind and the feelings of the victim. The victim becomes a psychological prisoner, accomplished through utilizing a variety of methods. The first is isolation. When the victim is isolated from all social support, they depend on the victimizer for everything. The second way is "monopolization of perception." They eliminate anyone who may compete or interfere with the control of the capture. They insist on compliance regarding food, clothing, money, the house, conversation and appearances. They make their victim feel as if they are walking on eggshells. As in the cycle of abuse, according to Biderman, there are "occasional indulgences." The victim receives some type of motivation for compliance, either affection or a night out; it's identical to the honeymoon stage in the cycle of domestic abuse. Biderman's final component is "devaluing the individual." The victim feels unable to make a decision. They doubt themselves and lack faith in their own abilities.

In the book and website, *Malignant Self Love - Narcissism Revisited*, author Sam Vaknin's description of a malignant narcissist provides a frighteningly accurate profile which depicts John's thought process. Described as manipulative and selfish, the malignant narcissist is this and more. Vaknin describes the malignant narcissist as someone who controls his wife/family in every aspect. John could control, manipulate, and mislead people as he twisted arguments to make others appear to be at fault. Yet in a moment's notice, he could turn around and show his public self as charming. His public personality was a sharp contrast to his private reality.

To get inside John's head would be to feel a superior attitude, which he freely communicated. When John announced he was king of the castle, he truly believed he was the ruler. As a rule maker, he was highly demanding of Skylar. He had a huge sense of entitlement, primarily because he made the money; therefore, his wishes should be granted. She was his possession. That was the crux of the abuse; when the possession misbehaves, you beat them into submission.

John denied he was abuser, which wasn't uncommon. Until an

abuser is willing to face their behavior and attend counseling, he will remain blind to his persona as a batterer. Hopes for therapy to address a narcissistic personality disorder are even less likely. The reason is simply because the narcissist does not believe there is anything wrong with him.

Chapter 11

Always trying to please John, Skylar planned a birthday celebration for his thirty-fourth birthday in May of 1994. She cashed in a bond and purchased tickets for a dinner cruise in Boston Harbor. Hoping to surprise him, she opted to drive. As she backed the car out of the driveway, John asked with a smile, "So, where are we going?"

She smiled back. "You'll see when we get there." She had arranged a wonderful evening and wanted to keep it a secret until they arrived at the dock.

But he demanded, "I wanna know where we're goin'. What if I don't like it? What if I don't feel like goin' there?" He began an argument that continued the entire way into Boston.

Did John perceive himself as important enough to discard an expensive night out his wife had provided? Did he perceive himself as so small and unimportant he had to control everything in order to feel worthwhile? This is a tremendous example of both narcissism - having a grand sense of self importance - and abuse/control.

John had no control, as Skylar had made the plans and was, literally, in the driver's seat. It was almost intolerable for him to even give up that small bit of control. Skylar tried to ignore him and concentrate on driving as she thought back to another birthday outing she had arranged and the disaster she had averted.

In 1987, just prior to their wedding, she had made reservations to an elegant restaurant in Boston which featured dinner and comical theater performance that had received rave reviews. She arranged for a cake to be brought out as the cast members' sang their rendition of *Happy Birthday*. His reaction to the restaurant had been lukewarm and his attention to the show was that of boredom.

After dinner, he turned to Skylar and said, "I hope you didn't have a stupid idea to have someone come out and sing 'Happy Birthday'!" She managed a smile. "I need to go to the ladies' room." She rushed out and looked for the maître d'. "I need to cancel the cake I ordered!" She saw the cake ablaze with candles.

"No, no, no!" Skylar was panicked. "Please, can you just cut a slice and bring it to him? No candles and no singing!"

The cake was whisked back into the kitchen and she forced herself to breathe easier. She returned to the table with a smile. John got his one slice of cake in a silent observance of his birthday.

Skylar thought back to that evening and to the panic she felt at almost ruining his birthday. This time, it was perfectly planned. John loved boats and loved to eat. She smiled, thinking of the beautiful night ahead until his voice broke into her thoughts.

"I don't wanna wait 'til we get there. I wanna know now!" Skylar's smile began to fade. "Wipe that stupid smile off your face and tell me!"

Skylar glanced sideways at John. His face was red. She felt the sweat on her palms as she tried to hold the steering wheel. Close to tears, she stubbornly refused to disclose their destination. "Please, John. I really want to surprise you."

"Well, I might not be in the mood to go to where you planned. I hope this isn't another idiotic place," he replied, making a veiled reference to the dinner show of a few years prior.

At least he wasn't yelling, so Skylar told him, "I already paid for this, and I know you'll like it." She began looking at the street signs. "Let me see...I think I need to take a left over here." She attempted to concentrate on driving in an attempt to refocus John from insisting she divulge her secret location. She pulled into the parking lot.

When John saw the boat, he became interested, so he stopped the insults. He reached for Skylar's hand. "Hey, this could be good!"

She returned the pressure on his hand but felt as if she had been beaten up. She felt a sharp pain in her head as she held back her tears. She walked quietly and regained her composure, determined to put on a festive front for the remainder of the evening.

John's birthday heralded the start of summer. Everyone in the Bauers house seemed happy and healthy, except all the children as well as Skylar were bothered by itchy scalps. They were constantly scratching their heads. One Sunday, when John and Skylar were lying on the couch, Joshua lay down alongside Skylar for a cuddle. She stroked his head, running her fingers through his hair and suddenly saw tiny little bugs crawling all through his hair.

"Oh, my God! We have lice!"

Upon examination, they found the children and Skylar were infested with lice.

John calmly said, "You go get the stuff to kill the lice and I'll grill some burgers."

After dinner, they began the procedure. It was tedious eliminating lice, not only from four people, but also from the bedclothes, pillows, and stuffed animals. Mattresses needed to be vacuumed. Brushes and combs needed to be boiled. John went to work on the children, and Skylar began stripping the beds and doing laundry. In between loads, she would help with the children. The boys whimpered and Jillian cried, screamed, and kicked. It was a long and laborious process. John went through the process too, although he didn't have one bug or one nit in his hair. It took hours. After the children went to bed, Skylar showered and lay down on the clean sheets. John came in the room and took her towel away.

"Now," he said, "my reward for doing such a good job."

Skylar smiled. She was relieved he had helped and felt grateful that he willingly took on the laborious task of picking the nits out of her hair as well as the children. It was probably the only time she felt they were really a bonded family.

Everyone was lice-free in time for a visit from John's sisters. Cara arrived first from California. She asked Skylar if she would drive to the airport a few days later to meet Audra, who was arriving from Ohio with her toddler son. She suggested having dinner in Boston, prior to meeting Audra's eight-thirty flight. John agreed to stay home that evening. Just before Skylar left, she reminded him to check on Joshua because he had a slight chest cold.

Audra's flight was late and there was a lot of traffic, so Skylar didn't get home until after eleven o'clock. She went upstairs and saw John in bed watching television.

"Hi," she greeted him, and then asked, "did you check on Joshie?" John replied, "Umm, no. I forgot."

She turned and went into the boy's bedroom to check on Joshua. He felt cool but his breathing was rapid and shallow. She returned to the bedroom and got the telephone.

"I can't believe you forgot to check on him! I told you he was sick," she admonished as she called the pediatrician.

She described Joshua's symptoms to Dr. Kemble. He was concerned about Joshua's breathing difficulties and told her to take him into Children's Hospital in Boston.

"I have to take Joshie to the hospital. Please," she stressed to John, "take care of Cary and Jillian until I get back."

She helped Joshua into a sweatshirt and sneakers, buckled him into his car seat and drove to the Hospital. In the emergency room, Joshua was examined and diagnosed with bronchiolitis, the same as Cary had in 1990. Joshua received several Ventolin breathing treatments. Skylar kept up cheery chatter with him so he wouldn't be afraid. They ate popsicles between the treatments. By the time they left the hospital, it was sunrise. Joshua fell asleep in the car. He recovered in time to visit with his aunts and cousins, before they flew back home.

At the end of the summer of 1993, Skylar planned a birthday party for Joshua and Cary, who would be celebrating their fifth and third birthdays respectively. The night before, Skylar blew up balloons and tied them to dowels, which she stuck in the ground all over the yard.

She bought a piñata and stuffed it with candy. She made lunch plates for the children and wrapped them in colorful plastic wrap and made several salads for the adults. For entertainment, she hired a mobile gym. The company would be bringing gymnastics equipment and an obstacle course to set up in the yard. There would be two instructors who would provide music and structured games for the children. It was going to be a great party.

Skylar enlisted Lori to help her with the festivities while John sat on the far side of the yard, smoking a cigar with his friends. When the guests left, John announced he had to go to work for a while so Lori offered to stay and help her clean up the yard. When they were done, Skylar put the children to bed. They were exhausted and fell asleep quickly. She joined Lori, and they went out to the sun porch with a glass of wine. When John came home, he found the women on the sun porch and offered to barbecue. He lit the barbecue and poured himself a glass of wine. He and Lori smoked a joint as they waited for the grill to get hot enough.

Lori announced, "I have a joke!" She recited, "A man saw a sign in a clothing store which said 'We sell everything!' The guy walked up to the clerk and asked her for some glass pants. The woman replied, 'Sorry sir, we don't sell those.' The man argued the sign stated that the store sold everything. The woman remarked that glass pants did not even exist. The man went home, did some research, and found glass pants. He went back to the store wearing the pair of glass pants. The man said triumphantly, 'See, I told you they existed!' The woman said, 'At first I thought you were crazy, but now I see you're nuts!'" Lori laughed uproariously.

Skylar groaned. "That was awful!" she said, giggling.

"Glass pants?" said John. "That would be kind of cool. I wonder how they'd look on me! Probably something like this…" He stood up and unbuttoned his jeans and let them fall to the floor. He stood there in his grayed BVD's and Security Safe t-shirt.

Skylar was shocked and speechless. When she recovered enough to speak, she firmly said, "Okay, John, you've made your point. Now please get dressed."

He said, "No, I think I like being like this. I want to barbecue this way." He stepped out of his jeans and took off his shirt. He went outside and put the steaks on the grill.

Lori didn't comment on John's semi-nudity. She randomly started talking about the weather. "I don't want winter to come at all. Maybe if we run around the yard naked, we'll be able to keep the warm weather here longer."

John exclaimed, "Great idea!"

Agitated, Skylar said, "Sorry, I'm not getting naked. John, *please* put your clothes on!"

He replied, "No, I'm comfortable like this." He ignored her and continued grilling.

When dinner was ready, they sat at the table in the backyard. Skylar was embarrassed that John was clad only in his underwear, but was relieved that he was covered by the table.

Once they finished eating, Skylar said, "I'll clear the table. John, put your pants on." He ignored her, got up and carried some plates into the kitchen. "John!" she urgently whispered. "Please get dressed!"

Just then, the telephone rang and he grabbed the phone. "It's Paul!" he announced.

Skylar whispered, "Invite him over." She thought Paul's presence would be an incentive for John to get dressed. She went to Lori in the sunroom. As John spoke to Paul on the kitchen phone, he stretched the cord so he was able to walk down the stairs into the playroom. He tried to entice Paul to come over by telling him Lori was going to run around the yard naked.

Lori overheard him and surprised Skylar when she started yelling, "Naked!"

As John talked to Paul on the phone, he slipped off his underwear and stood there completely nude. It was at that moment Lori stood up to use the bathroom and walked past John. She didn't flinch or say a word. It was as if she was used to seeing him undressed.

Skylar was mortified and shocked at seeing John standing there without a stitch of clothing. For a second, she couldn't breathe. She couldn't talk. She was horrified, yet puzzled at the lack of response or reaction from Lori as she walked past him. Skylar closed her eyes to the probability of a relationship between John and her best friend. It just wasn't possible. Lori had been her support during all the abuse. She would listen to Skylar and she comforted her. Although the behavior that evening may have been apparent to a stranger, Skylar refused to acknowledge any intimacy between her husband and her best friend.

The rest of the evening was a nightmare. Paul's appearance at the house had no effect on John, who continued to walk around as if he were fully clothed. He flaunted his nudity as he sat on the couch, spread his legs, and grinned while ignoring Skylar, who implored him to get dressed. Paul and Lori sat there laughing.

Skylar had never been more humiliated. She wanted to grab her keys, get into her car, and leave. The only thing that prevented her from doing so was the distressing thought that John would take her absence as an opportunity to have sex with Lori in her own house. She couldn't bear the thought, so she sat there and allowed him to degrade her until one-thirty in the morning. As John walked everyone to the door, Skylar stayed where she was, too stunned to move.

John returned to the sunroom and jumped on top of Skylar, pulling at her clothes.

"Get the fuck off of me!" she screamed.

"You're my wife!" John spat as he struggled with her.

"And you're a pig!" she screamed as she continued to fight back.

John froze for a second. Then he stopped fighting, stood up, and walked upstairs. Skylar didn't move. She curled up on the couch alone, finally dozing off, and slept fitfully.

She awoke to the nauseating odor of frying bacon John was cooking for breakfast. The children were watching cartoons in the playroom, so she doled out hugs and kisses, and then walked into the kitchen where John was slicing strawberries at the counter. She had to know.

"Why did you do that last night? What the hell were you thinking?" she demanded.

"I thought it would be fun if you and Lori had sex together," he replied casually.

"We've discussed this over and over, many times," she reminded him.

"Well, don't blame me. It was Lori's idea. I told her to let me get the ball rolling and do it at my pace. I figured you'd get into it," he answered.

She became tearful. "But you're my husband. You already knew I wasn't interested."

"Well, I *am* interested, and I thought you'd change your mind." John replied, sounding smug. "Besides, you should be mad at Lori, not me. She came up with the idea."

Skylar's voice quavered. Keeping her voice low so the children wouldn't hear, in an angry whisper, she explained, "Even if it was her idea, you already knew I would not go along. You're my husband! You're supposed to protect me!" This felt like the ultimate betrayal.

He harshly answered, "Yeah, and you're my wife – and you're sup-posed to do what I want! I *am* interested in being with two women and I hoped I could convince you! I guess I'll have to find it someplace else!" He changed his tone. "Kids! Come have breakfast!"

It always amazed Skylar how easily he could go from a vicious argument to sounding absolutely pleasant. She went upstairs to the bathroom, locked the door and turned on the shower. She stepped in, turning her face to the hot water as she allowed the tears to flow.

Their rekindled love since the Marco Island trip died in John's betrayal. That was the moment when Skylar lost all respect for him.

Chapter 12

In September of 1993, Cary started preschool. He was an adorable three-year-old with blonde hair, blue eyes, and long lashes. He was endearingly mischievous and would laugh with gusto at his own antics in the classroom. Because he was extremely energetic, his teachers suggested additional activity would benefit him so Skylar enrolled him in a gymnastics program, sure it would be a good fit for her son who was small, agile, and fearless. There was an hour class, one afternoon per week. In the middle of the fall semester, there was a demonstration day held for the parents. John agreed to meet them at the gym. When Cary noticed his father there, he excitedly ran to him. He briefly acknowledged him. Unsmiling, he turned to Skylar.

"See, he's doin' nothin'. I'm leavin'." He turned and left her standing there with Cary.

According to Dr. Martha Stout, author of *The Sociopath Next Door* writes, *a sociopath cannot derive pleasure from being with his children or watching them grow.*

Skylar could feel her heart swell with love as she watched her children run and tumble in a field of grass. She frequently displayed her interest and affection toward her children and couldn't understand John's apathy. His indifference to his son was a sliver of his sociopathalogical behaviors, which had been gradually increasing in word, deed and attitude.

After the incident with Lori, Skylar didn't think John's conduct could get any crueler. She was wrong. It began in November, when Skylar began feeling some discomfort in one of her teeth so she made an appointment to see the dentist.

When she informed John of her upcoming appointment, he glee-fully crooned, "You'll probably need a root canal!"

She ignored his sardonic comment. The morning of her appointment, the dentist examined her tooth and took X-rays. He determined the pain was from an old filling so he refilled the tooth and reassured her that the discomfort would subside in a day or so.

That evening, when John came home, he eagerly asked, "Do you need a root canal?"

"No, I don't. He just replaced my old filling," she answered.

His face displayed obvious disappointment. "Too bad!"

"It sounds as if you were hoping I needed a root canal," she looked confused.

He looked her straight in the eye and gritted his teeth, and in a low voice stated, "I had to have them. You should know what that kind of pain is like."

Shocked and disgusted at his comment, she turned and walked out of the room. She didn't want to be near John.

From Skylar's journal on, Saturday, November 28, 1993: *Now I guess I must not put it off any longer, so here goes. I am most seriously contemplating a divorce. John is impossible, mean to me, selfish and shows me no loyalty. Everyone else comes before me. I guess it really came to a head when he took off all his clothes in front of Lori (9-11-93). It was sickening! He wants me to do a 3-way scene with him and another woman. I really lost respect for him. I lost a lot of my feelings at that point. I just want him to leave. He's done too much damage and has been too emotionally abusive to me. I don't know if I can really love him again.*

In early December, John went to New York for a weekend event sponsored by Cigar Aficionado magazine. Attendees would have a chance to sample various cigars and enjoy a gourmet meal.

He told Skylar, "You wouldn't want to go. The place will be filled with smoke because everyone will be smoking cigars. And you know you can't eat rich food."

He was determined to make it sound as unappealing as possible be-cause he already had an escort for the event. In addition to the woman in Florida, he was also dating a girl from Connecticut, who was attending the event with him in New York.

For Skylar, it was a respite when he was not home. There was less stress when he wasn't there. And the fact it would be a whole weekend was a pretty pleasurable thought. She cared for the children and enjoyed them even more, knowing the house would be quiet and calm for three full days. John flew to New York but never called home. Although Joshua and Cary were accustomed to his absence, Skylar had hoped he would call to talk to his sons. She wanted to talk to him as well, and share her news she was certain would please him. She had scheduled an interview for a part-time position as an instructor at a modeling school.

From Skylar's journal on, Wednesday, December 1, 1993: *I told John about my interview for the part-time position at the modeling school. He said, "You can pay the baby-sitter if you work." I said, "If I'm making ten dollars an hour and pay the baby-sitter seven dollars, I'd be working for three dollars an hour." He said, "Well, you'd better decide if it's worth it. You just want the money so you can go out and buy frivolous things." He's such an ass! I have a head cold so Mom picked up the boys at school My cold is timely as I was able to watch Sally Jessy Raphael's talk show on TV. Her show was about men who try to control their wives. I wished I taped it, but I did take notes. The whole show was my life! There was a psychotherapist who said that women are stronger of the two sexes, and these men who control don't want wives - they want slaves! The women used words such as "trapped," "no freedom," "he's like a father," etc... The same words I used! The therapist also said, "What kind of wife, mother, and person is she going to be if she's treated like that?" John tells me I'm an unhappy person, which is simply not so! He's trying to shift the blame on me. If I had any doubts as to the problems in this marriage, I sure as hell don't now. Perfect example of his selfishness: Last night, I'm sick and can't breathe and I asked him. "Will you rub my back?" He said, "Okay, and while I'm rubbing your back, can you rub my front?" Can't I just relax without having to do something to him too?*

Skylar interviewed for the instructor position without John's approval and was offered the job. She informed him that evening. "I was offered the job for Saturdays, and I'm taking it. You can either stay home or pay the babysitter."

He didn't respond; he mentally calculated how much money he would deduct from the grocery money if he had to pay a babysitter so Skylar could put extra money in her pocket. He knew his silence appeared to be his consent so he needed to remind her who was boss. He retaliated to her disobedience by spending three days in Connecticut, telling Skylar he had a job there for a new client.

From Skylar's journal on Sunday, December 5, 1993: *John was gone all weekend. He didn't call on Saturday night or all day today. I don't have any feeling left for him which is not an unusual occurrence when one is living with an abusive person. I can't love someone who's so mean and cruel and doesn't care about his children. When I tell him he should be home more often, his response is, "If you didn't want to work so hard, you shouldn't have had so many kids!" Hard to believe someone can say that about their own children. He doesn't care for them or for me. The marriage is over. The stress is getting worse week-by-week. He nauseates me. He's sick and getting sicker.*

Just prior to the holidays, John told Skylar, "I'm goin' to Florida. I need to talk to this handyman that Paul told me about. He has Christmas off, so that's the only time we can talk. I'm gonna expand my business to Florida. It'll be great, because of all the new construction and repairs after that hurricane. And, I'll have the best of both worlds, winters in Florida and summers in Massachusetts."

Disbelieving, she asked, "Where are the children and I going to be?"

"You'll all be here. You can come down on vacations. I'll have to go back and forth."

He was gone for almost a week. She hoped the time apart would promote a surge in paternal feelings toward the children and hoped he would miss them. But when he returned, it was obvious he hadn't changed. Because she was earning a meager paycheck, John felt he could reduce the amount of money he was giving her for groceries. He implemented a new rule: if she needed groceries, she had to present him with a shopping list so he could approve it first. She refused and they argued. It seemed as if one argument blended into another. Finally, she stopped talking to him and he just glared at her all the time.

From Skylar's journal on Sunday, January 16, 1994: *Now John says if I file for divorce, Paul Redmond will testify I had an affair/sex with him while John stripped that awful night of September 11th. Hopefully, my documentation of that event will prove the truth. He's a very sick person.* That could have become the most critical journal entry she had ever written.

The following Saturday, Skylar taught six classes at the modeling school and got home a little after five o'clock. When she opened the door, she discovered John had moved out of the house. He took televisions, stereo systems, and the piano as well as decorative items. Terrified, she ran upstairs to see if the children's rooms had been touched. All their clothes were there. John's father, George, brought the children home a few minutes later. He and Nora had been watching them while John cleared out the house.

From Skylar's journal on Saturday, January 23, 1994: *When I came home, I discovered John had cleared out the house. Unbelievable! He called tonight and said, "I still love you but I don't know if you love me." He said he did it because he saw "the writing on the wall" and thought I'd throw him out first. He said, "Believe me, I don't want to hurt you, and I could have taken everything. I'm not trying to be mean." He refused to tell me where he is staying.*

Despite the abruptness of his sudden departure, Skylar enjoyed the solitude of living in the house just with the children. Everything was clean and tranquil. All the stress was gone from her life. John called her often. He was polite and charming and expressed his desire to move back but Skylar was very content with his absence. He told her how much he loved her and promised he would do anything to make the marriage work.

From Skylar's journal on Tuesday, February 1, 1994: *John moved back in but he didn't bring his clothes or furniture or the piano. He said he wants to work on marriage and told me he loves me. I guess we'll see. We decided to begin marital counseling.*

Although she believed he wanted to make the marriage work, part of his decision to return was due to her pending inheritance from her great uncle. His will was still in probate, so during the time they were apart, John asked Attorney Liz Lewin, who was the sister of his friend Phil, to go to the probate court house to read the will.

"Find out what she's getting and when." John told Liz. He was determined to get his hands on her inheritance.

From Skylar's journal on Wednesday, February 23, 1994: *I asked John to pick up diapers for Jillian and he refused to go unless I gave him money for the diapers as well as gas money! He's still incredibly selfish. He made a mess of the house. He refuses to participate in any children's activities unless he can be with his friends. Then he tells me he wants custody! That's ridiculous! He said his friends would say whatever he tells them to say in court. He said he'll say I'm an unfit mother, which obviously isn't true. One just needs to read my journals to know the truth. I'm not worried one iota. He's still buying, dealing, and smoking pot. He went to his dealer's house on Friday night and made deliveries to Paul Redmond, Phil Lewin, and Lori. There are huge bags of pot in the freezer. He insults me constantly and asks, "Why don't you have a tummy tuck?" Maybe I will, but not for him.*

At the end of February, Skylar received her inheritance. She bought a computer for the family and a home gym. She allowed herself an extravagance of a modestly priced fur coat, which infuriated John. He hadn't purchased any clothing for her since they were married yet he was angry she bought a coat.

He screamed, "Why don't you put the thousand bucks in my pocket? You just spent a grand on a fur coat! I should get somethin' too!" Angrily, he grabbed his jacket and left the house, slamming the door. He returned with two pairs of boots. He boldly displayed the price tags which showed $500.00 and $300.00.

"John, are you nuts? Eight hundred dollars for boots?" she was flabbergasted.

He justified his spending by hotly declaring, "I couldn't find any boots I liked! You just bought a coat. I can buy boots!" His escalating anger signified the start of another cycle of abuse, which was unbearable as it was directed toward the children.

One March evening, Skylar was in bathroom upstairs and John discovered the boys had gone into the downstairs bathroom and squirted water on the carpet in the playroom. Infuriated, he grabbed five-year-old Joshua and began hitting him on his rear end, back, and legs.

"You fuckin' little bastard! I'll teach you!" He kept hitting him, ignoring Joshua's screams. Then he grabbed Cary, who was a tiny three-year-old and started beating him until Cary shrieked in pain. John's eyes were blazing. Hearing the cries, Skylar ran downstairs. She scooped up a sobbing two years old Jillian, who was frightened after witnessing John's assault.

"Stop it, John!" she pleaded.

He shouted, "Get her out of here!" Skylar believed John knew he was out of control and if he hit Jillian he would kill her. "Get the fuck out of here!"

Jillian was screeching in fear as Skylar took her out of the room. Suddenly, the boys broke away and ran upstairs. They clung to their mother, sobbing. She bent down and gathered them in her arms. John stormed past and left the house, slamming the door and leaving her to comfort three hysterical children. She wanted to call the police or the Department of Social Services but she didn't know what he would do if she made a complaint against him. Mostly, she was afraid her children would be taken away from her for her inability to protect them.

She didn't realize how badly they had been beaten until the next day. Sable stopped by the house early in the day while Skylar was dressing the boys. As she removed Cary's pajamas, Sable noticed he was black and blue from his back to his legs.

Sable gasped. "My God, Skylar! What happened?" She picked up Cary and held him close.

Shocked, Skylar looked at Joshua's back, and he was just as bruised.

"Oh, my God, Mom, John beat them yesterday!"

"You need to report this!" Sable firmly stated, lightly rubbing Cary's tiny arms.

She tearfully replied, "I thought about it, but I'm afraid. What if they blame me because I let it happen? They'll take the kids away. And what will he do to me if I report him?"

Calm and reasonable, Sable told her, "Skylar, you're not going to like this, but I told you not to marry him. He's crazy."

"I know, but maybe if I talk to him..." She suggested, her voice fading off.

"You need to get away from him!" Her mother implored.

Skylar sighed, "I can't."

When John came home that evening, he was rational. So, she took a chance and told him about the bruises on the boys.

"John, they are all black and blue! I can't believe you did that to them!"

He was very calm, and looked deep into her eyes and said, "I swear I won't do that again." He provided the classic batterer's response and as a typical victim, Skylar believed him.

However, a week later the boys were annoying him as they were playing and screeching in glee. John wanted quiet and they annoyed him.

"That's it!" he screamed. He grabbed the boys by their arms. "Go into your room. I want to you to pack your clothes!" He glared at Skylar. "Stay the fuck out of this." John reached under the sink and got two plastic bags. "Put your clothes in here. GO!"

The boys looked at Skylar, sobbing. "Mommy!" Tears rolled down their little faces.

Her heart was breaking. She pleaded with John, "That's enough, John! Stop it!"

He took a step toward her and his fist hit the wall with a loud bang. She flinched, her eyes widened in fear.

Through gritted teeth, he hissed, "Shut your mouth, bitch, or you can go with them." He turned back to Joshua and Cary. "I said, Get up to your goddamn room!"

The terrified little boys ran into their room. Their wails of fear could be heard reverberating through the house. He followed them upstairs, his footsteps loud and furious.

Jillian began whimpering, and Skylar held her tightly.

They heard John shouting upstairs. "Now you'll learn to behave, you fuckin' little bastards! I'm takin' you to the home for bad children!" The boys' wails turned to terrified shrieks as their father slammed the dresser drawers.

Skylar heard them coming downstairs. They each carried plastic bags that held their clothing. Tears rolled down their faces. Cary was gasping for breath, he was so frightened. Both boys ran to Skylar and clung to her legs, screaming and sobbing.

She dropped to the floor with Jillian in her lap and gathered the boys close with each arm. These were her children. John may have hurt her, choked her, abused her, and humiliated her, but she wasn't going to allow him to do the same to her children.

She whispered words of comfort to her sons, "Don't worry. You are staying right here with Mommy."

John appeared in the doorway, his eyes bulging in anger. He stopped when he saw all three children clinging to Skylar, panic on their little faces.

"Let go of them, Skylar. Get up, Joshua! Let's go, Cary!" The boys screamed in fear.

Skylar firmly said, "John, stop it now!" She stood up, tucking the children behind her in the corner of the kitchen.

"NO! They need to learn a lesson! Get up now! Bad children need to be in a home for bad children!" He took another step forward.

"John, you need to chill, right now! Leave them alone! Go in the other room!" She stood her ground, defiantly. When he didn't move, she looked at the children huddled in the corner. "C'mon kids, let's go put your clothes away. You are not going anywhere." She got up and nudged the children in the direction of the stairs. The boys started moving toward the stairs. She scooped up Jillian and began following them. Over her shoulder, she glared at John as she walked upstairs with the boys. Although she presented a brave front, she was alarmed he would follow. Instead, she heard the kitchen door open and slam shut.

Robin Shaye

John often would sit in his boat in the cold garage and smoke a joint. She sighed in relief. She knew he would be there for a while.

She took the plastic bags and put the clothing back in the drawers. Once all the children were in their pajamas, she read them a story.

"Daddy isn't taking you anywhere, so don't you worry." She reassured the boys as she tucked them into bed. She put Jillian in her crib and handed her a pink teddy bear before she turned the light off and walked into her own bedroom.

Silence permeated the house.

The arrival of warmer weather and fragrant breezes were usually pleasant for Skylar as she could take the children on outings, but that spring was a time of barely holding on. John was scarcely there, and when he was, he was insulting, argumentative, and selfish.

From Skylar's journal on Monday, May 16, 1994: *John decided that seventy-five dollars is enough money to get me through the week. However, he bought a little convertible for himself because he "needs" it. He's still a selfish asshole and will never change.*

From Skylar's journal on Thursday, May 26, 1994: *I've had enough. I am just exhausted by the whole situation and John's abuse. I must survive for my children and that's the only important thing. I really can't go on like this. He's so selfish. When he was gone, I was so happy. The house was immaculate, there was no stress, the kids were great, and I was content just being here with my children. Then he had to move back in and ruin it.*

Although she expressed great anger at John, in her heart, she hoped he would want to change and make the marriage work. She just wanted a family and didn't feel she was asking for a lot. She made every effort to reason with him. She tried to explain to him in soft tones that his treatment of her and the children was unacceptable.

When John didn't respond, Skylar said, "I am trying to make this work for the family, but you are offering me no other choice. I think you are going to have to leave."

John's replied, "*You* have problems. I work hard and deserve my free time, without kids."

"But they're your children too. Don't you want to spend time with them?" she asked.

"I see them on weekends."

"Barely. You see them at the lake, with your friends." she explained.

"Why do you need a distraction? Why couldn't we do something as a family?" She begged.

He sneered, "Like what? Go to a zoo? It's boring. I don't like to be bored. And I am home sometimes. Your job is to take care of the children. After I work, I don't want to come home and be bothered by kids. What don't you get?" He asked through gritted teeth.

Skylar said everything possible in an attempt to get through to him. She felt she did everything possible to reach him, even handing him five hundred dollars from her inheritance to help defray the cost of the preschool. But no amount would have been enough because it was for the children, not for the cigarette boat that John desperately wanted. The most important thing to him was fulfilling his egotistical desires and being with his friends. She could never do enough. Therefore, she felt she had no other option. There was no reason or compromise. She needed to separate her children and herself from the abuse, neglect, and selfishness.

The thought of what she needed to do filled her with fear. In the morning, she went to the probate court in Dedham and filled out the necessary paperwork for a restraining order, which would which would protect the family from further abuse and get John out of the house. She was terrified, thinking about his reaction when enraged. However, after she spoke to the domestic abuse advocate and the judge, she felt a calming sense of relief. It was indeed the right decision. She returned home, packed his clothes in boxes and put them in the closet by the front door.

At five o'clock, Sable pulled up in her car. Skylar brought the children's car seats out and frantically secured them in the car.

"Grandma's taking you to the toy store!" she called to the children. They ran out of the house and Skylar buckled their seatbelts. She told

Sable, "After you're done shopping, call me. I will let you know when it's over."

Sable looked concerned.

"Don't worry." Skylar reassured her. "See you soon, kids!" She waved to the children, who were excitedly wiggling in the back seat. Sable's car pulled away and headed to the center of the toy store in the center of town. Skylar did not want the children there when the police showed up.

Her heart was pounding in fear. The timing was everything. If John chose not to come home that evening, it wouldn't work. Ten minutes later, she heard John's truck pull into the driveway. He got out and began cleaning out the back of his truck. He ignored Skylar, who was standing at the front door. She saw the police cars coming down the street so she closed the front door and peeked out the window.

Two police cars pulled up in front of the house. One officer approached John and served him with the restraining order. After he read it, both officers escorted him to the front door.

Skylar opened the door and said, "Your clothes are in this closet." She pointed to the front hall closet. This was the first time she had blindsided him and he was furious.

He picked up the boxes. As he left, he paused to look her in the eye. "You'll be sorry." He said. He hooked his boat up to his truck and left.

Skylar closed the front door and sighed in relief. It was over.

Chapter 13

There was a dreamy tranquility in the atmosphere when Skylar awoke. It was the start of a new day with the total absence of stress. She did some gardening as the children played in the yard. She cleaned the house thoroughly and made several trips to the town dump. Later that evening, she gave the children dinner and baths and tucked them in to their freshly washed sheets. As the children fell peacefully asleep, Skylar felt her decision was well overdue. She felt relaxed and calm, knowing she now had control over her life.

From Skylar's journal on Sunday, May 28, 1994: *Lori called and said, "I told my mother what happened. She said even though she only met John briefly a long time ago, she thought he was very pompous and pretentious. She thought there was tension between you two and that he treated you like a child." Lori's mother hit the nail on the head.*

From Skylar's journal on Wednesday, June 1, 1994: *I have to go to court tomorrow and face John. I am nervous so I called Lori. She was on her other line talking to John! He called her because his lawyer said he was not allowed to call me. Lori said he spent the weekend at a former girlfriend's house, helping her put up a dock. When Lori told John I was on the other line he said, "Tell her I love her and want this to work out. I'll stay away and go for therapy." I don't understand it; if he loves me, why did he spend the weekend with an old girlfriend?*

What John said and what he did was completely different. After he left the marital home, the first thing he did was contact Sally and her husband, who lived across the street from the Bauers' home. He asked them to watch the house and tell him if Skylar went out at night or to get the license plate number of any car parked there. John's behavior was typical of an abuser.

Although an abuser can be removed from the marital home, the abuse can still continue. This behavior is called, "Abuse by Proxy." According to Sam Vaknin:

> Rejected stalkers are intrusive and inordinately persistent. They recognize no boundaries — personal or legal. They pursue their target for years. Oddly, they interpret rejection as a sign of the victim's continued interest and obsession with them. They are, therefore, impossible to get rid of. Many of them are narcissists and, thus, lack empathy, feel omnipotent and immune to the consequences of their actions.

Skylar's first day in court took was scheduled in early June 1994. She had hired attorney Roger Woodman, who was referred by the Massachusetts Bar Association. John's attorney was a statuesque blond woman named Zoe Powers. Instead of defending John, she told the judge Skylar had a history of instability. Skylar was shocked at the lie. She had an idealistic view of the judicial system and naively believed that everyone took the oath seriously and told the truth.

Nevertheless, the judge continued the restraining order against John for a year. He said, "Mr. Bauers can return to the marital home with a police officer to get the rest of his clothing. If Mrs. Bauers allows it, he may telephone her." Skylar agreed to talk to John on the telephone.

From Skylar's journal on Friday, June 3, 1994: *John calls and tells me he loves me very much and he wants to work it out, and he promises he'll go for therapy. He said his lawyer told him to quickly leave the courthouse the previous day so he couldn't be served with the divorce papers. He told me he wants his family back. He promised to see the children on Sunday.*

On Sunday morning Skylar got up and got the children ready. They were eager to see their father. But by noon, he still hadn't called. The children were disappointed, so Skylar took them to the zoo for the day. They had an amazing day, despite the precarious beginning. When they returned from the zoo, she saw she had no phone messages. John never called.

Skylar stood stoically at her next court date as her attorney presented the motions regarding child support. The judge said he would take everything under advisement. The judge made an order allowing John to visit the children that weekend.

He boldly retorted, "I am staying at my parents' house, so I can't take them overnight. They don't like having kids there and making a mess in their house."

Later, he called Skylar and said, "I am too busy to take them overnight. And, by the way, is you can date, so can I!"

"You've always been too busy for them," Skylar snapped. "And I didn't throw you out so I could date. I am just trying to end your abuse!" She slammed down the phone. She pulled out a piece of paper from her night table drawer. It was a list of over thirty ways he had abused her, tried to control her, or degraded her. She used the list as a reminder of her life with John so he couldn't convince her to slide back into a relationship.

Despite that, she was peaceful. The house was immaculate. She loved walking downstairs into the kitchen and seeing everything in its place. No hardened drops of ice cream on the counter. No little hairs all over the bathroom from John's razor. Everything was clean and shiny and tidy. Anything that was floral and feminine was prominently displayed. She had made the place her own for her and her children. Since John never brought back the piano his parents had given them, Skylar went to a used piano sale at a local college and purchased a small, inexpensive spinet piano with her inheritance money. The children loved hearing her play, and she liked sharing her music. She thought about starting to teach again and hoped that Joshua would begin playing as well. She felt free, relaxed and finally in control of her own life. No more rules, no more humiliation, no more insults, no more abuse.

She walked down the hallway to check on her sleeping angels. Joshua would soon be six years old. He was sleeping on his side, his hands tucked under his pillow. His dark brown hair was sticking up, and his dark lashes rested on his chubby cheeks. He was a handsome boy with dimples and a tiny cleft in his chin. He was a typical first child. He was a bright student, popular, and good at sports. He was even-tempered and cautious.

In the other bed slept Cary, who was almost four years old. He was the most angelic looking of the three children, especially in sleep. He was a beautiful boy, with blonde hair and incredibly long lashes, now closed over bright blue eyes. Although small-boned, Cary was anything but frail. He was active, daring, and original. Although sometimes a challenge, he was bright and funny. His personality was effervescent. In sleep, his exuberance was at rest. Skylar bestowed a kiss on each boy's cheek.

She turned to go into the smaller bedroom where Jillian, two and a half years old, slept soundly in her crib. Her hair fell in loose, almost raven waves around her strikingly beautiful face. Her resemblance to Joshua was noticeable, but Jillian had the most incredible turquoise eyes, while Joshua's were chocolate brown. Skylar smoothed her hair and kissed her goodnight. This was her nightly ritual.

She opened the glass slider in her bedroom to get some fresh air, and got into bed.

Suddenly, the phone rang. "Hello, Skylar. How are you?" John politely asked.

"I'm fine," she answered cautiously.

"And how are the kids?" he asked her.

"They're all fine," she was abrupt but kind.

"I have something to tell you. It's bad, Skylar. It's so bad. And I want to protect you from it." Uncharacteristically, it sounded as if he were crying! She had never seen him cry. She was a very soft touch when someone cried. Sometimes, she would start to cry as well.

"Oh, John. What is it? It can't be that bad," she asked tearfully.

"It's about the taxes I've never paid. I don't want you to get punished for my mistake. I told them you weren't responsible. I'm gonna have to make a deal with them." He paused. "Skylar, I need to see you. Are the kids asleep? Can I come over? Maybe in an hour? Please."

She felt very badly that he sounded as if he were in so much pain.

"Okay," she whispered. "Come by at nine o'clock." She hung up the phone.

He arrived promptly at nine o'clock with a bouquet of red roses. Cool and arrogant, he presented no sign of the weeping voice she had heard on the phone.

"In retrospect," Skylar later informed her attorney, "it was one of his best performances. Definitely Oscar worthy. He proclaimed his love. I didn't let him in; we just talked by the door. He just wanted me back so we could sell the house and relieve him of that liability."

From Skylar's journal on Thursday, July 14, 1994: *I ran into John on Monday. He lectured me about going out too much.*

Was Skylar going out too much? She was definitely going out and having fun. She wasn't drinking, taking drugs, or picking up men. She was getting dressed up, meeting people, listening to music, and dancing up a storm. She was behaving as any victim of control and abuse who was suddenly free.

It was a confusing time for her as well.

Lori would call and say, "Skylar, don't feel guilty about going out. All you are doing is dancing. John is out all the time and getting plenty of sex. He called me. I know this. Don't feel guilty. You are doing nothing wrong."

Yet, John would call her and declare his love for her. He would appear when she was picking up Joshua from summer camp. The children would be excited to see them together. They would shout, "Daddy, kiss Mommy!" And he would kiss her passionately. But, she wasn't sure what to believe. He would kiss her one day and then there would be no contact for days.

Unbeknownst to Skylar, he was in constant contact with Lori and he knew Skylar's every move. He received reports from the neighbors which included the times she went out, what time she retuned, and what she was wearing. Some nights, he would call and beg to visit her once the children were asleep. He brought her flowers. He told her how much he appreciated her giving him three children. He said all the things she had wanted to hear for years. Paradoxically, when she would see him around town, he would brag to her about his new girlfriend.

Although a constable was still trying to serve him with divorce papers, he actively avoided being served. He was determined to evade service. He even moved out of his office in Newton because there was only one way in and out. He moved into an office in Needham, which had multiple egress, so if John saw the constable waiting for him, he could leave through a different exit. Despite the fact he had nightly trysts, he did not want to divorce Skylar.

Trying to move on and break free of John, Skylar accepted a date with a very cute man she met one evening. They saw each other several times. Finally, she told him about John.

He became very uneasy and told her, "Skylar, I want to continue to see you, but I'm very nervous about your psycho husband. I'm afraid of what he may do to me."

Skylar wasn't terribly upset. Her few dates were an adjustment to single life, and she found the transition easier than she thought. Because of all the abuse she had endured, she didn't need time to mourn the end of her marriage. She was more than ready to move on.

In early August, she heard a quiet knock on her door at ten o'clock. She looked outside and saw John's truck. She opened the door, and John stood there with a huge display of red roses. Because the children were fast sleep, she invited him in and they talked for hours.

"I've been thinking about a lot and I don't want to lose my family," he told her.

Skylar's feelings had been wavering for over ten weeks. She enjoyed her alone time, but she also deeply wanted her family, including John, intact. That night, passion reignited, and they decided to reconcile.

They planned a romantic celebration dinner for the next evening. Skylar asked Maree to babysit. John arrived an hour before Maree so he could spend time with the children. Skylar was happy to see him playing with the children. She felt so much optimism that this time it was going to work. Suddenly, his cell phone rang. He brought the children inside and took the call on the far side of the yard. He stood there for forty-five minutes, talking to a woman he had been dating during their separation. Skylar waited for him to come back into the house. She started feeling a little sick to her stomach. Disheartened, she knew this was a mistake. How long did it take to say, "I am back with my wife and children."?

When John finished the call, he walked back to the house and embraced Skylar and kissed her tenderly. "Hey, you look great except for one thing." He took her left hand and asked, "Where's your wedding band?" He kissed her hand. "Go put it on." He turned his attention to the children. "I love your mom! Who loves Mom?"

The children were yelling, "We love Mommy!" Skylar smiled at the children as she went upstairs, retrieved her wedding band from her jewelry box, and placed it on her finger.

The American Judges Association reports one of the most common reasons for resuming a relationship with an abusive partner is the fear the abuser will act on threats of taking the children. In fact, studies show batterers have been able to convince authorities the victim is unfit or undeserving of sole custody in the majority of challenged cases.

Maree was there when Skylar got back downstairs. She kissed the children good night and Maree brought them upstairs. John put his arm around Skylar and they walked outside.

Once they were seated in the car, John announced, "Honey, I love you so much. If I had to do it again, I'd marry you tomorrow."

Although still stinging from his forty-five minute phone call with the woman, she hoped the separation had convinced John his family was to be cherished. She was unsure if the separation had changed him but she was willing to try again. She felt that they *both* wanted their marriage to work. They had weekly meetings with a therapist. They planned more family activities, even going to the zoo. Maree babysat the children so Skylar and John could have adult time together. Everything seemed to be working.

The fall of 1994 was lovely and loving. John took Skylar for dinner to an elegant restaurant. He took her hands from across the table.

"I really love you, honey." Skylar smiled. "So, I talked to my accountant, and he said we should sell the house and move into a rental house for a year. It will help with my tax situation."

She was surprised at this abrupt change in the direction of the conversation. "What? Move into a rental? How will that help?" she asked.

He said, "If we sell the house, I can go to the IRS looking poor. If they see we don't even own a house, they'll probably make a deal so I won't have to pay much. After I pay the IRS, we can buy another house."

Skylar was skeptical. "But we've only been in the house four years, and we still owe a lot. I don't know why selling the house would make a difference. We still need a place to live."

"Skylar, trust me. That's what my accountant said. Ya think ya don't see me now, just wait. We'll end up losin' the house, I'll have to work night and day, and we won't be able to send Joshie to camp!" His voice began to rise. Noticing the look on her face, he lowered his voice and played his final card. "If we sell, we can move to Newton or Needham, like you always wanted." He knew he had said the magic words.

John hadn't changed. He was still a manipulator who would lie to get what he wanted. He knew he could only play the boring role of a faithful husband and father for a short while. If Skylar threw him out again, he would be stuck paying the mortgage for her. Or, they would have to sell the house, and she would get half the money. No, he had to play it straight until they sold the house.

That weekend, he called a real estate broker who came by to look at the house.

After looking around, she said, "You need to make this look as uncluttered as possible. Can you pack up what you aren't using at the moment and perhaps put it in storage? Also, move as much from your storage area. A potential buyer will appreciate a very large storage space." John answered, "I can put it in my parents' basement."

Skylar packed all their china, crystal, and wedding gifts. She packed her treasured record albums. She had boxes of books from her childhood and artwork she had done throughout high school. She had a box filled with mementos: funny post cards written by her deceased father, letters from John, souvenirs from trips, and her yearbooks from camp, middle school, and high school. She put all of her photo albums in storage, albums of the photos she had taken of the children, her own baby photographs, and photos of her grandparents. The items she had inherited were packed as well. When all the packing was finished, John took the boxes and brought them to his parents' house in Needham. When they were done, Skylar saw the boxes that represented her whole life, stacked in George and Nora's unused basement.

That was the last time she would see her belongings.

Chapter 14

From the New Testament, Jeremiah 13:23: "Can the Ethiopian change his skin or the leopard change his spots?" It is an allusion to the pessimistic rhetorical questions and a well-known cliché. A leopard doesn't change his spots; this is referred to as an idiom, meaning people cannot change their character traits, particularly the negative ones.

On a warm September evening in 1994, John made arrangements to meet his friend Phil for dinner. It was Phil's first date with someone he had recently met, and he was nervous. When they got to the restaurant, Skylar found Phil's date attractive and well spoken. Her anticipation of a nice evening was shattered when Phil enthusiastically gestured to John and loudly announced to his date, "This guy is wild! Johnny has to have sex all the time. When these two were separated, he had sex with four women!"

John chimed in, "Yeah – in ten weeks!" He and Phil laughed boisterously.

Skylar was mortified. She excused herself, went into the bathroom, and vomited. As she composed herself in the ladies room, she sadly thought, *This isn't going to work.*

As the briskness of autumn approached, she was still teaching modeling and had received an invitation to a party at the studio of the head photographer of the modeling agency. She was excited when John agreed to go, as it was going to be a fun event.

However, as she was dressing for the party, John suddenly announced, "I'm not in the mood to go to a party with people who think they're special because they model." He struck a pose, mockingly. As a narcissist who needed to be the center of attention, attending a party where the focus would be on the models was more than John could bear. He berated models because they effortlessly would take the spotlight. Skylar went to the party alone.

Their marital therapist didn't seem to think John was wrong because he didn't attend the party, which wasn't unexpected as he sided with John the majority of the time. He felt John deserved his weeklong trips to Florida without his wife, but he announced that Skylar's desire to go to a health spa for a weekend was "shitty and selfish." Skylar questioned the therapist's ability to remain unbiased.

According to Sam Vaknin, *"The narcissist sends a (nonverbal) message to his psychotherapist; there is nothing you can teach me. I am as intelligent as you are. You are not superior to me. Actually, we should both collaborate as equals in this unfortunate state of things in which we, inadvertently, find ourselves involved."* Because the narcissist is so charming, it would be difficult for a therapist, with training only in couples counseling, to detect someone with this type of personality disorder.

The cycle of abuse and humiliation was ending, and another honeymoon phase began. In November of 1994, John took Skylar for a romantic weekend to a resort in Stowe, Vermont. They went roller blading, had candlelit dinners, and enjoyed side-by-side massages. The trip was perfect. It prompted a trip to the New Year's Eve celebration in Orlando.

Orlando was equally as wonderful. They visited the theme parks, went out for romantic dinners, and took an intimate boat excursion. At Planet Hollywood, he told her, "I'm gonna buy you a leather jacket." When he took out his credit card, he turned to her and added, "Since I'm nice enough to take you on this trip and buy you a jacket, I deserve one, too." He told the clerk he was purchasing the man's jacket as well.

The honeymoon phase of the cycle of abuse is aptly named. While many couples who aren't in abusive relationships enjoy their mates on a fairly even keel, the couples in abusive relationships can only experience the very highs and the very lows. The highs are fueled by intense love and generosity. It is a phase of courtship. Everything appears as if the couple was actually on a honeymoon. In sharp contrast, the lows are periods of physical abuse, mental abuse, emotional abuse, humiliation, and despair.

Upon their return from Florida, Skylar was basking in the warmth of the honeymoon phase contrary to the bitterly cold winter of 1995. She didn't mind, as it gave her the chance to organize the house. As she went through the drawers, she found the picture she had taken right after John had thrown her down and choked her. The marks on her neck were painfully prominent. It hurt her to look at them. She took the pictures and carefully shredded them as they were a reminder of another time. She felt so sure they were really going to make it that she didn't want any negative reminders.

John reinforced her confidence when he called from work and said, "Business is so slow and it's really freezing. We should all go away on a vacation to someplace warm. What do you think?"

She was surprised and thrilled. A family vacation sounded wonderful! Being with her husband and children were all she ever wanted.

John made last minute reservations. The following afternoon, the Bauers family boarded a plane for Miami. They spent several days there, going to the beach, taking a boat ride through Coconut Grove and exploring the area. A few days later, they drove to Key West.

One afternoon, they went to the beach. Skylar played with the children in the clay-like sand, while John sat on a chair and smoked a cigar. She asked him to watch the boys while she took Jillian to the restroom.

John responded, "Yeah, yeah, I'll watch them."

When she returned, Cary was missing. She ran all over the small beach, her heart pounding wildly as she frantically hunted for him. It was a flashback to the time John promised to watch Jillian in a department store but ignored her, and she toddled away. The desperation was the same as that day, searching the store for Jillian in tears. Reminded of this, she was greatly relieved when she found Cary playing in the sand with some children. As she picked him up and held him close, she promised herself to remember the fact that she already knew: she could never fully trust John with the children.

Later that day, John declared, "Since I spent my money taking the family on the trip, I deserve a special gift." It was reminiscent of their honeymoon and searching the jewelry stores for the right bauble. He dragged the family into every jewelry store in Key West until he finally found an old coin from a shipwreck, framed in gold and encrusted with emeralds, hanging from a thick gold chain. He paid the jeweler three thousand dollars and put the necklace around his neck.

When they returned to Boston, Skylar attempted to continue the family togetherness by suggesting taking the children to an ice skating show at Boston Garden. But the honeymoon phase doesn't last forever and the energy had just about faded.

"I don't want to go to a boring ice show," John retorted.

She didn't want to anger him by insisting, so she opted to take the children alone. When they arrived at Boston Garden, she saw a little boy from Jillian's preschool class sitting with both of his parents. Seeing the family together, highlighted John's indifference to a traditional family outing. Skylar felt like crying, but instead she smiled, waved to the family, and tried to convince herself she was happy. She was attempting to turn the charade into reality.

As the crocuses began peeping up their heads in March, everything began a downward spiral. There were no more family trips or outings. There were no more date nights. The glow of the family times faded into a gray sadness. John was barely home, but when he was, he was sexually insatiable. It was the only time Skylar would get any sweetness out of him and therefore she complied.

In mid April, John suddenly began telling her she should be on Prozac, to "help with your mood swings." Skylar was puzzled; she didn't *have* any mood swings. At his suggestion, she bought a book on Prozac. After reading it, she could clearly see she didn't fit into any category of the depressed patient. She didn't feel unhappy or anxious but he was really pushing her hard to take the drug. She told him she didn't feel she was a good candidate for anti-depressant medication. She was very happy with the children but not with John and she didn't feel that drugs were the way to achieve happiness with him. It would be as if she was repressing the symptoms but still had the disease.

There were reasons John kept hidden from Skylar as to why he wanted her to take Prozac. He had met someone who was going to provide him with a very easy lifestyle. He knew the children meant everything to Skylar, and there was no question regarding her care of the children, so he would have to take another route and try to prove her as unstable by utilizing every method possible. He had a back-up plan to teach her a lesson she would never forget. He needed to be patient, get all his ducks in a row, and then seal the deal. He had someone waiting in the wings, someone who would keep her mouth shut, and was willing to take on the responsibility of the children as well as paying half the bills, someone who was just the kind of compliant woman he needed. Physically, she wasn't even close to what he found appealing in the least, but her willingness to help him castigate his wife made her very attractive.

He had met her in early March of 1995, when he walked into a potential client's office. He was anticipating obtaining a good account with steady work from a pest control company. The office was located in an older building above a restaurant. The hallways were dark with worn linoleum floors. He entered the office located at the end of the corridor.

The bland office contained a lone metal desk in the front of the room. There was a door leading to another room on the back wall. Out of that back room, carrying an armload of manila folders walked a woman.

"Can I help you?" she asked in a short clipped voice. She put the pile of folders on the desk at the front of the office.

He smiled. "I'm John, from Security Safe. I have a nine o'clock appointment."

The woman replied, "I'm Maryanne. He's running late, but he should be here soon. Why don't you have a seat and wait for him?" She sat down at the front desk.

John took one of the chairs against the wall. Maryanne was staring at him.

"You look familiar" she said, smiling broadly at him. "Do you ever go to O'Malley's?" she asked, naming a small restaurant which was located on the border of Newton and Needham.

"Yeah, I've spent some time there. Do you go there?" he asked.

"My mother's house is right around the corner."

"So, you're from Newton?" John asked. "My wife is from Newton."

"Who's your wife?" Maryanne asked.

When John mentioned Skylar's name, the smile faded from her face. She remembered Skylar well. She was one of those stuck-up Newton bitches who ignored her during high school. Yes, she remembered Skylar walking through the halls, her long brown hair swinging down the back of her cute little sweaters and tight jeans. Skylar, giggling with her girlfriends or walking down the hall with her boyfriend, the same boy Maryanne had her eye on since stepping foot into the high school. As she watched them kiss between classes, Maryanne burned with jealousy.

Maryanne Szalony had been a loner in high school. She was short, thickset, and plain with over-bleached blond hair. Her only friend Joan was her physical opposite. Tall and gangly and noticeably contrasting to squat Maryanne, they would walk the halls, each clutching their books to their chests. Groups of students would make fun of the mismatched duo as they made their way to their classes.

Now, twenty years after high school, Maryanne was heavier by twenty pounds. Still a light blond, her hair was cut very short and styled with spikes of hair sticking up. Maryanne kept a broad smile on her face and looked at John with intense interest.

"So, how is Skylar?" Maryanne asked, her voice overly sweet.

"Skylar is a bitch." John frowned, remembering the previous evening, when she was upset because John hadn't returned home until after eleven o'clock that evening. She had turned her back on him when he reached for her in bed and he was still irritated at her refusal.

"I'm divorcing my husband," Maryanne announced boldly. "Maybe we could have lunch someday?" she suggested. "It would make us both feel better." Maryanne kept smiling flirtatiously, displaying huge, horse-like teeth.

Just then, the front office door opened, and Maryanne's boss walked in. "John, come on in." He walked to the rear office.

"Call me," Maryanne whispered, as John stood up and walked to the back office.

Instead, she made the first move and contacted him. They made arrangements to meet for dinner. John was not particularly attracted to her. He found her exaggeratedly animated and too loud for his taste, but there were several things about her which he felt would compliment his lifestyle. She had her own income and a house near the lake in Natick. She had two teenage daughters who could help baby-sit. She was sub-missive and would let him do as he pleased. John was accustomed to ac-quiescence and dominance. Deep within his soul, he wanted Skylar but he was overcome with intense anger as she wasn't the obedient wife he required. She made her demands. She fearlessly spoke her mind. Skylar was vocal in her wish for an equal partner in marriage, contrary to John who wanted a concubine. His narcissistic view of himself was skewed because she expressed unhappiness. It was unfathomable that she didn't find him as wonderful as he saw himself. It would have been easier just to leave Skylar the first time she challenged him, but everything about her intrigued him, and that was why he couldn't let her go.

By the summer of 1995, Maryanne was demanding more time with John. He would make excuses and tell her he needed to spend some time with his family so he wouldn't arouse suspicions. He began to spend time with his family at the lake. One afternoon, Skylar surprised him when she announced she was going to learn how to waterski. He watched in admiration when she caught on quickly and skied around the lake. The children were applauding and screaming when John helped her back on the boat. He was overcome with emotion.

"You did great!" he exclaimed, covering her with kisses. They skied together as often as they could.

But by August, he knew the end was near if he chose to move forward. His ducks were lined up in a perfect row. They had a buyer for the house and the closing was imminent. Maryanne was urging him to leave Skylar so he could move in with her. John had decisions to make.

Skylar began looking for rental properties. One rainy Sunday, she excitedly showed him an advertisement for a duplex in Needham located across the street from his office. The rent was three hundred dollars less than what he was paying for the mortgage. Upon touring the unit, they found it tasteful and spacious. John had to agree it was perfect in every way, except he was determined not to rent the unit. When he spoke to the owner, he was rude and demanding.

Finally, the owner told him, "I don't think this is the right space for you."

Skylar was puzzled, as she knew he usually tried to charm everyone he met and this behavior was uncommon for him. She didn't realize his brash behavior was to insure they weren't accepted as tenants. He did not want his wife and children in such close proximity to his office, which also served as the site for his extracurricular trysts with Maryanne.

Further searching led them to a lovely single-family house in Newton. The owners were planning to sell the house in September of 1996. But Skylar was so excited at the thought of Joshua attending her former elementary school that she didn't carefully consider they would have to move again in one short year.

She didn't question John when he suggested, "Why don't *you* write a check for the security deposit? After all, we are moving to the town *you* wanted and you'll get the money back in a year." Thrilled to be living in Newton, she happily complied.

It was a decision which ended up costing Skylar everything.

For John, everything was contingent on Skylar agreeing to sign the papers for the sale of the Medfield house. He needed to romance her until that time, so he took her to New Hampshire, where he reserved the honeymoon suite of a Victorian bed and breakfast.

They visited his friends who live on a nearby lake. He was very loving and attentive toward his wife and his friends commented, "You two are the most perfect couple."

Skylar later perused her actions and added an undated entry in her journal: *I was behaving as an ostrich, with my head in the sand. I knew we were in the honeymoon phase of the abuse cycle. I was just waiting for the explosion. I was foolishly trying to convince myself my marriage was blissful.*

A few days after they returned, Skylar drove to the real estate office to pass papers on their home in Medfield. John was already there. He told her they had no equity in the house, therefore they wouldn't be receiving any money for the sale of the house.

The minute they passed the papers, he began to change. Skylar would suggest going to the lake for a quick ski, and he would refuse. He made Skylar unpack and arrange the house.

"I don't have time to do this! I have to work extra hard to afford the rent because *you* wanted to live in Newton!" He would yell. It didn't make sense because the rent was less than their mortgage. They were now living closer to his office, yet, he was never home for dinner. Then the abuse cycle began with a vengeance.

In late September, he took the family to Maine to visit Tom and Heidie. When they arrived, Heidie's friend was there, waiting for her to return from an errand. John began to flirt outrageously with this woman he had just met, as Skylar sat there, leafing through a catalogue.

"Do you like to golf?" he asked, smiling invitingly. "I love using my putter. I bet you'd like to use my putter too," he offered suggestively.

"That would be fun. Do you have balls too?" she boldly flirted back.

"Maybe we could check out my balls. I always keep my balls with my putter."

Skylar was disgusted as he continued his conversation, filled with sexual innuendoes. Nauseated, she left the room. She was fuming but went to bed.

When she confronted him later, he said, "I was just being nice. Her divorce was just finalized, and she was upset."

"So that's how you cheer her up?" Skylar asked. "I wonder how you cheer up women when I'm not there."

He left the room and proceeded to ignore her for the rest of the weekend. He didn't speak to her or spend any time with her. When she asked him to stop the truck so she could look in a gift store, he said, "I need to know what you want to look at so I can decide whether it's important enough to stop."

After a nightmarish weekend, they returned home. When they entered the house, the telephone was ringing. It was a friend of Skylar's. John came in, grabbed the phone from her, and slammed it down. "When I am home, you don't talk on the phone!" he screamed.

From Skylar's journal on Monday, September 11, 1995: *For the past week or two, I've had terrible chest pains. Either I'm very sick or suffering from tremendous stress. In any case, I think I'm going to have to see an attorney again. John is totally nuts, and he's killing me. I shouldn't have to live like this. No one should have to live like this. No other married, thirty-eight year-old woman should have to ask permission to go out for dinner with friends. No other woman has to beg and plead for her husband to allow her to look in a store window.*

She made a doctor's appointment for a physical. The doctor examined her and, although surprised at her request, ran a cardiogram. The test was normal.

John began encouraging her, once again, to consider getting a prescription for Prozac, so Skylar called a psychiatrist. She told him about her life with John, and then asked, "Would you advise me to take a drug if someone else was creating the stress in my life?"

He replied, "No. People take Prozac to take the edge off a tragic event or if there are unexplainable mood swings. If someone is creating intense tension for you, maybe you should not be with that person. Prozac won't give too much help."

She didn't want to take a drug in a futile attempt to escape from the situation John was creating. With the psychiatrist in full agreement, she opted not to take the drug.

She tried to avoid stress by lowering her voice to a hint above a whisper. If John called to say he would not be home for dinner, she would purr, "Okay, darling, I will see you later." Instead of calling the children inside to eat; she would go outside and quietly tell them dinner was ready. She tried to keep calmness and tranquility in her life, especially as John was being particularly cruel and unreasonable.

He appeared preoccupied when he was at home. Skylar was unaware of another plan he had secretly been plotting for a very long time. She thought they were still fighting to keep their marriage together. She didn't know they were fighting very different battles.

Chapter 15

In November of 1995, Skylar was anticipating attending her twentieth high school reunion.

Prior to the reunion, John randomly announced, "Phil Lewin is going to your reunion. He's dating one of your classmates; this girl named Maryanne."

She couldn't remember anyone named Maryanne, so she looked in her current school directory. She saw the name Maryanne (Szalony) Dziwka. Skylar's memory of her was vague, albeit unflattering. She mainly remembered Maryanne having only one friend and speaking in short, clipped words as if she was angry.

She told John, "I can't believe he is dating her. She was odd, and kind of an outcast."

It was strange because Phil usually dated attractive, personable women. But if he was dating Maryanne Szalony, Skylar assumed she had probably changed a lot since high school. However, Phil was always John's puppet, and he would do whatever he asked. John's motive was primarily to satisfy Maryanne and keep her where he wanted. He knew Skylar would never suspect Phil was merely attending the reunion as a cover for John's relationship with Maryanne. The fact that Skylar was the mother of his children didn't enter his thoughts as he planned this ultimate act of disrespect.

The night of the reunion, John began rushing Skylar as she was getting ready. "Hurry up! Let's get going! I'm hungry!" He threatened, "If we don't leave now, I'm stopping at Legal Seafood to get some oysters."

"Okay, I'm done." She finished brushing her hair and shut off the bathroom light. "One second." She ran to the playroom and gave the children a kiss goodnight.

Upon arriving at the reunion, John didn't look for food; he looked for Phil. They found him sitting at a table with Maryanne. Skylar noticed that Maryanne was heavier than she remembered. Her bleached hair was very short and spiked. She didn't look happy.

Skylar was friendly as she greeted her. "Hi, Maryanne! How are you?"

Maryanne didn't make eye contact with Skylar. She looked straight ahead and said, "Hi," in her short, choppy way. She sat there staring straight ahead with her arms crossed over her chest.

Skylar rolled her eyes. She took John's arm and said, "Let's walk around."

Begrudgingly, he accompanied her as she greeted her old classmates. Most of the women looked fantastic. The men appreciated it and doled out the compliments.

After twenty minutes, John announced, "I'm gonna go talk to Phil."

"But I want you to walk around with me," she said.

"Look, Skylar," he said, "I don't want to just stand there and listen to all these men tell you how beautiful you are."

John walked to Phil and Maryanne, who had not moved from their spot. As John sat down, Phil approached Skylar and led her away, saying, "Skylar, introduce me to someone."

"Phil, I thought you were with Maryanne." She stated.

He said, "No, I don't like her."

Skylar didn't want to spend the evening of her reunion trying to find a date for Phil Lewin. Several of her friends were there, and their husbands were seated at tables as their wives mingled, so she didn't find it strange that John didn't accompany her. She barely noticed that he was seated with Maryanne the whole night. She barely noticed that Maryanne didn't move from her seat even when the photographer got everyone together for a class picture.

"Is your husband here tonight?" One of Skylar's former classmates whispered to her as the photographer lined everyone up for the picture.

"He's sitting over there," she gestured. "At the same table as Maryanne Szalony."

The woman grimaced. "*She* hasn't changed much. Maybe she likes your husband."

Skylar returned an odd look.

"Just kidding, Skylar." The woman said, with a laugh. "I would hardly consider Maryanne Szalony a threat to your marriage."

Skylar agreed and promptly put the thought out of her head.

However, by then, John had been in a relationship with Maryanne for at least seven months.

According to Sam Vaknin,
> "*Narcissists are people who fail to maintain a stable sense of self-worth. Very often, somatic narcissists (narcissistic who use their bodies and their sexuality to secure narcissistic supply) tend to get involved in extra-marital affairs. The new conquests sustain their grandiose fantasies and their distorted and unrealistic self-image.*"

After the reunion, John gradually began replacing items in the house. He removed the new stereo and replaced it with an old unit, explaining to Skylar it was easier for her to use. He took out the glass end tables and replaced them with older wood tables from his parents' house, explaining he was afraid the children would get hurt if they broke the glass. It was easier for her not to question. She merely accepted his explanations as a way of keeping the peace. She was still trying to get that ostrich thing right and closed her eyes to these odd changes.

In December, her lifelong friend, Lindsay and her boyfriend came by for dinner, bringing a large order of Chinese food. As Skylar arranged the food on the table, John grabbed the containers, filled his plate and began eating, smelling each item before he put it in his mouth.

Joshua asked, "Dad, can I have some spare ribs?"

He yelled at Joshua, "You cannot eat until after I am done!"

Lindsay flinched and looked at Skylar, questioning. Joshua, frightened at his father's outburst, began crying. Skylar comforted him and quickly served the children. Once they were eating, she got a plate for herself. John didn't look up from his meal.

John took an intense, almost abnormal joy in food. He would bring home steaks and salmon and cook dinner for himself at ten o'clock. Skylar suggested he come home instead of shopping and she would heat up that night's dinner.

He sneered, "I may not be in the mood for what you cooked."

John would first smell his food before tasting it. He had very specific needs regarding food. Because he liked the butter soft, he insisted on always leaving it on the counter, where it would become rancid. He would buy an apple pie and refuse to refrigerate it. He would have one piece and then let it sit on the counter until the apples were covered with green mold. Skylar would throw it out and he would scream at her and threaten to make her pay for the moldy food she had discarded. He put a second refrigerator in the garage with a lock so no one else could open it. He loved the little butter cookies with the cherry in the middle, which he would buy at the bakery. He refused to share them with the children and kept them in the locked refrigerator.

A harsh chill was in the air as 1996 began. Skylar had hoped the new year would herald a new beginning, but John seemed lost in thought all the time. The van he purchased for work was stolen when he left it running as he got a cup of coffee. He reported it to his insurance company, claiming the van was locked. Skylar expressed her sympathy. She was doing everything she could to hold her family together, even consenting to an intimacy she did not feel.

On January 3rd, she was in bed and John joined her with a glass of wine. She was trying to muster up the courage to ask permission if she could go out with Lori for dinner on Friday night. That night, he brought up the subject first.

"The sitter called when you were bathing Jillian. Are you going out on Friday night?"

"Oh, Maree called? I wanted to go out for dinner with Lori," she waited nervously.

In a calm voice, he answered, "If you go out, you'll have to pay for the baby-sitter."

She felt the knots begin to grow in her stomach. "Why?"

He explained, "Because I work hard, and you do nothin'."

His answer infuriated her, but she kept her voice even. "I work, too. I am taking care of the children, the house, and the laundry all day and night. You would rather go out for sushi with Phil instead of coming home and having dinner with us."

John, in a most arrogant tone, haughtily stated, "I should be able to spend the money on myself and not for your good times." He sneered at her. "If you didn't want to work so hard, you shouldn't have had three kids."

Her heart was palpitating. "My children have nothing to do with this. I *like* having three children. You don't want to be a part of this family! I've had it with your selfishness! I want you to leave!"

John slowly got out of bed and placed his wine glass on the night table. He unplugged the lamp on the night table. "I need this," he said, purposefully taunting her.

Jumping out of bed, Skylar walked around the bed to where he was standing and boldly stated, "You've already taken enough from this house!"

He approached her slowly, and then suddenly shoved her against the wall. He put his face close to hers. With his teeth gritted he looked her in the eyes.

"I'll take whatever I damn well want, bitch!" The last words were screamed into Skylar's face and he punched the wall near her head.

She cowered on the floor with her arms and hands covering her head and face. Scared, she still found the courage to yell, "Leave the lamp alone!"

It wasn't that the lamp was anything special; it was just that she had enough of the years of abuse and control. Her heart was pounding and

Skylar had never felt as intense an anger in her life. It was as if all the years of abuse and neglect had come to a head.

She screamed, "Get the hell out of here! You are a loser and I can't stand the sight of you! You are a piece of shit!"

She stood up, grabbed the lamp, and faced him. Visions of swinging it at his head crossed her mind, but she knew he would kill her if she made one move toward him. She stood her ground with a defiant stare and he glared back. She opened the closet and tossed the lamp in, and then she moved to the other side of the bed.

He approached her. "Now you've done it! You don't EVER talk to me like that. We'll see who is leavin', you fuckin' cunt!" He shoved her hard against the wall.

She bravely screamed, "Get out, loser!" She had enough of his abuse.

Surprised that she didn't back down, he changed his tactic and declared, "No, I'm calling the police!" He picked up the phone in the kitchen and called 911. In a very calm and rational voice, he said, "There's a domestic dispute in my home." As he put the phone down, he approached Skylar, grabbed her shoulders, and pushed her down on the floor. His eyes were blazing and through clenched teeth he snarled, "You are going to be so fuckin' sorry. I wanted to relax tonight! I should beat the shit out of you!" He drew one arm back, his hand clenched into a fist.

She cowered on the floor, trembling in fear. Just then, the doorbell rang and the police officer could be seen through the window.

Skylar began to sob in relief. John opened the door, and the police came in. They assessed the scene and saw Skylar on her knees, crying, shaking and visibly traumatized. They saw John standing, with his public face, his calm demeanor, and arrogant stance. They told him he would need to leave. Without a word, he hooked up the boat to his truck and left the house.

Alone, Skylar locked the dead bolt on the door and dismantled the electric garage door.

She called Sable who told her, "You better call a lawyer. You need to protect yourself against him."

Late at night the phone rang. When Skylar answered, there was dead silence. It rang continuously until midnight. She was terrified all night and couldn't sleep. As she lay awake, she thought about what had occurred. She felt John had pushed her over the top that evening. She had never felt such extreme fury. She felt like one of the abused women whose stories flooded the media on how they fought back and finally killed their abusive husband. At one blind moment, she felt like she may have been one of those women. She was at the end of her rope and hated him with a passion for the years of abuse. Yet, after he left, she felt such a feeling of calmness wash over her. There was no sadness, no anger, just sweet relief. After years of abuse, when her abuser was out of the picture, the stress was gone. Her home was quiet. The fear was gone. The rules were gone. Skylar had the opportunity to take control of her life. Only when she came to that realization was she able to finally sleep. The tears were gone, and in their place was utter tranquility.

That weekend, Skylar had planned a birthday party for Jillian, who was now four. She concentrated on the task at hand and began to prepare for her party. She had small child-sized tables and chairs delivered and had set them up in the playroom. She decorated the room, assembled goody bags, and baked a special cake, shaped like a girl, for Jillian. On Sunday morning, she picked up dozens of colorful balloons then went upstairs and helped everyone get dressed for the party. The telephone rang just as she finished dressing the children.

It was her sister-in-law Audra, calling from Ohio. Skylar was accustomed to her calls attempting to get information. She wasn't very good at pretending she was just calling for idle chitchat.

Audra asked, "Are my parents still invited to Jillian's party?"

"Of course they're still invited. They're Jillian's grandparents." Skylar smartly answered.

"What about Johnny?" she asked.

Skylar replied, "Come on, Audra. He's her father. Of course I'm not keeping him away from his daughter."

John's parents attended the party, sitting there woodenly and they didn't mention John. Lori and her boyfriend arrived and helped gather the winter jackets of Jillian's friends. All the children gathered on the living room floor to watch the puppeteer Skylar had hired. The children were giggling, and Skylar kept up with the merriment, despite John's absence.

"Did he call?" asked Lori.

Skylar shook her head. "Are you kidding? If he called or came by, he'd have to pay for this. That's why he's not here." She felt quite sure that was the reason.

"I guess you're probably right on that one." Lori stated. "Look at your kids." she said, changing the subject. "They look so happy."

Skylar looked at her three beautiful children laughing at the puppets. The fact that John wasn't there meant nothing to them, as his absence was a too common occurrence.

After the puppet show, the children went downstairs for cake and ice cream. Skylar hoped John would come by to see Jillian or at least call, but he didn't appear and the phone remained silent.

As the winter snows began in earnest, without a call from John, Skylar knew a divorce was eminent. She began dating a gorgeous man named Jake English. She had noticed him one evening when she was out having dinner with Lori. Jake was a man you couldn't help but notice. He had sandy brown hair, green eyes, and a strong face with chiseled features. He was tall, standing well over six feet all. He had a long and lean physique from years of martial arts. That evening, he noticed Skylar as well and sent a round of drinks to her table. Talking to him after dinner, she found him strong, yet gentle. He was educated, well-spoken, and most importantly, very respectful.

His first date with Skylar was an offer to come to her house and shovel all the snow. She was not used to a man who was so considerate and she liked it. They saw each other quite often before she introduced him to the children. They adored Jake. He loved them and played with them, behaving like a father. The children weren't used to male attention, and they would scream with joy when Jake came to the house. They would beg him to sleep over, but he agreed with Skylar's belief it was not appropriate for him to spend the night when the children were there. He explained it wasn't proper and she appreciated his traditional values.

Unlike John, Jake was a secure man and secure with their relationship. He was not threatened by Skylar's newfound independence. He supported her interests. He warmly congratulated her after she auditioned for a dinner-theater production and was offered a role as a permanent cast member. He assured her he would meet her after the show each weekend if he didn't attend the performance.

She was still receiving anonymous phone calls late at night, which frightened her. Jake advised her to get a restraining order against John. She went to court and easily got a 209A restraining order, which documented his physical abuse, threats and practice of stalking her.

John immediately violated the restraining order by picking the new lock Skylar had installed in the house. He only wanted the video tapes of his friends waterskiing and left the videos of the children. He stopped by the preschool school to see Cary and Jillian. He called Joshua when he was visiting his friend Jed, who lived across the street, and asked him if "Mom had any strangers in the house." He made no attempt to contact Skylar or go into court to arrange a visitation schedule. He wanted to see the children on *his* terms, not a court order. He was too busy getting his new life arranged. It began the day he left the house in Newton when he made a phone call as he drove away.

"It's done. I'm out," he said.

The woman on the other end gasped in delight. "Finally! When can I see you?"

"How 'bout Sunday? Phil is having some people over to watch the football game." Sunday was Jillian's birthday and party.

"I'm getting rid of him tonight! I'm throwing him out of the house! You can move right in!"

"Maryanne," John cautioned, "give it a little time! Let your kids get used to the idea."

"No! This is my decision!" Maryanne screamed. "I've waited long enough! Either you move in now, or you can go back to her!" she threatened.

"Okay, Maryanne. Get it done." John sighed wearily.

She replied, "I'll do it tomorrow. You can move in on Sunday."

That weekend, she told her husband she wanted a divorce. He packed a suitcase and moved to his parents' home in Framingham. On Sunday, John brought Maryanne to Phil's to watch the football game on television. He made no attempt to participate in Jillian's birthday celebration.

Skylar was filing for divorce as well. She hired her former attorney Roger Woodman.

Instead of his former attorney, Zoe Powers, John hired Phil's older sister to represent him. Liz Lewin was a petite yet masculine looking woman with short, dark hair. Her lifestyle choices ranged from controversial to bizarre. Professionally, she was completely unethical. In 1995, she was sanctioned by Judge Shauna McGowan for her misconduct while acting as the attorney for a man in a divorce proceeding. Liz exacerbated the proceedings and abused the court process by directing her client not to cooperate with the guardian ad litem (custody investigator), which she acknowledged in court. She undermined the legal process and challenged the integrity of the judges and appointed experts who did not agree with her.

From the docket on caselaw.com, Judge McGowan stated: *"Ms. Lewin made a mockery of the legal proceedings by filing so many vexatious and harassing motions, so many motions for reconsideration, vacating, review, etc., such constituting an egregious abuse of the court system. She did not attempt to exercise proper control and guidance of her client and had become so enmeshed with her client that she lost her professionalism in advocating for a client. She made the husband's tirade a crusade of hers as well."*

Ironically, Liz had met Skylar at a barbeque at her parents' house in Needham. Liz knew how attentive and loving Skylar was with her children. Liz's own mother complimented Skylar when she saw her caring for the children. Alternately, she knew what kind of person John was, as her father, attorney Herb Lewin, had represented him when he was arrested for possession of cocaine. Although she was well aware of the characteristics of all the players, in order for Liz to be an effective attorney for John, she would have to lie. Since John was a family friend, his attorney fees were negligible; he only had to pay court fees.

Liz summoned Skylar into court to review the child support order. She claimed John was paying above the recommended guidelines according to the income he claimed. She didn't ask for a visitation schedule with the children.

Skylar's attorney Roger resubmitted the Complaint for Divorce from June of 1994. He listed the reason for divorce as irreconcilable differences.

Skylar said, "Irreconcilable differences are not the reasons I am getting a divorce. I am getting a divorce because of his abuse. I want this changed to cruel and abusive behavior."

Roger told her, "We can't change it. Someday, your children may come to court and look at the file. Do you want them to know their father was abusive? They're young enough now, so they will forget anything they saw. You don't want a reminder for them in court documents."

She replied, "All I want is the truth." It seemed as if irreconcilable differences was a benign reason. The synonyms for irreconcilable differences were incompatibility, opposition, contradiction, and diversity. It was much milder than the synonyms she used to describe John, who choked his wife, kicked car windows, ripped clothing, and tried to force his wife to have sex with another woman. Accurate synonyms could include malicious, violent, sadistic, and perverted. Skylar was divorcing John due to cruel and abusive behavior and nothing less.

When she wasn't gathering her papers for her pending divorce, Skylar was working. In addition to her teaching job, she was performing on Saturday nights throughout New England. Her pager beeped one evening as she was in the dressing room preparing for the performance. She saw it was the baby-sitter, Connie Taylor. Because Maree wasn't always available to babysit, John had introduced Skylar to Connie the previous year. Although John knew her since high school, he told Skylar he met her when he changed the locks at the daycare center where she worked as a teaching assistant. He didn't tell Skylar that Connie was a customer who bought her marijuana supply from him.

Skylar called home, and Connie told her, "Jillian has an infected finger."

It seemed odd and sudden, as Jillian had not complained. It was especially strange as Skylar was meticulous with the children's health issues. If Jillian had an infected finger, it was indeed puzzling.

"It should be checked. I can take her to the hospital," she offered. It didn't sound like an emergency but Connie insisted and Skylar was being cued by the show's director.

"Okay, take her. I'll call you after the show." Skylar didn't give her best performance that evening, as she was preoccupied with Connie's message about Jillian. She called home after the show. Frightened when there was no answer, she grabbed her bag and rushed home. She found Connie at the house. She reported that Jillian had an infection. The doctor had soaked her finger and applied an antibiotic cream.

Baffled, Skylar asked Connie, "How could this have happened?"

"I slammed Jillian's finger in the door last week and forgot to tell you." she replied. "Also, I had to call John so he could sign the consent forms to allow treatment at the hospital."

At that moment, John was sitting outside of Maryanne's house smoking a cigar, almost giddy with glee at how well the evening went. Connie had been a brilliant accomplice, and now he had the doctor's report and pictures he needed to make Skylar look as if she were neglectful in her care of the children. It was the first step of his complex and convoluted strategy to take away her children.

Chapter 16

On Monday, Skylar took Jillian to the pediatrician to examine her finger. It was rapidly healing without complication. After returning home from the doctor, she received a telephone call from her attorney. He informed her Liz had filed a motion for John, seeking an emergency change in custody. She was stunned. It was preposterous that he was attempting to get custody.

What court would take custody from a mother who was the sole caregiver and place them with a man who was uninvolved with the children because he was never home? she thought. Her family and friends thought the motion was ridiculous. Her attorney was unconcerned. It was simple; Skylar's parenting skills were beyond reproach. She was the consummate mother with a pristine record. John was a drug dealer with a criminal record. He would never get custody.

Barry Nolan, veteran television journalist and Emmy winning commentator who covered the tragedy of 9/11, Waco, Oklahoma City, and the Republican Convention, attended the 6th Annual Battered Mother's Custody Conference in Albany on January 15, 2009. The Battered Mother's Custody Conference is a national public forum to address the many complex issues facing battered women and their advocates as they strive to protect themselves and their children in and out of family court during divorce, custody, and visitation disputes.

In his article, Barry Nolan stated: "Pretend you are a woman who has finally left an abusive relationship, taking your children with you. If your controlling, soon-to-be ex-husband sought to get full custody of the children as one last slap at you, what would you say? Okay? Sure, that sounds fair? Fat chance."

Undaunted by John's motion, she drove to the hearing. Upon her arrival in court she was surprised to see the babysitters, Maree Labarini and Connie Taylor, and Jean, the mother of Joshua's friend Jed, who lived across the street, standing there. Skylar asked them why they were there and they replied, "John subpoenaed us to come in."

John and Skylar were called to the family advocate's office. The advocate was a tall, attractive blonde woman so John turned on the charm. He smiled at her as if she was a very appealing date. His blue eyes stared into hers and his flirtation was outrageous. It was almost a seduction. She, in turn, responded to the allure he was generating in her direction. He related the story about Jillian's finger dramatically embellishing every detail to make it sound as if Skylar were purposefully neglectful. Skylar was stunned when he ended with, "There were two reports made to the Department of Social Services on her already!"

The woman asked Skylar if she thought John was a good father. She thought, *John was an absentee father and abusive. But if I say no will I be judged harshly for allowing my children to be subjected to John's abuse?* She didn't yet understand that *she* was a victim. She remembered his help when the children had lice, so she murmured, "When he's there..."

The woman asked John if he thought Skylar was a good mother. He loudly answered, "No!"

Jolted, Skylar looked at him in utter shock. He had never complained about her care of the children! If she had been such a bad mother, then why wasn't he ever home to monitor this?

Linda Martinez-Lewi, PhD, of San Diego has extensive clinical training and experience in narcissistic and borderline personality disorders. She has worked for many years with clients dealing with relationships with narcissists. She is the author of *Freeing Yourself from the Narcissist in Your Life*. Dr. Martinez-Lewi states: *"Narcissists become particularly shameless during a divorce. They accuse the other spouse of neglecting the children when the reverse is true."*

This was a sharp contrast to the first time they had separated in 1994 when, John moved into his parents' house. He refused to take the children for any overnight visits. During the days he had them, he would plan activities with other people so they could watch the children. He never took them anyplace without assistance.

Skylar thought, *There has to be some ulterior motive as to why John is asking for custody now.* One of the reasons, she later discovered, was that he did not want to pay child support. His own extended family knew that was a reason he pursued custody, but they didn't suspect all the motives that drove him.

Dr. Lenore E. Walker is referred to as the "mother" of the battered woman syndrome due to her research in the late 1970s. She has helped women and has educated individuals to better understand why battered women have such difficulty in getting out of domestic violence relationships. The author of *The Battered Woman*, Dr. Walker states:

> *Batterers commonly engage in child custody battles. For some batterers, it's a way of prolonging the inevitable disintegration of their family. Others use child custody as a weapon to keep the woman from going through with a divorce. The abusive/controlling man feels that they still need to control their ex-wife. They feel as if she is still their possession. Abusive men who try to get custody of their children are successful 90% of the time.*

Maree, Connie, and Jean had submitted written affidavits, prompted by Liz and then left the courthouse. Skylar read the affidavits in shock, horror, and disbelief. Maree and Connie wrote Skylar would lock the children downstairs, although the door did not have a lock. They wrote the house was filthy, smelled, and was full of used diapers. Both Maree and Connie wrote, *Skylar drinks too much.* Jean had written that Joshua was always hungry and that she heard some unusual language coming from him, but she did not elaborate.

Judge Crown was an older male judge who usually sat in the

probate court in Salem. Many family attorneys knew he often made decisions thoughtlessly and they would groan when they heard his name. It was Skylar's misfortune that he was sitting in Dedham that day. He said he was going to assign a guardian ad litem (GAL) to their case who would investigate each side by meeting with the parents, children and collaterals. Once they gathered the information, they would write a report with a recommendation regarding which parent was best suited to have custody of the children. Judge Crown ordered the cost of the investigation to be split equally.

Skylar wasn't worried as she had sufficient documentation, in addition to her journals, as evidence who should retain custody of the children. She was however concerned about the cost of the investigation. She had no doubt the court would find in her favor, but it seemed unfair she would deplete her savings on an investigation she found irrelevant.

From Skylar's journal on Friday, February 16, 1996: *After court, Roger came to my house to pick up a check because I didn't have my checkbook with me. When he came into the house, he said, "Where's the mess? Where's the smell?" He looked around the whole house and couldn't find any indication of what Maree and Connie had been talking about. Later, I confronted Jean, in front of her house, about the kind of language she had heard from Joshie. She told me that she heard "weenie sucker" and "penis sucker" coming from Joshua. I asked Jean if she thought her affidavit was vague and if she had written those words, wouldn't her affidavit sound kind of silly? I asked her if she thought I was using those words, and she said, "No... Liz Lewin specifically told me not to write those words on my affidavit."*

During the day in court, John never asked for a visitation schedule or if he could see the children. Audra called to tell me Nora and George said I was going to accuse John of sexually abusing the children. I told her they were stupid. I didn't have to make up anything when the truth about John's abuse, neglect or disinterest in being a father was apparent.

Skylar called the Department of Social Services (DSS) to get information about the alleged reports John claimed had been filed. She learned of reports in October of 1995 and January of 1996. The DSS routinely followed up on all complaints. Each report on Skylar was dismissed on the very same day and she was never contacted. The October 1995 report stated: *The children were crawling out of their bedroom window, which was on the first floor.* One major discrepancy was the children's bedrooms were never on the first floor, not in Medfield and not in Newton. Who made these complaints? Was it someone who had genuine concerns, or was it someone John Bauers convinced to call in order to build his contrived fight for custody?

Skylar later discovered that John had persuaded former Medfield neighbor, Sally Beaux, to make the first complaint with the Department of Social Services.

Attorney Liz Lewin made the second complaint.

On Friday, February 23, John brought Skylar back to court for a contempt charge. He claimed she wasn't letting him see the children. It was a frivolous contempt because there was no court order regarding his visits. She revealed this to the family advocate.

"Well, Mrs. Bauers, we can create a visitation schedule beginning this evening. John could pick the children up tonight and keep them until Sunday morning."

"Where are they staying?" Skylar asked.

"Well," laughed John, "they can stay at my girlfriend's house."

"No," she firmly stated. "This would be confusing and inappropriate. In fact, that needs to be written in the visitation agreement as well."

"That goes for you too!" he sneered.

She shrugged. "I don't have a problem with it. Write it." she told the family advocate.

"My girlfriend wants me to bring the kids to her house. Skylar knows her."

Skylar asked, "Who's your girlfriend?" John ignored her.

Liz told Skylar, "John's girlfriend is Maryanne."

"Maryanne? I don't know anyone named Maryanne." Skylar said.

"You went to high school with her," replied Liz.

Skylar was shocked. John's girlfriend was Maryanne Szalony Dziwka. She had been at the high school reunion with Phil Lewin, Liz's brother, posing as her date.

From Skylar's journal on Sunday, February 23, 1996: *When the children came home from their visit with John they were acting up and telling me that I am a bad person. "Dad said we'd live with him, and dad's friend Connie, would pick us up from school" Joshie declared. "What have you bought me for over $100.00 like the remote control car that Dad bought for me?" Then Jillian told me that she had two summer dresses at Maryanne's house. Why would he try to confuse them by promising they are going to live with him? Why would he buy an expensive toy for Joshie now? Is he trying to buy his affections?*

The stress continued on Monday when Skylar went to Temple Beth Shalom in Needham to pick up Cary and Jillian from preschool. The principal stopped her and informed her "Unless the tuition is paid by Friday, Cary and Jillian will not be able to continue in this school."

When she returned home, she placed a call to John's parents. George and Nora had been in the group of founding members of the temple when they first moved to Needham. She couldn't imagine them allowing John to smear their name within their temple community by not paying the bill. George answered the telephone.

"Hi, George, it's Skylar. Cary and Jillian are going to get kicked out of preschool unless the rest of the tuition is paid. John won't pay it. Do you think you could take care of their tuition?" Skylar got to the point immediately.

George slowly said, "They don't need to go to preschool."

"Yes, they do," she patiently explained. "They need the stability of the same routine. Also, I use the time they are in school to go on job interviews."

"Why do you need a job? You didn't work during the marriage," George responded.

Oh, my God, thought Skylar, *What an idiot.* Keeping her voice even, she stated, "Your son is not giving me enough money to live on, and therefore, I have to work."

George contemplated this request. He told her, "Well, I'll have to ask Nora."

Skylar hung up. She had her answer. She was on her own.

Despite their reputation in the synagogue and the fact these were their grandchildren, they refused to pay the tuition, and Cary and Jillian were terminated from the program.

The second ax fell when Skylar received a call from the insurance agency. They informed her that the homeowner's insurance was canceled. They provided her with the cancellation date. John had called up to cancel it six days before he left the house.

Skylar felt it was important for Cary and Jillian to keep the same daily routine, so she began making telephone calls to different schools in the area. After much searching, she found a school with a similar curriculum as their former school located in a beautiful brand new building in Newton. The director invited her to visit. After her tour, Skylar felt the school was perfect fit. A partial scholarship was available and Skylar was thrilled. She had managed to maintain their stability for her children. When Cary and Jillian saw the sunny classrooms with the large windows and the modern playground, their eyes lit up and they laughed in delight. It only took a week until Cary and Jillian felt comfortable and happy at their new school.

It was for the benefit of her children that Skylar gave her entire support check to keep them in school. Utilizing every resource available, she registered with the local food bank and began receiving free food every other week. She used her small salary to buy fresh fruits, vegetables, and meats. She was tenacious in her search for a fulltime job. She realized that teaching at the modeling school on the weekends wasn't sensible because she needed to work when the children were in school. Although she had limited skills for an administrative job, she had a good background in sales, albeit over eight years old. But, she was keeping her options open and was willing to work in almost any area geographically.

At the same time, she was looking for an apartment, which was difficult because every landlord asked for names of previous landlords. She had no rental history. Her income was only from a part-time job, and most of that money went to a local college girl, she had hired to babysit. In addition, the "lead paint law," which stated any child under six years of age could not live in a rental unit that contained lead paint, prohibited her from some rentals because Jillian was only five. She was looking everywhere for a new home and new employment. Whatever she found first, a job or an apartment was where they would settle.

From Skylar's journal on Saturday, March 2, 1996: *Received an anonymous phone call yesterday. It was from a girl who told me she knew I was getting a divorce. She said she had information for me. She told me John was seeing someone in Florida who was "devastated" when he broke up with her because he "wanted to make his marriage work." She said he was dating someone else in Connecticut. She told me he met Maryanne at her job.*

The girl didn't want to reveal her name. Skylar knew the information wasn't going to help her with her divorce, yet the information was a revelation. She had always suspected infidelity from John, and now she was sure. The anonymous telephone call gave her the reassurance that divorcing John was the right decision. She reveled in her own strength for heeding her instincts. She was going to get through this, and the children were going to stay with her.

Chapter 17

Skylar had her first meeting with the guardian ad litem (GAL) in early April of 1996. In preparation for her meeting, she copied approximately fifty pages from her journals. She also provided notarized copies of records from doctors, dentist, hospital, and school conferences where she was the only parent listed. In legal jargon, it would be considered supporting evidence. She did not consult with her attorney in preparation for the meeting.

The court appointed Julie Ginsler as the GAL. Julie had a law degree and a degree in social work. She was a tall, thin woman in her late fifties. Her hair was red, but her skin was almost colorless in its pallor. Her features were plain, her demeanor was bland, and her affect flat. She spoke slowly and quietly, with little inflection.

"Tell me about your situation," she asked.

Skylar related her daily involvement with the children and as well as John's incessant absences, from the house providing an example of an occasion when John came home from work early and was surprised to hear Cary speaking in full sentences. He hadn't been home enough to know his son had started talking.

Julie didn't question Skylar's parenting skills or her ability to care of her children. She seemed more concerned about her relationship with Jake. She asked whether he slept over when the children were present.

Skylar was surprised at the question but she responded, "Jake is a gentleman. He's very proper, and the children love him." She was honest and candid as she had nothing to hide. She felt optimistic as she left Julie's office.

Robin Shaye

The second visit occurred a few weeks later in Skylar's home. Julie noticed the piano and asked Skylar to play. She played several pieces and Julie complimented her ability. She asked if she could speak to the children privately so Skylar left them in the downstairs playroom.

Joshua later related Julie had asked them what they eat. Joshua told her, "Mom makes good meals. She always cooks, but once the food was too spicy, so we got pizza." The children reported about Skylar's participation in school events and extracurricular activities.

Before she left the house Julie asked for a list of collaterals to speak with in regard to Skylar's involvement with the children. Skylar thought it was wise to give her a list of unbiased, professional people whose words would hold more weight than friends. She provided the names of teachers, the director of the preschool, and the pediatrician. Julie wanted to speak to Jake. Skylar also gave her Lindsay's number, as she had witnessed John's callous interaction with the children. She was sanguine about the outcome of Julie's investigation.

The sun was shining, and the weather was warm. Skylar was in high spirits, as she had transferred to the sales department at the modeling school where she had been teaching for four years. It was a more lucrative position with a weekday schedule. She was also eagerly waiting for word on a prospective apartment, which was logistically very close to her job on the north side of Newton. The owner of the apartment was checking the place for the possibility of lead paint. Everything in her life appeared to be moving in a positive direction.

John was irked when he was greeted by a cheerful Skylar each time he picked up the children for a scheduled Thursday night dinner, in addition to every other weekend.

I gotta wipe that smile off her face, and I know the best way to do it, he thought.

One Thursday evening, Maryanne accompanied him when he brought the children home. Perfect, John thought when he saw Skylar unloading her groceries from her car. Maryanne got out of the truck to allow the children to climb out of the back. She boldly stood there, staring at Skylar mockingly. The children raced into the house to watch television. Maryanne glared at Skylar before getting back into the truck.

Skylar wasn't smiling. She was appalled. She yelled to John, "Next time, leave the whore at home!" She marched into the house.

John sat there, smug that he was able to get a reaction from her. He didn't care about Maryanne being the target of Skylar's words. It didn't matter who was insulted, as long as he was able to get a satisfying reaction.

Skylar was more appalled than angry to see Maryanne at her house. She found it incredibly tasteless. She called Sable to tell her how Maryanne had the audacity to come to her house. She repeated to Sable what she yelled to John.

"Did you really say that?" gasped Sable.

"Yes, I said it. The children were already inside and didn't hear me. I mean, what kind of woman who had been having an affair with a married man would go to the marital home? I call it as I see it. She's got no morals or scruples."

"I agree with you," Sable replied. "At least she should have a little shame."

Skylar sighed. "You know, I am so over him, and I really feel John is with someone who suits him. But it kills me that my children have to spend time with that trashy woman!"

"Skylar, don't get upset. The children are young enough. When they get older, they'll figure it out. You don't need to get yourself stressed," Sable said, soothing her daughter.

Maryanne never appeared at the house again. John began coming to the house alone. He changed his behavior toward Skylar and was softer and polite. He would greet her at the door when he picked up the children. He would bring them to the door when he dropped them off, sometimes coming in carrying a sleeping child. He would linger and talk to her. One afternoon, he called to tell her he would be a little late getting the children and offered to pick up a sandwich for her. When he arrived, the children were in the backyard.

"Here," he said, handing her a paper bag. "I got just what you like; turkey, mustard, and pickles."

"Wow, thanks," said Skylar. She turned to bring the sandwich into the kitchen.

"Honey," she heard softly and she turned around to see John standing there with his pants down to his knees. He began touching himself. "You miss my penis, don't you?"

Skylar was embarrassed and turned away. "John, pull up your pants! This is ridiculous."

He crooned, "It really misses you."

She turned and looked out the kitchen window. "The kids are coming in."

He quickly pulled up his pants and fastened them as Skylar watched the children playing on the swing set. She turned to face him. "You should wait in your truck. I'll get their sweaters and bring them out to you," she said, walking toward the front door. She wanted to usher him out as quickly as possible so he wouldn't realize the children were still happily playing outside.

The following Thursday, John brought the children home from an early dinner. Skylar usually let them watch television in the playroom after a visit with him in order to wind down a little bit before she put them to bed.

John came in and said, "Hi." He smiled and swaggered toward Skylar. "Let's go upstairs." By then, he had Skylar backed up against the wall.

"C'mon John, you're being silly. Let me go." She tried to keep her voice light. She didn't want to anger him.

"Please." He took her hand and forced her to touch him. "Feel how much I want you."

She tried to get him to stop but he was too strong for her. In a terse whisper, she hissed, "John, stop it. We're getting a divorce, and we're both with other people." She ineffectively tried to push him off her, but he just laughed. He was easily able to grasp both of Skylar's narrow wrists in one hand and hold her tightly.

"That doesn't matter," he said. By then, he had unzipped his pants. He had his full weight against her, pressing her into the wall.

"John, get your goddamn hands off of me!" Her voice came out in a panicked, tearful squeak. "Please stop!" She tried to keep her voice quiet so the children wouldn't hear. Sobs wracked her body as she struggled against him, as he held her wrists as tight as a vice. She was unable to move at all.

With his full body weight on her, he was able to tuck one of her hands behind her back, pressing her against the wall so she was unable to move. He took her free hand and forced it inside his underwear, pressed her hand on him, and moved it back and forth quickly.

Skylar closed her eyes. Her tears streamed silently. "Don't do this, John."

He ignored her. She felt him breathing hard in her ear. "You're a good girl, Skylar." Suddenly, it was over. John loosened his grip on her and she was able to release her hand.

She reached up and tried to wipe her hand on his shirt. He jumped away from her.

"Hey! We don't need *her* to find out." He closed his eyes briefly, as if in bliss and smiled, "Mmm, that was nice." He handed her the dish-towel from the kitchen.

Skylar took it woodenly and wiped her hand. She couldn't look at him.

He took her silence as acquiescence. "Should I come back after the kids are in bed?"

His words seemed to shock her back to reality. "No! I want you to go!"

"Fine." John looked in the mirror and arranged his hair. "See ya." He opened the door and walked out, whistling merrily.

Skylar thought she was going to be sick. She sank to her knees and retched but held it in. She felt violated. She told herself, *Hold on, the children are here.* She strained to take long deep breaths. She glanced in the mirror and forced herself to smile. *Okay, I look normal. The children won't be able to tell.*

Robin Shaye

"Kids!" She forced a smile into her voice. "Bedtime."

After she put the children to bed, she took a long, hot shower which drowned out the sounds of her sobs. She scrubbed her hands and arms with her nailbrush until her skin was raw.

The morning dawned bright and sunny. Skylar's sole focus was on the children and keeping their lives as normal as possible. She signed Joshua up for the Little League baseball team and managed to get the fee waived by writing a letter to the recreation department.

Liz Lewin instructed John to get involved with the children's activities, so he signed up to be a coach for the team. He would appear at the games on the days that the children were with Skylar. On the days the children were with him, he would skip the game and take them to the lake.

Julie Ginsler called Skylar just once during the summer. "Skylar, I think the children should stay at Maryanne's during visits. After all, she is John's fiancée."

His fiancée? For a moment, Skylar was puzzled. Then she realized John's ploy was an attempt to convince Julie he was in a permanent relationship and would provide a more stable environment for the children. Skylar had no choice but to let the charade slide and do as the GAL suggested.

Since John was now "engaged," Skylar hoped he wouldn't touch her. She didn't trust him and did her best to keep him out of the house, but some nights, when she unlocked the door to let the children in, he would enter the house as well. He would usher the children to the playroom and approach her. She would try to stop him, but he was simply too strong. Although her attorney was aware of John's actions, he refused to go back to court.

"No one is going to pay any attention. The last time we filed for divorce, you two got back together. The judge will just think this was an attempt to reconcile."

One night, John took his assault on Skylar a step further. "C'mon, Skylar. I know how much you miss us. Let me touch you."

"John, get out!" Skylar loudly stated, stamping her foot.

"Mom?" called Joshua from the playroom.

"It's nothing, Joshie," yelled John. "Go watch your show." He turned to Skylar. "You little bitch. You want the kids to see this?" He threw her on her back upon the steps leading up to the bedrooms. "You wanna scream again?" He kissed her roughly as he reached inside her shorts, roughly fondling her until she bled. He then rubbed himself on her stomach until he was satisfied. "You're a disgusting mess. Go wash up."

Skylar stumbled into the bathroom. Blood was everywhere. She heard the front door slam as she grabbed a washcloth and cleaned up as best as she could.

"Mommia!" She heard Jillian's little voice calling her by her personal nickname.

"Breathe, breathe," she whispered to herself in the bathroom. "Calm, calm." She took a deep breath then called out, "Mommy's in the bathroom, sweetheart. I'll be right out. Go wait in your room." She grabbed her robe from the hook, and brushed her hair into a neat ponytail. She forced a smile to her reflection in the mirror. She opened the door. "Bedtime."

The children were tired and Skylar quickly tucked them in. She took the phone to the basement, went to the very back of the laundry room, and called her attorney, on his cell phone. She told him what had happened with John. She screamed and sobbed into the telephone, "How can you let him continue to do this to me?"

Roger said, "Skylar, we can't rock the boat until the GAL report is completed. It's a good sign she hasn't called me. Usually, they call if they are going to change the custody arrangement. You're gonna win, Skylar! Just hang tight."

That night, she took a long, hot bath. She couldn't move. She lay in the tub until the water was tepid and she began to shiver. The bleeding had stopped. She took the clothing she had been wearing and threw everything in the garbage. She curled up in her bed still wearing her robe and fell asleep.

This time, the bright, sunny morning didn't make her forget John's assault. Roger's reassurance that everything looked good didn't alleviate her anxiety. Her stress level was so high that when she learned there was lead paint in the apartment she had been hoping to rent, she broke down and sobbed. When she thought things couldn't get any worse, her sales position hours were changed to a late afternoon and early evening schedule. She couldn't accommodate that schedule without compromising her time with her children. Determined not to break, she began searching for another apartment and another job.

She was discouraged and felt it was ludicrous she was even en-meshed in a custody battle. She had lost faith in her attorney as he wasn't stopping the abuse and didn't attempt to get an increase of the meager child support she got based on John's unsupported testimony of income. She called Lori to vent. "My attorney is not doing the job."

"So get someone else." Lori advised.

"But, who? Do I just randomly pick a name out of the phone book?" she asked, frustrated.

"Let me ask my boss if he knows anyone." Lori told her.

She waited a minute after hanging up the phone then picked up the receiver and dialed a number. "Yeah, it's me. I was just talking to her, and I have some information...but it's gonna cost you," she said flirta-tiously. Lori paused for effect. "She's looking for another attorney."

"Oh, that's perfect! I know just the guy. She'll never see it coming. I will see you tonight. You deserve something special."

"What about Maryanne?" Lori asked.

John chuckled. "I'll tell her I'm workin' late." He clicked the but-ton on the phone and dialed another number. "Can I speak to Nathan Hillman? Nate, hi! It's John Bauers. I have a little business proposition for you..."

The next evening, Lori called Skylar. "Hey, my boss has the name of an attorney for you. He's in Needham. His name is Nathan Hillman."

Skylar called Attorney Hillman in the morning. She related the details of the case.

"Yeah, I handle cases like this pro bono. It's good PR for my firm to take on one or two per year."

After a brief meeting, she fired Roger and hired Nathan Hillman.

A Needham resident, Nathan had an ongoing professional relationship with John. He had been a patron of George's hardware store for years, and John had installed all the locks in his office and was installing decorative hardware in his home, pro bono. Nathan did not reveal this to Skylar.

Despite her new attorney, Skylar's nerves were raw, and she couldn't eat. Her clothes hung on her, but she kept forging ahead, hoping to conclude the custody battle and move on to happier times. She was experiencing symptoms typically associated with post-traumatic stress disorder, or PTSD. According to the National Center for Post-Traumatic Stress Disorder, PTSD is an anxiety disorder that can occur after enduring a traumatic event. There is a feeling of fear and helplessness. The years of domestic abuse Skylar endured was a key contributor to her PTSD. The gauge was the intensity of the trauma, the amount of time it lasted, how much control she had over the events, and how much support she was able to obtain.

Skylar fought hard to stay strong and show John he hadn't beaten her down. The next time he came to the house to pick up the children, John smiled engagingly at her.

"Hey, don't you remember what it was like with me?" He said, still smiling.

In order to prevent any physical contact, she kept the screen door locked when he came to pick up the children. Feeling safe with the locked door between them, she forced a fake smile.

"Yes, I remember what it was like." She let the smile leave her lips and continued, "You tried to control me, you abused me, and you cheated. I think that sums it up."

She caught him off guard and he didn't like it. The surprised look on his face was worth it as she bravely continued, "By the way, I'm not impressed with your selection of…your *fiancée* is it?" Referring to the old, vulgar joke, she innocently asked, "Do you put a paper bag over her head when you fuck her?" Her smile was genuine this time as she asked this question. She let a small giggle erupt.

With annoyance in his voice, John replied, "You know, you're just like Phil. You think if a girl is not pretty, I shouldn't go out with her."

She was very surprised at his response. "Wow. I thought you'd be defending her."

John continued, "Maryanne and I agree on everything. She lets me hang my pictures on the wall, and we agree on which pillowcase to put on the bed."

Skylar knew she had hit a nerve. "This sounds like a serious relationship." She burst into laughter. It felt good seeing John confused and vulnerable as she found his weakness.

His face scowled. "You little bitch." He reached for the door handle and found the door locked. It was infuriating for John the narcissist, who had once bragged to about his reputation of being seen with thin, good-looking women, when Skylar touched upon his vulnerability.

According to Sam Vaknin, *"It's devastating to point out a fact to a narcissist which contradicts his inflated perception of his grandiose self."*

Skylar shook her head. "You're such an idiot."

There were footsteps on the steps. "Daddy!" Joshua, Cary and Jillian came running upstairs. "We saw Dad's truck outside the window," said Joshua.

"Daddy's here. Give me a kiss." Skylar bent down for hugs and kisses from her children. She unlocked the screen door. "Have fun!"

Joshua and Cary ran to the truck with Jillian trailing. John had to put his anger aside, and he followed the children to his truck.

By the end of the week, Skylar found a job opportunity with a computer school as an admissions representative. There was growth potential, and the schedule would allow her to work during the children's school hours. Although she had no experience in that industry, the manager found her intelligent and articulate. At the second interview, he offered her the position. She was elated and eagerly anticipating starting her new job in mid-September 1996.

Skylar began her apartment search assiduously in communities north of the city. But she was a red flag to landlords. She had just returned to work, and divorcees were often a risk as well, so she kept running into dead-ends which discouraged her incessantly.

Tension was high as everyone waited for the results of the GAL report. It seemed to be certain the report would be in Skylar's favor. However, Sable was less sure as she told Skylar, "You know what John is like. You know his act. What if she likes him?"

"Mom, there is no way she's going to give the children to him. It's just not a possibility," Skylar answered, positive the children would remain with her.

John was considering his options as well. He knew what he was up against. Skylar *had* been that perfect mother with a stellar reputation. But, Skylar still didn't realize what she was facing. John was a master manipulator with an unscrupulous attorney. His act had been perfected, but was it enough? What would happen if he couldn't get the children from her? He did not want to pay child support. He was unhappy living with Maryanne, despite her devotion to him. She was melodramatic and exhibited embellished affectations in her mannerisms and speech. She had a short fuse. But she was a guarantee of providing him and the children a cheap place to live as well as childcare help. He couldn't handle taking care of three young children, and at first, he thought the tradeoff was worth it. But the longer he knew Maryanne, his doubts grew. He began to consider asking Skylar for another reconciliation. That seemed far more appealing.

The next time he brought the children home, he stood at the locked door chatting with Skylar. He was polite and charming, telling her funny anecdotes about the children. They talked at the door for an hour. After he left, he drove to his office and called her immediately.

"Hi, it's me." he paused. "Didn't we have great sex?"

"What?!" She was puzzled at his odd question. She asked, "John, where are you?"

"At the office," he replied. "Didn't we have great sex? I mean, wasn't it just the best?"

"John, you can't talk to me like that anymore. We are both involved with other people."

He said, "That doesn't matter to me. Skylar, does it matter to you? Are you so in love with Jake that you can't remember how good it was between us?"

She exhaled into the phone. "I'm not having this discussion. I'm hanging up now."

"Wait! I'll stop. Skylar, I was thinking maybe we should try to make it work for the sake of the kids." He began talking very fast. "Where are you working? Woburn? We could live in Waltham or Belmont. It would be a central location for both of us."

"I think you are getting a little carried away," she told him.

Keeping his voice very soft, he asked, "Don't you miss me?"

Skylar hesitated. "I don't know... I like not having you controlling me all the time."

"Well, maybe we can work this out, especially since you will now be working full-time and bringing in your share." He sounded as if he had everything all planned.

Skylar silently visualized her life with John. It no longer appealed to her.

His voice interrupted her thoughts. "I have it easy at Maryanne's house. She pays half the bills, and her daughter's baby-sit. And it's near the lake. But there's a lot missing in my relationship with her. We should be together. I miss you a lot."

Skylar shook her head sadly. "Oh, John." She sighed. Then very slowly and quietly, she said, "I think we both need to get on with our lives." She gently hung up the phone and unplugged it from the wall. She didn't want to hear from him again - ever.

On Thursday, September 5, 1996, John was taking the children to dinner. Joshua's birthday was that Saturday, and the children were spending the weekend with John. This was the first birthday she wouldn't share with Joshua so she bought a small birthday cake for an early celebration when John brought the children home that evening.

She reminded him, "I have a surprise birthday cake for Joshie since I won't see him on his birthday. Please don't be late."

"That's really nice of you. Sure, I'll bring them back by eight o'clock," he promised.

Skylar cleaned the kitchen and put a festive table cloth on the dining room table. She set out the plates and forks. She taped up a cardboard sign that read, "Happy Birthday!" She sat in the kitchen and had a small bowl of chicken soup for dinner. After she finished, she sat on the couch with a magazine. She was engrossed in an article when she heard the telephone ring. Looking at the clock, she noticed it was eight fifteen. She ran for the telephone, sure it was John telling her he was running late. She picked up the receiver. "Hello?"

John's voice answered cheerily. "Hi. I am running a little late."

"When do you think you'll be here?" she asked.

"Well, I'm still at the restaurant with the kids and Maryanne. We are just waiting for the waitress to bring out Joshua's birthday cake," John said matter-of-factly.

Skylar's heart sank. "John, I told you I was having a cake for him tonight."

John laughed. "Well, I guess that's too bad. See ya." The phone went dead.

Skylar wanted to scream in frustration. Why was John ruining Joshua's birthday? Why was he taking that away from her? She returned to her magazine but couldn't focus. It lay on her lap as she stared at the wall.

The sound of John's truck broke into her thoughts. She looked at the clock. It was nine-thirty.

The following day, Nathan called her and said, "We have to go to court. The GAL report is in, and it is not in your favor." *There had to be a mistake!* The words screamed through Skylar's head. Holding back tears, she called Julie Ginsler, but Julie refused to take her calls. So she wrote a five page letter and faxed it to Julie's office. She expressed her shock at learning Julie's recommendation for custody when everything appeared to be going smoothly. She described the myriad of events she suffered at the hands of John Bauers in great detail. This was not something anyone could make up. She tore her insides out with her passionate plea to make Julie realize her mistake and save her children.

Julie did not have any training in domestic violence or the knowledge of how to determine a victim. She wasn't skilled in finding the truth in an investigation. She had no knowledge of personality disorders. Julie had let a barrage of one-sided correspondence from Liz Lewin, albeit unethical and the absence of a rebuttal, determine her decision.

Three years later, the *Battered Mothers' Testimony Project* at the Wellesley Centers for Women located in Wellesley, Massachusetts, began the first human rights initiative in the United States to address domestic violence and child custody issues. The goal of the study was to assess whether the Massachusetts family court system acted in accordance with internationally accepted human rights standards. The report was published in 2002.

Through numerous interviews with judges, guardian ad litem and others, the important issue that was revealed was the lack of understanding about abuse, especially as it is manifested once the couple has separated. In the report, one guardian ad litem expressed an opinion that most battered women lie about abuse. Although many of the guardian ad litems were not as forthright, much of the findings indicated that skepticism was more prevalent than it appeared. This was a critical area of concern because, according to the study, guardian ad litem are not held to established standards when evaluating custody disputes involving abuse allegations; instead, they are free to make judgments based solely on their own opinions and perspectives.

The judges were equally lacking in knowledge about abuse. In the report, one judge drew a line between abuse and battering. He stated that abuse was perhaps name calling, pushing, and shoving, while battery was something physical which would result in hospitalization or medical treatment. However, the definition of battery is not only physical abuse; battery also consists of emotional, verbal, psychological as well as physical abuse. Ignorance in issues of domestic abuse led to horrifically wrong decisions in court, which ultimately destroyed families.

Reading the final guardian ad litem report proved even more preposterous than learning Julie's recommendation. Skylar provided teachers, school principals, and doctors as impartial collaterals who would offer objective opinions. John gave the names of his friends. He didn't give the names of anyone who could be relied upon as unbiased.

Coincidentally, both parties provided the names of women who worked as hairstylists. John suggested their former neighbor, Sally Beaux, who stated, "Skylar was delusional. She thought she was someone else." Sally had a license to cut hair, not a degree in psychology.

Skylar's friend Lindsay was a hairstylist as well, and she had described John's refusal to feed the children until he ate, ignoring their cries. She touted Skylar's loving care of the children and confirmed John's usual absence from the house. Julie didn't document Lindsay's comments. *Why did one hairstylist's word make it into the report and the other's was omitted?*

Incredulously, the report read as if Julie only spoke to John's collaterals. When writing about the information received from Skylar's collaterals, Julie inserted John's name when Skylar was complimented. She wrote that pediatrician Dr. Kemble had commented, "They seemed like a nice family" but Julie wrote this as, "They (Skylar and John) seemed like a nice family." The pediatrician clearly wasn't referring to John in that statement, as he had never met him.

According to the *Battered Mothers' Testimony Project*, the guardian ad litem produced reports that favored the abusive father over the mother. They held the battered mothers to higher behavioral standards than fathers. They discriminated against battered mothers. Sadly, they stereotyped the battered mothers as hysterical and unreasonable.

Janet Normalvanbreucher, researcher and writer, reveals the truth about the Father's Rights political agenda in a 1999 article, *Stalking Through the Courts.* Ms. Normalvanbreucher states in her article,

"Already victimized once by the batterer, the woman seeking to escape from an abusive relationship becomes victimized a second time when her abuser places her 'on trial' in the eyes of the community."

Although the report was written in John's favor, when it was presented to Judge Irena Shaver, she said, "I read the report. There is nothing in this report that warrants a change in custody. I feel there is no reason the children need to be taken from the mother's residence. However, if she doesn't find a place to live by next week, I will give the children to the father."

Although Julie tried to write a report favoring John, she didn't have any reasons which would hold enough weight to remove the children from their home and their mother.

Skylar called Jake, who said, "I will help you in any way I can. We've got to get you into a place. I will co-sign the lease for you."

Time was of the essence so they proactively made an inquiry at a complex rather than chase advertised rentals from the newspaper. Jake knew of a complex which was secure, child-friendly, and only fifteen minutes north of Skylar's job. Security was crucial due to John's history of stalking. Even during the GAL investigation, John boldly recited Jake's full name as well as his address when he picked up the children. He had copied his license plate and was able to track him.

Skylar had asked John why he was so curious, and he replied, "I need to know who you are dating." Anticipating a move to a gated complex made Skylar feel safe.

According to Sam Vaknin:

> *Abuse by proxy continues long after the relationship is officially over. The majority of abusers get the message, however belatedly and reluctantly. Others — more vindictive and obsessed — continue to haunt their ex-spouses for years to come. These are the stalkers. They stalk their prey as a way of maintaining the dissolved relationship, at least in their diseased minds. They seek to "punish" their quarry for refusing to collaborate in the charade and for resisting their unwanted and ominous attentions.*

"…Until You Die": The Narcissist's Promise

Lenore E. A. Walker and Glenace E. Edwall, co-authors of *Domestic Violence and Determination of Visitation and Custody in Divorce*, p. 130 (1987) states: *"Violent men will likely seek new means of control when old ones fail. Batterers use the legal system as a new arena of combat when they fail to keep their wives from leaving."*

Linda Matchan, author of *The Militant Divorcee*, wrote an article in the Boston Globe, December 15, 1998. She interviewed David Cherney, President of the Massachusetts Chapter of the American Academy of Matrimonial Lawyers. He described litigation as a *"symbolic gesture to regain control of the ex-wife. You see custody battles launched not for the child's best interest but to exploit weakness in the spouse. I've seen fathers who travel three days a week and clearly have no ability to care for their kids on a daily basis, yet they'll file for full custody, either to get leverage or put the fear of God in the mother, or to get her to accede to his demands on the financial end."*

Skylar was determined never to let John control her again. Jake drove her to the apartment complex located in Andover. There was a vacant three-bedroom townhouse which was available immediately. It was perfect. She filled out the lease, and Jake co-signed below her signature. She took pictures of the grounds and took a copy of the lease and floor plan so she could bring it to court. Driving through the gates of the complex, she was overjoyed with the direction of her life in anticipation of a new beginning with her children.

In court, Judge Shaver looked at the signed lease, floor plan and photographs. Liz Lewin angrily presented the GAL report again.

Once again, Judge Shaver denied Liz's motion. She looked at Skylar, smiled, and said, "Have a nice move."

Chapter 18

Skylar was thrilled, happy and relieved. She brought the children to Andover to register Joshua for second grade and Cary for kindergarten at the elementary school. She drove to the preschool program to show Jillian her new school. The program also featured an after-school program for the elementary school. There was a bus that went directly from the elementary school to the after-school program.

They left the school and went to tour their new home. Skylar showed them the grounds, the playground, and the pool. The children were excited seeing all the amenities. In preparation for their move, she set up phone service and cable television. After being a stay-at-home-mom for eight and a half years, Skylar had managed to begin a new career, find housing, and maintain stability in her children's lives. She was proud of what she had accomplished. She was a self- sufficient woman and excited about the future.

Five days before the schedule move, Nathan called. He told her she had been summoned to appear in court that Friday. Liz had filed a third motion to change custody, utilizing an unethical tactic referred to as judge shopping. According to a 2003 memorandum from the National Center for State Courts: *"Judge shopping is not an isolated problem, and it has happened in courts everywhere over the years."*

There were several methods of judge shopping. In this particular instance, judge shopping occurred when an attorney practicing in a court with a master calendar system filed a series of motions before different judges, with each such motion only nominally different than its predecessor, until she obtained a favorable ruling.

A remedy for this would be meticulous record keeping so each motion filed was monitored in detail and the results of each hearing copiously documented, thus promoting greater consistency among each judge's rulings.

By judge shopping, Liz was able to bypass Judge Shaver, who had denied the motion twice after reading the GAL report two times. Liz was able to land them in front of the judge from Salem with the reputation for making wrong, uninformed decisions. They were in front of Judge Crown, who originally assigned a guardian ad litem to the case.

Julie made an appearance, but the only thing she said was, "When Skylar gets upset, she thinks of herself." She wasn't asked to explain her comment. What did she mean? Did Skylar sit down and think? Did she tell the children she was too busy thinking to care for them? Did that simple, benign sentence warrant a change in custody?

Liz began by telling Judge Crown, "John is all prepared to take the children. He had them registered in school and an after-school program. The GAL wants them with my client."

John didn't have a court order deeming him the custodial parent. He didn't have the children's birth certificates. He hadn't transferred Joshua's school records. How could he have done this?

Skylar had presented all the needed documents to Andover insuring the children could start school on Monday morning, without a disruption in their schedule. But Nathan stood there quietly, head bowed. Skylar frantically whispered, "Say something!" as her attorney remained mute. He didn't rebut, object, question, or defend. She wanted to scream at him, but she didn't, even when Judge Crown ordered the change in custody. Nathan Hillman remained silent.

According to Mo Therese Hannah, Ph.D., professor of psychology at Siena College in Loudonville, New York and chairman to the Annual Battered Women's Custody Conference states:

> *"A growing numbers of protective, non-offending, loving, and fit mothers are losing custody of their children to their or their*

children's abusers. Women who seek to exit bad or even dangerous relationships are often met with retaliatory suits for child custody. Many women who try to leave an abusive partner find that the family court system can become a place where the abuser is enabled and even facilitated in further victimizing her and her children."

Skylar left the court numb. She felt as if her children had died. It was unfathomable that a judge gave John Bauers custody. She saw nothing as she drove home. She pulled into her driveway and forced herself out of the car. She needed to get into the house, the empty, quiet, and child-less house before she started screaming. She didn't hear the incessant chirping of the birds; all she heard was her heart pounding so loudly she thought it might burst out of her body.

Her hand was shaking badly and the tears began to blur her sight but she managed to slide the key into the lock. Once inside, she closed the door and collapsed on the carpet. She sobbed in rage, frustration and grief. Daggers of pain riddled her as her stomach knotted.

"Oh God, why?" she cried out. "What have I done to deserve this? I want my babies!" She cried for her children until there was nothing left.

The sound of the telephone rang piercingly. It was Sable. "Skylar? How come you didn't call me? What happened?"

Skylar whispered, "They're gone. The judge gave him my children."

"Oh, no! How did this happen?" Sable's voice echoed in disbelief. Her voice broke into sobs. "How could a judge give custody of those children to that monster?"

"I'll call you later, Mom," Skylar whispered. She dropped the receiver on the floor.

A sharp knock on the door broke into the fog of anguish. "Skylar! It's me! Open the door, baby!" Jake was at the door. She had promised to call him after the hearing, and when he didn't hear from her, he drove to the house.

She opened the door. When Jake saw her tearstained face, her disheveled hair, and wrinkled dress, he knew what had happened. He gathered her in his arms and picked her up. She sobbed into his shoulder. He sat on the couch with Skylar in his lap.

"My God, how did this happen?"

As she related the hearing, he kept shaking his head in disbelief. "But I see you with those kids. You are such a good mother!" He got up and began pacing the floor. "I don't believe it. Those kids are everything to you. Why couldn't they see it?"

Ever since he had met the children, they had formed a special bond. He was the one who took Joshua to his very first Red Sox baseball game. He played ball in the yard with Joshua. He gave piggy back rides to Cary, delighting in his exuberant laughter. Jillian was especially fond of Jake and would play dress up and dance for him. They had touched his heart. Jake wiped the tears from his eyes.

Skylar rose from the couch and approached him. She swayed and almost fell. Jake grabbed Skylar. "Have you eaten today, baby?" he asked.

"I couldn't get anything down this morning." She told him.

"I am going to get something to eat. I'll get some pizzas and be right back. You've got to keep your strength up. You've got to be strong so you can fight for your kids." Jake picked up his keys. "I'll be back in fifteen minutes. Will you be okay?"

"Yes. I'm just going to sit on the back porch and get some air."

When Jake left, Skylar opened the back door. As the brightness of the day faded and the sky turned dark, she sat on her back porch, oblivious to the chill in the air. She looked at the stars twinkling in the night sky.

When he returned, she was still on the porch. He brought her in the house, and they sat on the couch with the television on low in an attempt to distract Skylar. Jake broke off small pieces of pizza and fed them to her. She didn't eat much, but at least he was able to get some nourishment in her. They spent the remainder of the night on the couch staring at the television but seeing nothing. He held her in his arms. Her deep breathing told him she had finally drifted off to sleep. He picked her up and carried her into her bedroom.

After tucking her into bed, he whispered to her. "Skylar, listen to me, baby. In the morning, you are going to feel even worse, but I want you to get up and get dressed. You have to keep going for the sake of your children."

She heard Jake's words and felt his kiss on her cheek. He left the house, closing the door behind him. She was all alone and she fell into a deep, dreamless sleep.

The phone ringing at seven o'clock woke her. She was nauseated, but she reached for the phone. She heard Cary's sweet little six year old voice.

"Hi, Mommy! Dad said we are going to live with him now because the judge said he was the better parent."

The words tore into Skylar's heart as John had hoped they would. But she couldn't say anything to Cary and refused to let John know how he had destroyed her.

She softly said, "Cary, Mommy loves you very much and I'll see you soon." She hung up the phone.

Ten minutes later, the phone rang again. Unable to sleep, Sable had called Skylar.

Sable was heartbroken. She knew this was John's first step in destroying her relationship with her only grandchildren.

Skylar asked her, "Did I do something I am unaware of? Should I have done something differently?"

Sable replied, "The only thing you are guilty of is marrying John Bauers."

John was vindictive, but ripping the children from their mother didn't sate his appetite for vengeance. He called the owners of the rental house. "This is John Bauers. I moved out of the Newton house and have custody of my kids. I'm not paying the rent anymore because I'm not living there. If you want to start eviction proceeding's against Skylar, I can help you."

By Monday, Skylar summoned up enough strength to complete her due diligence. She drove to the Middlesex probate court where Maryanne had been divorced. She wanted to read her divorce file, hoping she would find something that may help in her custody battle. When she got the file, she discovered the dates of Maryanne's separation coincided exactly with Skylar's own separation dates. She found the telephone number of Maryanne's ex-husband, Ed Dziwka. Perhaps he could shed some light on the situation and provide Skylar with the ammunition she would need to get her children back where they belonged.

She called Ed that afternoon and introduced herself.

"Skylar, I am so happy you called!" Ed replied. "I wanted to call you, but your telephone number is unlisted. I have a lot of background information for you. Can we meet?"

On Wednesday, she met him at a local Chinese restaurant. He was a tall man with a kind face. They went into the virtually empty restaurant and sat down. He began talking as she avidly took notes.

John and Maryanne had started seeing each other since approximately May of 1995. John had been living in Medfield with Skylar at that time. Their relationship began when he had called Pest-Away to exterminate carpenter ants in the house. When the owner of the company learned about John's business, he invited him to come to his office, telling him he may have some steady work for him. John met Maryanne in the office, the same way he had met Skylar.

Ed Dziwka was a nice, uncomplicated man, but Maryanne was always looking for excitement. It was common knowledge in Natick that Maryanne was having an affair with a local police officer. He wasn't her first indiscretion, and he wasn't her last. Maryanne used to carry her diaphragm, in her purse, so it would be handy during any impromptu liaison. She purchased a cell phone and would go into the bathroom, turn on the water, and call her liaison of the moment. Ed had been aware of her affair with John for months prior to their separation.

Ed confided Maryanne would take the credit cards and go on shopping sprees. One of the items she purchased was an expensive briefcase. When he chided her for her extravagant purchase, Maryanne told him she wanted to look as if she was important.

Ed shared, "Maryanne wanted a maid. She was a terrible cook and couldn't keep the house clean. Her Aunt Dita would come to the house to cook, clean, and change the bed linens."

He believed Maryanne had low self esteem. "Maryanne told me she wanted to be Jewish and be a JAP, a Jewish American Princess. She didn't have any friends, even at our wedding. I think she was really lonely and sad because she used to sit for hours and look at the neighbor's houses and tell me she wondered what was going in their lives."

After their conversation, Skylar had better insight on Maryanne. Indeed, Ed was accurate in his assessment. Maryanne wanted to be like the Jewish girls she envied years ago in high school. She wanted to be Skylar. Having an affair with Skylar's husband was a coup for her. She didn't consider how calculating and cruel John was toward the mother of his children because she thought she had found the importance she craved being with John, despite his constant focus on Skylar. Nothing else mattered.

Skylar and Ed agreed to keep in touch and share any relevant information. Ed wished her well on her visit with her children that week.

On Thursday evening, Skylar was able to take her children out for dinner. She pulled her car beside Maryanne's house. The door opened, and the children ran out. Joshua was leading the group and reached her car first. He opened the door and happily climbed into the car.

"Hi, Mom." He hugged Skylar and kissed her cheek.

Jillian screamed, "Mommia! Mommia!" and climbed over Joshua. She put her arms around Skylar's neck, hugged her tightly, and began crying.

She rubbed Jillian's back and murmured, "Mommy's here, sweetheart." Jillian grabbed fistfuls of Skylar's hair and sobbed into her neck. John appeared in the doorway of the house and began walking toward the car. He looked angry. In a stern voice, he said, "Jillian, you need a sweater."

Skylar gave her a kiss and said, "Go get a sweater, honey."

Jillian released her grip on Skylar and looked into her face. Her lower lip trembled, and her turquoise eyes were still teary.

"It's okay," Skylar whispered, wiping the tears from Jillian's cheeks before she climbed out of the car and ran into the house to get her sweater.

"Mommy!" screamed Cary. He had just appeared at the doorway of the house. He had one sneaker on and was holding the other one. He began giggling and running for the car.

"Cary!" John's voice stopped Cary in his tracks. "Get back in the house and get those sneakers on right now, young man!"

"John, I'll do it," Skylar called out.

"No! Maryanne can help him. She's gonna be his stepmother anyway." He smirked at Skylar, knowing the thought of Maryanne as a parental figure would upset her. He shooed Cary back into the house and John followed him inside.

Skylar sat in the car with Joshua. She asked him about his new school, and Joshua began describing his teacher and his new friends. She listened but was anxious to get away from that house with the children. Finally, Jillian and Cary appeared at the door with John. John walked between them, with an arm around each child, firmly holding their shoulders.

Skylar called out, "Climb in, kids."

John said, "We had a talk, and they don't want to go with you. They want to stay with me and Maryanne. You can take Joshie."

Skylar firmly said, "John, let go of them." She saw he had re-gripped each child by their upper arms and they began to whimper.

He gritted his teeth and snarled, "They don't want to see you, Skylar. Just leave or I'll take Joshua back too. I'm in charge now."

Skylar's eyes began to water. She didn't want him to see her tears, so she slowly began to drive away from the house.

As she slowly drove down the street, she heard Cary and Jillian pleading, "Mommy! Mommmia! Come back! Mommy, please, Mommy!"

Skylar stopped the car and looked back. She saw Jillian and Cary, free of John's grip, running after her with tears streaming down their face.

Robin Shaye

"Mommia!" shrieked Jillian with sobs in her voice.

Skylar put the car in reverse, but she saw John run after the children, easily catching them. He scooped them up, one under each arm and brought them into the house. Skylar still heard the screams and saw their little legs kicking. The door shut, and the light went off.

Bravely, she turned to Joshua. "Guess it will just be us tonight, pal. How about chicken fingers and French fries?" Joshua nodded enthusiastically. Determined not to let John's actions spoil Joshua's evening, she drove her car away from the dark house.

Ann Bradley, M.A, lives in Palo Alto, CA, and is a certified coach in Positive Psychology at the University of Pennsylvania. She is a coach on relationships and how to survive a difficult divorce. As a public speaker and consultant on divorce and narcissism issues, she helps people with divorce planning and survival tactics. Ann has twenty years experience as a business and academic writer, and she is the author of *Divorce: The Real Truth*, *The Hidden Danger: Surviving, Deception, Betrayal and Narcissism*, as well as websites on narcissism and divorce.

Ann believes, "Divorce is never good, but for a narcissist, it's a huge slap in the face." She states: *"Facing a narcissist/abuser and his lawyer you have a situation that can turn very quickly into an explosive, tenacious, battle. You will be hit with increasingly intense abuse. The legal system can be a very effective battering tool."* She provides a frightening analogy of the attorney of a narcissistic abuser. What she describes would be as if Liz Lewin asked John, "Shall I hit Skylar over the head with a 2 x 4?"

Ann goes on to state:

> *The legal system is adversarial and full of men (and women)*
> *with tremendous needs for power. The abuser becomes enraged*
> *when faced with a partner who has found the power to leave.*
> *The abuser feels justified in his behavior, sees nothing wrong*
> *with it, and has no realization of consequences. Often the*
> *abuser who sees he is losing control will escalate the methods*
> *of control and abuse. The lies will be bolder, and he will backstab*

and betray with more intensity. He has a fierce need to regain
power and control. Continued use of the legal system may now
be available to him. He will deplete assets to pay attorneys
to continue the battle.

The abuse can easily continue under the smoke screen of the legal system, which is a playground full of men and women with a tremendous need for power.

John had the connections and means to bring Skylar back to court time after time with repeated or frivolous motions. In doing so, he was successfully depleting her finances. He knew she had limited resources to pay for an attorney, but he didn't have to worry about his finances. He didn't have to worry about exorbitant legal fees with a close family friend acting as his attorney.

Therefore, he was able to have Skylar summoned to appear in court following her visit with the children. This time, he was requesting supervised visits. Doing so would put him in a very favorable light when the custody trial began. This court appearance was in front of Judge Shaver, the judge who ruled the GAL report didn't warrant a change in custody twice.

Liz got up and said, "Skylar tried to pull the children into the car. They ran away from her screaming, 'Daddy, I don't want to go!' Skylar needs to have supervised visits."

Although Judge Shaver had found in Skylar's favor after reading Julie Ginsler's report, on that day she ordered supervised visits. It was as if they had never appeared in her court. Skylar didn't understand how one day Judge Shaver announced there was nothing in the guardian ad litem report to warrant a change in custody, yet she was ordering supervised visits a few weeks later.

She voiced her protest and proclaimed, "I am a good mother!"

Judge Shaver actually sneered at her and sarcastically said, "Sure you are." Attorney Hillman merely stood there and didn't say a word.

This time, Skylar showed no emotion. She was baffled. She woodenly wrote down a list of people who could supervise her visits. She offered Sable, which was immediately rejected by John and Liz. So, she suggested Marci and Lindsay, her lifelong friends, adding Lori as an afterthought.

John reviewed the list, dismissing each person with an abrupt, "No, no," until he reached Lori's name. His face broke into a grin and said, "I'll accept Lori as the supervisor."

When Skylar informed Lori of what had happened in court, she commented, "Well, you know, Skylar, John is a good liar. He's very convincing. But it's a good idea that I can be the supervisor. I'll give a report there is no problem with you and the children."

Jake was livid at the outcome of Skylar's hearing and fumed, "This is ridiculous! You don't need to be supervised! Find a new attorney! Your attorney is terrible! There was no reason for the children to be living with him and not with you! You're a good mother!"

However, John was not finished with Skylar and she was summoned into court again.

Just prior to going her court date, Skylar signed a lease for a smaller, inexpensive apartment located on the ground floor of a house in Stoneham, minutes from her job. She had cancelled her lease on the townhouse as it was too large and unaffordable on just her meager salary. Her new apartment was older and quaint consisting of a large bedroom, den, kitchen, living room, and a large bathroom. There was plentiful storage, a washer and dryer, and a brick fireplace. The rent included all utilities. Jake offered to cosign, but the landlady liked Skylar and didn't require a cosigner. She felt lucky to find such a great deal. She felt fortunate as she already had her moving expenses from the security deposit she had given for the Newton house. John had received the check from the realtor and gave it to Liz. She had mailed it to Nathan and he planned on turning it over the Skylar at her next court appearance.

When they stood before Judge Shaver in court, John announced, "Skylar has not paid rent on the Newton house. I spoke to the owners and they are evicting her."

Skylar looked at him, shocked. Eviction? she thought. The owners had never contacted her. If she was being evicted, John was doing it independently and maliciously.

She stated, "Your Honor, I found an apartment. It will be available in three weeks, and I am in the middle of packing and cleaning up the Newton house."

Without any documentation regarding eviction, Judge Shaver ordered, "You need to vacate the premises this weekend. I am sure you can find a friend to stay with for three weeks."

Liz interjected, "Your Honor, Attorney Hillman is holding Skylar's security deposit for $1700.00. Since she still owes Julie Ginsler her guardian ad litem fee, that money should go to the GAL." Although Liz was not employed by the guardian ad litem as a bill collector, Judge Shaver ordered the check be given to Julie Ginsler. Court was adjourned.

Skylar was frustrated. Nathan suggested, "Why don't you get out of here? You don't need to wait around for the order. I'll call you." She left the courthouse and went back to work. When she was out of the room, John silently mouthed to Nathan, "Nice job."

That afternoon, Nathan called her at work. "I have the order and I can mail it to you. It's what the judge said in court." He purposely did not read the additional details of the order to her. "By the way, your trial is in a few weeks. If you get the kids back, they won't be able to fit into your new place. I would advise you not to take the apartment."

She considered how Nathan had represented her. He remained mute during the third custody hearing, and she lost her children without an argument or protest. He neglected to return her the security deposit check immediately, and she lost the money to pay for her moving expenses. He did not make an argument to allow her to remain in the Newton house for three more weeks. She did not trust him. She knew if she followed his advice, she would be homeless.

She answered, "I *am* taking the apartment because I am never getting my children back." She was learning about the legal system and was rapidly losing faith as they had failed her. And it was apparent to her that the court system had failed her children as well.

Skylar was somehow miraculously surviving the stress. She would tell herself, "At least I no longer have to be with him." She would repeat it over and over like a mantra until the pain and stress of the moment went away. She reread the list of the abuses she had written after her first separation from John in 1994. The list, containing over thirty instances of abuse, control, humiliation and neglect - was documentation to the way John treated her during their marriage. Her list kept her strong.

She still needed a place to live for three weeks so she called her friend Marci, who lived twenty minutes south of her office. Although Marci was a newlywed living in a tiny apartment, she and her husband graciously welcomed Skylar into their home until she could move.

Since John had custody of the children, Skylar wanted to make sure he followed up on the children's medical and dental appointments. She wrote a letter, dated October 1, 1996, documenting everything he needed to know regarding the children's medical history. Nathan forwarded it to Liz, who gave it to John.

Skylar included the name, address, and telephone number of the children's pediatrician as well as a reminder for their scheduled yearly check-ups. Cary had several medical appointments as well as evaluations for education plans within the schools. She provided a list of issues that needed to be addressed along with the doctor's contact information. The letter was thorough and comprehensive so John would be able to take over this new responsibility seamlessly.

Years later, it was discovered that John had ignored the entire letter. He didn't follow up with the endocrinologist for Cary's growth issues. What could have been rectified was not, and Cary grew to only 5'2" while Joshua towered over him at 6'2". John did not take any of the children to the dentist ever. Although their dentist was Skylar's uncle, who did not charge for their visits, John did not want the children to have any contact with her family, even if it meant free dental care. The children no longer had yearly physicals. This was the man who was telling the world he was the better parent.

Chapter 19

Skylar gathered whatever she needed for her three week stay with Marci and neatly stacked everything on the living room floor. Jake helped her pack the contents that weekend. She dusted and vacuumed so the house was immaculate. Jake rented a truck and moved the furniture and household items to Sable's garage. By Sunday night, the house was almost empty. Skylar arranged for a piano mover to pick up her piano on Tuesday and keep it in storage until she moved into her apartment. She was exhausted, so Jake advised, "Go to Marci's and pick the rest of the things up tomorrow after work."

It made sense as her car was filled to capacity. She would have to unload it to make room for the remaining clothing, vacuum, cleaning supplies, answering machine, coffee maker, photo albums, Nikon camera and her modeling portfolio still left at the house.

After work on Monday, she drove to Newton to collect her possessions. She put her key in the lock and nothing happened. She looked closely and noticed the shiny new hardware on the door. The locks had been changed. She peeked in through the small window and saw the living room was totally empty. *Oh, no!* she thought.

"It's not your house, bitch," she looked up. John had pulled up to the curb in his truck. "But I must say I found some pretty interesting stuff in there," he drawled mockingly.

"You had no right to change those locks. I want my things!" Skylar firmly stated.

"You lost your rights to everything," he replied smugly as he put the truck in gear and drove away.

If one could dig into the malignant narcissist's brain and extract the truth, the answer would be very simple. John regarded Skylar as chattel. He owned her, and, like a possession, he wanted her returned. But she clearly communicated that she had no desire to return to him, and that was a huge blow to his narcissistic self. Therefore, the malignant or abusive side needed to punish her. John lost his property and had to insure Skylar lost hers as well.

Disheartened, she drove back to Marci's apartment. She found being with her friend during the week extremely comforting. On the weekends, she would drive to the South Shore and stay with Jake. He was living in a house with his friend Pete. During dinner, Pete mentioned he had a friend named Jerry D. from Needham.

He said, "I told him my roommate was dating someone who had been married to John Bauers from Needham. Jerry told me he knew him and heard about the divorce. He said, 'That woman beats her children'."

Nonsensically, Jerry D. was on a slanderous rampage. Although he had never met Skylar, he relished any opportunity to malign her. At a local bar after work, he met Skylar's friend Lindsay. She told him she worked in Needham and he replied, "My friend, John Bauers is from Needham. He's going through a tough divorce because his ex-wife is a bitch."

John persevered in abusing Skylar in what narcissism expert Sam Vaknin describes as abuse by proxy. It is the way to continue the abuse after the relationship is over.

Sam states:

> One form of control by proxy is to engineer situations in which abuse is inflicted upon another person. Such carefully crafted scenarios of embarrassment and humiliation provoke social sanctions (condemnation, opprobrium, or even physical punishment) against the victim. Society or social groups become the instruments of the abuser.

Abusers often use other people to do their dirty work for them. These - sometimes unwitting accomplices belong to three groups: The abuser's social circle, the victim's social circle and the system — comprised of therapists, guardian ad litem and judges. The abuser uses his charm, his ability to manipulate and his impressive thespian skills to paint a picture of his victim, which appears as bizarre as a Picasso portrait.

The October air was crisp and fragrant the day Skylar moved to Stoneham. Her new apartment was cozy and felt like home. She found it peaceful and was eager to get home from work each day, light her candles, put her feet up, and enjoy the tranquility. She was anxious for the children to visit. She suddenly remembered she had to be supervised when she saw the children that weekend. But Lori was serving as the supervisor, so she was confident her supervision would end after the weekend.

On Saturday, Lori picked her up and they drove to Natick to get the children. Skylar was so happy to see them as they piled into Lori's car. But when she tried to talk to them, Lori kept interrupting, monopolizing the conversation. She behaved as if it were *her* visit. Each time Skylar tried to say something, Lori would interject.

At lunchtime, when the waitress came to take the order, Lori announced, "My kids will have chicken fingers and French fries." She turned to Skylar, "Just kidding, Skylar."

After lunch, Jillian turned to Skylar. "Mommia, I need to go to the bathroom."

"I'll take you, Jillian." Lori got up, took Jillian's hand, and led her to the ladies room.

Although agitated, Skylar focused her attention on her sons. "How's your lunch?"

"Really, good!" Joshua enthusiastically exclaimed. "I was starving! I didn't have dinner last night."

"Why not?" asked Skylar

"Daddy sent him to his room!" shouted Cary.

"Shut up, Cary! I'm telling!" Skylar had never heard Joshua talk to Cary that way. "Mom, I was fooling around and threw something at Cary. It hit Maryanne on her neck. She started yelling, 'Did you see what that little bastard did?' She was really screaming!"

"She screams all the time, really loud!" interjected Cary.

"So, then what happened?" asked Skylar.

"Dad told me to go to my room without dinner," Joshua said matter-of-factly.

Skylar couldn't believe what she was hearing. Before she could respond, Lori was back with Jillian.

"Mommia, I love you." Jillian threw her arms around Skylar's neck. "I love you too." Skylar hugged her back. "And I love you, and I love you." She stood up and gave Joshua and Cary warm hugs as well.

On the ride home, Skylar said, "Who wants to stop at the toy store?"

"We do, we do!" Excited screams reverberated from the back seat.

When they walked into the toy store, Lori grabbed Jillian and pulled her over to a display. "Jillian, why don't you get this Barbie doll?" She shoved a doll in Jillian's hand. "Joshie and Cary, come with me. I'll help you pick out a toy."

"Lori! Please! Can you back off a little? I would like to be able to pick out toys with my children." Lori stared at her. "Please." stressed Skylar.

She walked through the store with her children until everyone selected a toy. She paid at the register and they walked back to the car. When the children were dropped off, they hugged and kissed her before going into the house.

On the ride home, Skylar felt awkward. She wanted to ask Lori why she interfered with her visit but she refrained. She didn't want to confront Lori. *If I start an argument, she may give a bad report to the GAL,* she feared. So she remained silent. When Lori suggested they get together that night, Skylar feigned exhaustion and told her, "Jake is coming over to watch a movie." She did not want to spend another minute with Lori.

On Monday, Julie Ginsler called her at work. "Skylar, how did the visit go?"

Skylar diplomatically replied, "It went well. We took the children for lunch in Boston and went up to the Prudential skywalk. Before they went home, I bought them each a toy."

"Really? Lori said it didn't go so well," Julie stated, her voice sounding condescending.

Skylar felt her heart sink. "What are you talking about? There is no problem with my children and they had a great time." Her voice rose in panic. What is going on? she thought.

Julie continued, "Lori told me that children did not want to be with you. She told me they clung to her. And she said that you didn't want to select toys at the toy store, so she had to help the children and she paid for them because you refused."

"Oh no, that's not what happened at all!" she cried. "That is totally untrue! Lori was kind of overbearing, but other than that, everything was fine." Her voice caught in her throat.

Patronizingly, Julie said, "Skylar, you can't handle the children. I am going to recommend you still have supervised visits." She hung up the phone.

Skylar felt her heart pounding. She wanted to scream, but she was at work. She closed the door to her office and immediately called Lori.

"Hello?" purred Lori into the phone.

Skylar wasted no time with niceties. "Lori, I just got off the phone with Julie Ginsler. What the hell are you telling her?"

"Skylar, I didn't want it to seem as if you were so perfect, because then she'd think I was lying," she replied smoothly

"But you did lie! I have no problem with my children, and you know it! Why are you doing that to me?" Skylar kept her voice to an urgent whisper.

Sweetly, Lori chided, "Skylar, c'mon. I'm your friend. I just thought I should tell her it didn't go that well this time. But the next time I will tell her you are ready to see the children alone. It's more believable. Don't you agree?"

Skylar, hurt by the betrayal and disgusted by Lori's explanation, said, "No, I don't agree. The truth is what is believable. And you didn't tell the truth. You know that I shouldn't have had supervised visits anyway!"

Lori sighed. "Okay, Skylar, I get it. Don't worry. I will tell her what you want next time."

Skylar was not reassured and prayed that Lori would keep her promise.

That evening, Jake insisted she find another attorney. He was crazy about her children and was feeling the same frustrated disbelief. Although Skylar only had eight thousand dollars left, she was ready to part with all of it in the hopes of finding an attorney who she felt would save her children's lives. The following day, she asked the attorney from the legal department at her job for a legal referral. He gave her the name of an attorney who had an office in Boston. Skylar called Katherine Fabiano and made an appointment for a consultation.

Upon meeting Kate Fabiano, Skylar liked her right away. Kate was warm and articulate. After telling Kate about her life with John, she agreed that it was pretty clear Skylar had been a victim of an abuser, drug dealer, and absentee father. It seemed preposterous that Liz Lewin could continue this charade, especially going up against all the unbiased evidence they were presenting. Kate appeared to be an extremely competent attorney so Skylar hired her and handed Kate eight thousand dollars in cash. The trial would begin in less than two weeks.

Secure that she had retained strong legal representation, Skylar was looking forward to seeing the children that weekend. Lori was still supervising, so Sable insisted on meeting them for lunch. She planned to question Lori and find out what was going on in the mind of the woman who professed to be Skylar's best friend. They had devised a flawless plan for the interrogation. After lunch, Sable would go in Skylar's car when they returned the children to John's house. Once the children were out of the car, Sable would start questioning Lori. Sequestered in the car, Lori would have no place to run and would have to provide answers.

That Saturday, after a pleasant lunch with the children, Skylar asked, "Mom, want to come along for a ride?"

"Okay. I can leave my car here." Sable walked to her car and got in the back seat with the children, while Lori sat in front with Skylar.

Skylar drove to John's, kissed the children, and watched as they walked into the house. She began driving away from the house, and Sable immediately began to grill Lori.

"Lori, are you Skylar's friend, or are you doing this for John?"
Lori was flustered and protested, "I am Skylar's friend. I am not doing this for John, but Skylar doesn't know how good she had it."

Skylar interjected, "What are you talking about? You know what my life was like with him!"

"So he had control issues. But you got to stay home and not work. I think that's a fair tradeoff."

"A tradeoff? Life is not a tradeoff. So what that I didn't work? He tortured me! You know he was cheating. You know he was never home. You know he didn't give me money. Remember how he used to check my clothes when you and I worked together? You heard him screaming that night he didn't want me to meet you!" Skylar glared at Lori briefly.

Lori squirmed uncomfortably in her seat. "Well…I don't know…I think I should have custody of the children."

Sable leaned forward in her seat and touched Skylar on the shoulder. "Don't have her testify for you. She's working for him. Everyone told you not to trust her."

"No, no, no!" Lori's voice broke. She turned to face Sable in the back seat. "I love Skylar. She's my friend, and I love the kids! I'm going to court for her!"

Sable said, "If you aren't going to court to testify for Skylar, then please don't show up."

"I am going there for Skylar. But all I'm saying is that Skylar should think about maybe giving John another chance. Then she wouldn't have to go through this."

Skylar was livid. "Lori, you're crazy, and you're a bitch!" She looked back at Sable. "Mom, I don't want her testifying for me at all!"

"Skylar, I promise I will be there for you! I am sorry I made some bad choices about the GAL, but I am your friend. I know all about John. I know he was difficult. I heard his anger. He was controlling. He's a drug dealer. I think it will be good for the judge to hear this from someone else. Okay?" Lori turned and smiled at Sable. She brushed Skylar's hair back.

They had reached Sable's car. "Lori, I am telling you to think about this. I would rather have you not show up if you aren't going to testify for Skylar." Sable said. She turned to her daughter, "Skylar, I have something for you in my car. Walk over with me."

Skylar told Lori she would be right back. As soon as they were out of earshot, Sable said, "Look, I don't totally trust her, but she said she'd testify for you. If she tells the judge the truth about him, it could help a lot. I don't know what to think. I just don't think she would have the nerve to show up and testify for John."

Skylar hugged Sable and returned to her car. She gave Lori the best smile she could muster and began the drive home. There was no more mention of court.

That evening, Jake had dinner with Skylar.

She repeated her conversation with Lori.

He gripped Skylar's arms and looked deeply into her eyes. In a calm voice, he said, "I told you not to trust her. She's not your friend. Please, baby, I just want you to be very careful and think about this."

"Oh God, Jake, I just don't know what to do."

"Let's go sit on the couch."

Skylar walked to the couch and Jake lit the numerous candles she had all over her apartment. He joined her on the couch. She leaned back and he took her feet in his lap and began massaging them. Skylar relaxed.

"Hey, you'll never guess what I saw the other day: your ex's Toyota 4-Runner driving past the house. He drove back and forth for about twenty minutes and then left. Think he was trying to find me and beat me up?" He grinned, hoping to lighten the mood for her.

"As if," she murmured as his hands worked magic on her feet.

According to Pamela Kulbarsh, RN, Crisis Intervention Contributor at Officer.com:

> The most common form of stalking is "simple obsession". The victim of the simple obsessional stalker usually knows his/her stalker well and was in some form of relationship with him/her: an ex-spouse, ex-lover, friend, former boss, or co-worker. The obsessional activities begin after the relationship has ended or is headed for termination. The stalker

*often perceives that he/she was wronged by the victim. The
simple obsessional stalker's motivation is to mend the
relationship or to seek some type of retribution. Virtually
all domestic violence cases involving stalking fall under
this category.*

During the week, Kate and Skylar prepared for the trial. They made a list of witnesses and went through the paperwork. It didn't seem as if it would be a difficult thing to prove Skylar was the sole caregiver and John was never home. It was exhausting to have to list every instance of abuse in the marriage beginning with the daily wardrobe checking, throwing Skylar outside on the doorstep, locking her out of the bedroom, nude photos of ex-girlfriends, the cheating, the choking, the belittling, beating the boys, the sickening night when John tried to promote three-way sex and everything in between.

As Skylar related story after story, Kate kept muttering, "This guy is crazy."

It was with mind-shattering clarity, when everything was in front of them, to determine John was a man who was not only abusive to his wife, but he was abusive to his children as well. Unless he was going to blatantly lie in court, it would be a slam dunk. The amount of evidence and information Skylar had documented was staggering. And finally, after searching through her old photographs, she finally found the negatives of the pictures she had taken of herself. When the photographs were printed, it showed Skylar, her face blotched and tear-stained, disheveled hair and prominent fingerprints on her neck, the results after John threw her down and choked her. This would be entered into evidence.

Slam…dunk…score!

Chapter 20

The day of the trial dawned bright and chilly. It was November 18, 1996, when Skylar nervously arrived in the Norfolk probate court. She was dressed professionally in a white blouse, black slacks, and a black and white herringbone jacket. She wore her hair pulled back with light make-up and little jewelry. She smiled with relief as Jake walked through the door looking handsome in his suit and tie. Ed Dziwka, Maryanne's ex-husband, followed wearing a neat brown suit and striped tie. Minutes later, Sable appeared, accompanied by Skylar's friend Lindsay. Everyone gathered around Skylar. She began feeling less nervous surrounded by her supportive friends. They reassured her and encouraged her to remain strong. Finally, Lori entered the room. She walked to the rear of the courtroom and leaned against the back wall.

Skylar left her secure group and approached Lori. She looked directly into her eyes and asked, "Are you still testifying for me?"

Lori snapped, "I told you I would." She averted her eyes. Skylar followed her gaze and saw John enter the courtroom. He was wearing tight jeans, a Security Safe t-shirt, and heavy work boots. His cell phone hung from his belt.

Although a chill of fear ran through her, Skylar muttered, "What a slob."

Lori laughed. "Don't worry, Skylar." She moved away.

Sable approached Skylar. "What did she say?"

"She seemed angry, but she said she was testifying for me," she told her

"All rise." the court officer, Lucas Delmonico announced. Judge Daniel Copeland was presiding over the case entered the room. He was a nice looking man of average height, in his mid-fifties. In court, he'd vacillate by showing a sense of humor, yet other times he would wield his authority with a terse, no-nonsense attitude.

The first part of the trial was spent creating lists of witnesses and the tedious procedure of documenting and numbering the evidence which would be submitted during the trial. Included were certificates of completion from the required parenting classes. Massachusetts law deemed that divorcing parties with children attend a mandatory parenting class. The class provides information for the parents on helping the children deal with the divorce as well as teaching the parents how to set the guidelines as to appropriate behavior and conversation regarding their estranged spouse. Skylar had completed the two-day course three weeks after the original order. John completed his two-day program the previous night.

Once all the paperwork was completed, the trial began. Skylar's witnesses were scheduled to appear first. Ed Dziwka was the first person called to the witness stand.

Ed stated, "I was married to Maryanne, and we are presently going through a divorce. I discovered she was seeing John Bauers since May of 1995. As requested, I am providing a telephone bill as evidence to their relationship." He handed the telephone bill from May 1995, with numerous highlighted phone numbers, to Kate, who submitted the bill into evidence. He testified to the dates of his separation in order to build a timeline to illustrate how everything was calculated beginning with the sale of the Medfield house to the date of the final argument and separation. "There is a restraining order prohibiting any unrelated male from sleeping in our former marital residence while our daughters are present. My attorney has filed an order of contempt against Maryanne because she's allowing John to live in the house."

The trial stopped for a lunch break. Skylar's group opted to go across the street to a little luncheonette favored by the many attorneys and litigants appearing in court that day. Lori lingered behind, and no one realized she was not with the group until they were seated at a table. Jake offered to go back and find her. He returned within minutes, alone.

"I went back to get Lori, and she was standing on the steps of the courthouse talking to John, so I came back." Lori never appeared for lunch.

When everyone went back to the courtroom, Lori was sitting beside John. She stared straight ahead as Skylar passed and didn't make eye contact with anyone in her group.

Lindsay grabbed Skylar's arm. "What a bitch!" she whispered to Skylar. Look at what she's doing! I told you not to trust her!" Lindsay glared at Lori as they walked past.

Skylar felt a little hurt but was not surprised at Lori's betrayal. She felt it was better she learned the truth about Lori's true motives than to always be guessing.

The director of the new preschool where Cary and Jillian had been attending was called to the stand. The director testified she had many years of experience in early childhood development and held a Ph.D. degree.

She testified, "I met Skylar Bauers in April of 1996, shortly after the children had to leave Temple Beth Shalom. Skylar called our school seeking a scholarship for Cary and Jillian. We had several meetings to discuss the children's program and their classrooms. At that time, there was scholarship money available for the children and they began school that month. Skylar would drop off the children in the morning and pick them up in the afternoon. They were clean and appropriately dressed. The snacks Skylar provided were proper in keeping with the kosher dietary rules of the school. There were no behavioral issues with either of the children. I was in constant contact with Skylar. She was concerned about the children and their issues and attended all the parent/teacher conferences. Our school was open year round, but the children took one month off to attend day camp in July of 1996. Skylar told me she had applied for a camp scholarship and was approved for all three children to go to summer camp for four weeks. Cary and Jillian returned to school in August of 1996. Skylar kept me apprised of her plans to move from Newton. I feel Skylar is a good parent."

She stated only after the custody had changed was when she met John. "After Mr. Bauers got custody, Skylar was in contact with me about once or twice a week, asking about her children. She was a concerned parent. She came to school one day and had lunch with the children. The children seemed very attentive toward her." She concluded her testimony by stating, "My overall observations of Skylar and the children were good, and the children appeared to love their mother. Cary and Jillian are delightful children."

At the end of the day, Judge Copeland stated, "I feel that it's important for these children to have visits with their mother. I don't feel she needs to be supervised. So, I am making a schedule that Mrs. Bauers will have the children every weekend except the second weekend of the month. On Wednesday nights, she can take them to dinner."

As they exited the courthouse, Kate told Skylar, "I would say it went very well."

Upon entering the courtroom the following day, Lori stood with John. She had obviously coached him regarding appropriate attire. He was wearing a pair of slacks, a button-down shirt, and a tie. Lori was adjusting his tie. She grimaced at Skylar as she passed. Skylar ignored her.

Joshua's first grade teacher came in to testify. "I had initially met with Skylar when Joshua was transferring to the Newton school system. Skylar was concerned about his placement and the program. She wanted to make sure he was in the right class, which I described for her, and I answered all of her questions. She had enrolled Joshua in our after-school karate program. I would speak with her once or twice a week when she came to school to pick him up. Skylar attended the parent/teacher conference. She also volunteered and chaperoned a field trip for the class. Joshua was an excellent student and a wonderful little boy. He appeared happy, well cared for, clean, and appropriately dressed. I did not observe any behavioral changes in Joshua after the separation. I feel my observations of Skylar with Joshua were good." She paused, then took a long and puzzled look at John. She concluded her testimony and said, "I never met Mr. Bauers."

Lori Donnaccia was the next person called to testify. She was called as a hostile witness because she had originally come to court with the intentions of testifying for Skylar. Before she was questioned, Lori announced, "I spoke to John last night. He was kind of upset because his van had been keyed and 'Fuck You' was written on it."

"His van?" Skylar whispered to Sable. "What the hell is she talking about?"

Sable shrugged.

Lori began her testimony by describing her relationship with Skylar. "I met Skylar at work. Most of our socialization outside the house included John. I went to visit her in the hospital when Cary was born. I comforted her when she heard the news about Cary having some breathing problems. John was not at the hospital and I had to call him because she was too upset. During the week, I would speak to her on the phone. She would tell me about the activities she was doing with the children. I would visit a couple of times per month. I would observe Skylar doing the household chores, and sometimes I would help her. She arranged all the birthday parties for the children. She was their primary caretaker. I never saw her hit or yell at the children."

Lori described John. "John was never home. He was controlling. He wouldn't let Skylar out of the house. I thought it was weird when he put locks on all the doors."

The judge called for a short recess. Skylar remained in the courtroom with Kate while John and Liz went into the hallway. Lori grabbed her jacket and went outside. When the judge returned, Lori wasn't there.

"Miss Lewin, where is your witness?" he asked.

Suddenly, Lori came through the door. "Sorry," she said breathlessly. She took off her jacket and returned to the witness stand.

Kate resumed her cross examination. "Lori, what is your educational background?"

Lori giggled. Oddly, after the short break, her testimony had suddenly lost its lucidity. Kate's questions seemed to challenge her. Her demeanor had changed. Her eyes were glassy and she began fidgeting in the witness box. She began swaying and swinging her long hair back and forth. She managed to testify that she was not married, had no degree in early childhood behavior, and had no parenting skills or experience.

Kate asked, "Did you ever see John smoking marijuana?"

"Yes, all the time." Lori answered, and she guffawed loudly.

"And did you purchase pot from him?" Kate looked at her expectantly.

"Objection!" shouted Liz. "You don't have to answer that."

Lori exercised her Fifth Amendment rights and did not reply. However, she did enthusiastically state, "John provided marijuana for me. He got great stuff! When he got weed, it was primo. I mean, it was the best."

"Lori, what happened when you were at the Bauers after a birthday party?" Kate asked.

"Oh, John got undressed. He was walking around, and we were laughing. We were afraid that he would barbeque something that he shouldn't." Lori guffawed again loudly.

Judge Copeland laughed. Skylar cringed, and her stomach cramped listening to Lori's twisted version of that evening.

Kate moved on with her questioning. "Tell me about you and Skylar's boyfriend, Jake,"

Lori boldly replied, "I always get a lot of attention from men, and Jake was no exception. He was definitely interested in me so I told him, 'When you're with Skylar in bed tonight, you will be thinking about fucking me'. I think he was a little too serious about his feelings toward me."

"Let's move on. Tell me about Skylar and the children. Did Skylar ever lock them in the basement?" asked Kate, referring to affidavits of former babysitters Maree Labarini and Connie Taylor.

Emphatically, Lori answered, "The children were never locked in the Medfield or Newton basement. Skylar would play with the children. She had a really good life. She didn't have to work, and she could stay at home with the kids. But she wanted to be on stage, performing or modeling."

Kate said, "And your relationship with John Bauers? I mean, is there a relationship?"

Lori smiled and replied, "I'm not attracted to him, but he has really nice hair."

"Why did you suddenly change sides yesterday when you originally came in to testify for Skylar?" Kate looked at her curiously.

Lori giggled and said, "Nobody waited for me. And I was trying to end my friendship with Skylar anyway."

As Lori left the witness stand, Judge Copeland looked at Liz and said, "I hope she is not your star witness."

Several days later, Maryanne made her appearance in court. She showed up in mid-trial and made her presence known by flinging the door open with such force it would bang against the wall. Proceedings stopped, and everyone turned to see what had happened. She strutted to the front of the courtroom and sat close to John. Oblivious to modesty, she placed one hand between his thighs and with her other hand, she would begin rubbing his leg. She sat there and smiled as she loudly chewed her gum. It was the same scenario, each time she came to court.

Although she always smiled cheerfully, Maryanne's volatility was clearly exhibited during one court recess. As she turned around to pick up her coat, she saw Skylar facing her. Without provocation, she started screaming, "You bitch!"

Skylar and Sable looked at each other, shocked at Maryanne's random outburst. "Those poor children." murmured Sable.

The trial continued with Skylar's friend Lindsay testimony. She described her visits with Skylar when she lived in Medfield and Newton. She stated, "The children were always clean, well-behaved and happy. Skylar was attentive to the children and was a good mother. Anyone could tell she loved her children and the children loved her. She never yelled or hit them. I never saw her get angry. She was always busy cooking, cleaning or picking up after them. John was never home. I saw him there once when I was there for dinner with my boyfriend. We brought over Chinese food." She related the events of that evening.

"John took his food and started eating before anyone. Joshua asked him for some food, and John began screaming at him, telling him he couldn't eat until he was done. Skylar told Joshua she would get his food and made up plates for the children. Joshua appeared to be afraid of John. I was embarrassed for him to behave this way in front of my boyfriend."

Lindsay's testimony was completed, and court was adjourned for the day. So far, everything was going well. Skylar went home and got into bed early. She wanted to be well rested when she came face-to-face with the guardian ad litem, Julie Ginsler, in the morning.

Chapter 21

On November 21st, 1996, Julie Ginsler took the stand as a witness for Liz Lewin. She described, "The usual practices of a guardian ad litem are to contact and interview both parents, visit the homes, and talk to the collaterals. I did not deviate from the usual procedure in this matter. My first meeting with Skylar Bauers was in my office in Wellesley. Our second meeting took place in Skylar's home in April 1996."

GALs are required to limit their investigation only to the parents and their collaterals. Meeting with the attorneys who are obligated to fight for their own client is an unethical practice. However, ignoring ethics and the *Supreme Judicial Court Rule 3:07, Massachusetts Rules of Professional Conduct* for attorneys, Julie met with Liz immediately after her first meeting with Skylar.

Liz had no psychological training but told Julie, "Skylar is at risk." and recommended custody to John. Julie did not explain her interpretation of what Liz meant when she stated, "Skylar is at risk."

Skylar was not at risk by any means. She was coping beautifully under the circumstances. She dodged everything John was throwing her way. She was extraordinarily resourceful in maintaining stability in the children's lives. She was appropriate in every aspect in caring and relating to the children.

Liz told Julie, "Skylar does not want the kids staying at Maryanne's house overnight." She omitted revealing to Julie the existence of the court order prohibiting an unrelated male from staying at Maryanne's house. She informed Julie that Skylar had to move out of the Newton house and posed the question, "Where are the children supposed to live?" She didn't elaborate that Skylar's faultless difficulties obtaining housing were due to having no former rental history or recent employment.

Julie testified that she was concerned where Skylar finally obtained housing. Skylar found a safe home near her job, allowing accessibility to her children during the day, if needed. It was a sensible decision. On the contrary, Julie stated, "I felt she had made a poor choice as far as the children's needs were concerned." When asked to explain, Julie could not elaborate.

Julie described "good parenting skills in a divorce situation are when the children come first. Each parent needed to have an appropriate attitude and behavior toward the other parent. Skylar loves her children, but she is not able to put them first."

Julie boldly proclaimed, "John provided *plenty* of information." She went on to spout off a litany of lies provided by John, which she had documented in her GAL report. "John told me he was always home and had to take care of all the children's needs because Skylar was unable." However, in her report, she contradicted herself by writing, "Skylar's friends didn't have much to say about John because he was never home." Julie had written two opposing scenarios in her report. If John was always home, then why were Skylar's friends unable to provide information on him, thereby supporting Skylar's claim he was never home? Julie omitted the critical information contained in the medical records and school records which documented objective supporting evidence identifying Skylar as the children's sole caregiver.

Julie concluded her testimony, "Skylar does not have the ability to be consistent and flexible. She does not supervise the children. John is more flexible. The children seem happy. They are doing well in school. They enjoy being with John. The house is neat and comfortable. Skylar should seek counseling." She smiled warmly at John.

Kate eagerly began her cross-examination of Julie. "Julie, do you know if there is a court order restricting the location of Skylar's housing?"

"I read the court order prior to beginning my investigation. I didn't see anything that restricted where John or Skylar lived," she answered.

Kate nodded. "So, if the custody of the children was not contingent on logistics, why did you feel the move was a poor choice?"

"Well, the children would be in the car a long time when they would go from one parent's home to the other," reasoned Julie.

"But there was no order restricting location. And Judge Shaver approved Skylar's move. In fact, she denied a change in custody two times! Were you attempting to supersede a judge's orders? Was there something about the children making you feel that way?" Kate asked.

Julie admitted, "My visits with the children were limited."

"I see. And did you take into consideration the restraining order against John?"

"No, I didn't feel it was important."

Julie didn't feel Skylar's journal entries were important either. Oddly, Julie did not disclose Skylar's most telling entries, which showed John's premeditated plan to do whatever necessary to take the children from Skylar and destroy her reputation.

Entry from Skylar's journal Sunday, January 16, 1994: *Now John says if I file for divorce, Paul Redmond will testify I had an affair/sex with him while John stripped that awful night of September 11th.*

Entry from Skylar's journal Wednesday, February 23, 1994: *He says his friends would say whatever he tells them to say in court. He said he'll say I'm an unfit mother, which obviously isn't true. One just needs to read my journals to know the truth.*

Journals or diaries are personal documentation of true events and raw emotions. They are heartfelt and honest records normally intended to remain private. If Julie had acknowledged and entered excerpts from Skylar's journals about John's abuse, neglect, and threats to get custody, how could she write a report favoring John?

Kate asked, "Julie, do you think it's odd that John was living with Maryanne immediately after he left the marital home?"

"No, I don't," she tersely replied.

"So, you condone allowing the children to see their father sharing a bed with a woman who is not their mother, immediately after the father moves out. Interesting." When Julie remained silent, Kate asked, "Did you contact Maryanne's ex-husband, Ed Dziwka, in order to inquire whether or not Maryanne was a good wife and mother?"

"No, I didn't think it was important."

Kate pressed on. "And you have no idea if Maryanne worked full-time or part-time or what hours she was at home. Why is that?"

Julie answered, "I didn't feel that was important."

Kate summarized, "So, Julie, you wrote a report that recommended three children be taken from their mother, who had no history of drugs, alcohol, or being abusive in any way toward her children, and placing them in a home with a woman you knew nothing about and a man who had never been at home. Why?" Kate looked perturbed. Judge Copeland leaned forward, greatly interested in Julie's answer. Julie sat quietly with her hands folded in her lap.

"Well, I guess that's a difficult question for you," Kate remarked. "Tell me about your meeting with Skylar."

Julie testified, "I met with Skylar twice. The second time, I was in her home for two hours. The home was clean. The children's toys were neatly arranged on the shelves. The children were appropriately dressed and appeared happy. Skylar played the piano for me and she plays beautifully. She had a good relationship with her children. She stated John was never home and she did all the cooking, cleaning, shopping, and transportation of the children." Julie paused, "Oh, that wasn't in my report."

Kate flashed Skylar a quick smile. Julie was freely admitting the absence of important information. She neglected to include anything positive about Skylar, despite the myriad of positive, unbiased evidence presented.

Julie continued her testimony as she acknowledged, "Skylar selected the children's school and obtained scholarships for them. She transferred their records and acted like as responsible parent. She was a good mother. She was concerned with the children's welfare. She took care of all medical and educational needs. Joshua was doing well at school when he was in her custody. There were no issues there, and she never missed any parent/teacher conferences."

"What about extra-curricular activities?" asked Kate. "Skylar had the children involved in gymnastics, the Tiger Scouts, karate classes, Little League, and soccer." She referred to her list. "Did you ask Skylar about her involvement? Did John participate in any activities?"

Julie admitted she never bothered to ask about Skylar's involvement in the children's extracurricular activities. She admitted John hadn't enrolled the children in any activities.

"So, am I correct in saying that Skylar was the only one who addressed the children's education, medical issues, extracurricular activities, and summer activities?" Kate asked.

Julie didn't answer.

"Well, I think the inference is there," Kate stated, looking toward Judge Copeland. "Julie, were there any changes when Skylar was caring for the children after John left?"

Julie admitted that everything after John had left the house was status quo.

"And did you show your notes or review your findings with anyone after you completed your investigation?"

"No." Julie had made the decision to change custody unilaterally.

Her final piece of testimony at the end of the day pointed a finger at Liz, who had been in contact with Julie all summer. Liz had faxed undisclosed documents to Julie and spoke to her regularly, trying to convince her to suggest John get custody of the children. Julie stated she did not speak to Skylar during June, July, and August 1996.

It is not a legal practice for attorneys to get involved with the GALs for the purpose of prompting them in their decision of who would get custody of the children. This was evident to Judge Copeland as well as

Kate. Judge Copeland deemed the guardian ad litem report as being slanted and biased. He reprimanded Liz in the courtroom, but he was lax regarding any repercussion for her misconduct in court.

Although Liz was sanctioned in 1995 for unethical tactics in an earlier custody trial, she was still so enmeshed with her client that she lost her professionalism in advocating for a client. She made the husband's tirade a crusade of hers as well. Her method of representing a client was exactly the same when she was sanctioned, according to the 1995 docket.

The results of Liz's sanctions are unimportant. The public knows this sad fact: just because a person can be found innocent does not mean they did not perpetrate the crime.

Kate effectively dredged the truth out of Julie. Perhaps John had utilized his abilities to charm Julie to the point where she was unaware of how contradictory and inaccurate her report read. Perhaps Julie was no longer qualified to provide accurate investigations. One would have to wonder about the reason she wanted to become a guardian ad litem. Why would she want to have the power to make unilateral decisions which could potentially destroy a family? It was frightening that Julie stood by her report despite the blatant discrepancies from her own testimony. It is terrifying that three young children were wrongly removed from their home. It was heartbreaking that although Judge Copeland acknowledged the gross factual errors in Julie's report, he did not return Joshua, Cary, and Jillian to their mother.

Chapter 22

Having reverted to his usual attire of jeans, work boots, and Security Safe t-shirts, John Bauers swaggered to the witness stand on November 22, 1996. He began his testimony by opening his eyes wide and declaring, "My van was keyed last May by Skylar. She keyed the sides and carved 'Fuck You'." He presented pictures of an older van used by his employees, not the truck he had painted to match his boat.

Skylar immediately whispered to Kate, "I did not do this." They studied the pictures John had provided. "That is not my printing, and I can prove it." She showed Kate her notes taken during the trial. She pointed out the letter "u" was written on the van in lower case, with a little tail. Skylar's notes showed she printed the letter without a tail.

Kate considered the printing on the vehicle. The letters were bright and bold. Was it even possible someone could have scratched the letters with a key? She murmured, "This doesn't look like scratch marks. It looks like chalk."

John said he informed the Needham police and named Skylar as the suspect. He presented the police report, dated in May of 1996, six months prior to the start of the trial. There was no follow up on the complaint by the police in May. Skylar was never contacted. Interestingly, John did not tell Julie that Skylar keyed his van during the time she was gathering evidence and preparing to write her report.

John testified, "The police wouldn't check for her fingerprints, when I asked. I couldn't afford to have it fixed, so I buffed out the scratches and words as best as I could."

Kate asked John for a brief chronological account of his education and work history. He stated he attended Needham High School but did not attend college. He said he was a locksmith by trade, with an office in Needham and accounts in New England and Florida. He was the sole proprietor but hired extra employees as needed. He claimed his computer had crashed so there was no way to provide the court with documentation about his business. He did his own bookkeeping and maintained his own checks and bank statements. He testified he did not receive cash for his services. All his records were kept on his computer, including invoices, customer lists, and accounts payable/receivable.

John stated, "I was the one who was responsible for the family finances, checking account, and credit cards. I hadn't paid taxes since 1984, so I went to my accountant for help, and he told me to sell our house and go to the IRS looking poor so we'd get less of a penalty."

When asked about his relationship with Skylar, John denied everything Skylar had shared with Kate. He denied he left her when she was in labor with Joshua and smoked pot. He denied fantasies of seeing her in bed with another woman. He denied he controlled her. He got angry at Kate's questions and became defensive. He blamed Skylar for his behavior.

"I worked hard. She was home with the kids during the day. I did not want her going out at night. A few times when I allowed her to go, she wore miniskirts and low-cut tops. I didn't feel it was appropriate for my wife to be dressed that way. One time, I came home from work and heard her talking to her mother on the phone. I picked up the receiver, and Skylar was saying she wanted a divorce so she could put on sexy clothes, go to nightclubs, and meet men. She and Sable also talked about getting a hit man to have me killed."

He absolutely denied checking the cupboards or asking Skylar for receipts from her grocery shopping. He brazenly admitted spending three hundred dollars every two months on cigars and boasted he shopped for his clothing in the exclusive stores on Newbury Street. He admitted he purchased a competition ski boat without asking his wife, but said, "It's gone now. I sold it to a friend, but he said I could use the boat whenever I wanted." John stated he did not have any documentation as proof of this sales transaction.

When questioned about his drug use, he admitted he smoked marijuana but was wide-eyed as he denied selling it. He angrily denied using "half a lock set" as a code for half an ounce of pot in case someone was listening on the phone. He denied he kept marijuana in the freezer.

John acknowledged he kept his guns in a safe as well as nude pictures of a former girlfriend. When asked if he thought it was appropriate to have pictures of a naked woman in a safe in the bedroom he shared with his wife, he declared, "Those were my pictures." He admitted to locking a pregnant Skylar out of the bedroom but denied throwing his work boots at her hand.

He also denied any incidents of physical abuse during the marriage or sexual assaults on Skylar after their separation. He admitted he hit Joshua and Cary until they had black and blue bruises all over their bodies. He admitted telling his sons he was "taking them to the home for bad boys" and made them pack their clothing in plastic bags.

"John, can you describe the events leading up to the evening of the separation in January 1996?" Kate asked.

He began, "I got into bed with a glass of red wine from my collection. Skylar told me she wanted to go out to dinner with a friend, and I didn't want her to going out. She started screaming at me, so I called 911. I left the house and moved in with a friend. I met my fiancée, Maryanne, and moved into her house in March of 1996."

With regard to his involvement with the children, John sheepishly laughed as he stated he couldn't remember taking the children to temple, the museum, the zoo, or the movies. He admitted since the change in custody he had not done anything with the children, either in school or as extra-curricular activities. Court recessed for the day.

Liz waived cross-examination so Kate would not have the opportunity to question him further. Liz employed an attorney's trick of having her grossly fabricated case heard near the end of the trial so it would be in the forefront of the judge's recollection as he wrote his final report. This is usually done when the attorney knows they have a weak case and therefore excludes any recalling of witnesses to rebut the lies.

On Thanksgiving Day, Skylar found a chance to see the vehicle John claimed was keyed when he enjoying a holiday dinner with the children and parents. She drove to the office, where his van was parked. She carefully examined the sides of his van, and ran her finger over the side, feeling the faint horizontal scratches on the side of the van. She closely looked for the letters she saw in the pictures presented in court. There was no indication there had ever been letters or the words, *Fuck You* scratched on the van. The rest of the van was smooth to the touch.

Skylar called Kate and described the condition of the van. She suggested, "If we can prove he's lying and actually fabricating evidence, maybe the judge will realize he's lying about everything, and I will get the children back."

"Skylar, I think the judge knows he's lying about the van. John didn't report it to Julie because he didn't want anyone checking up on him. The judge has his number," Kate reassured.

John was a master manipulator who, it appeared, would use any means, honest or dishonest, to reach his goal. Therefore, Kate wanted to dig deeper. She felt the details of John's finances, were important. The way Skylar described John, painted a picture of an abuser. Kate needed to show the court he was an abuser in every capacity and, therefore, unacceptable as the custodial parent. She needed accurate information about John's income in the hopes Skylar would be awarded custody and child support. Digging into the way John manipulated his finances was paralleled to the dishonest way he controlled other aspects in his life.

On December 2, 1996, Kate summoned Sean McMann, an accountant, into court. He testified briefly about meeting John in 1994. He stated he had prepared John's tax returns from 1987 to 1994 but that they were never filed with the IRS. He testified John gave him the figures verbally. He claimed he did not see a shred of hard documentation, and there was no audit.

Accountant Earl Steves was the next accountant summoned into court. He testified, "In 1994, John asked me about filing a Chapter 11 or bankruptcy. I told John he should liquidate all assets. In August of 1996, he came in and asked me to prepare tax returns from 1987 to 1995. I prepared these with the verbal information he provided. I did not look at any hard material. John computed his own gross income, net income, and cost of goods sold. The tax returns were never filed. They were not audited statements."

During the cross examination, Earl Steves was asked whether or not there was a joint liability due to John's irresponsibility of not filing his taxes. Earl talked about an *Innocent Spouse Doctrine*. "Because they were married, John feels Skylar should share the penalty of the tax issues. Skylar would have to prove she was not involved and innocent."

Judge Copeland interrupted and immediately ruled that Skylar was, in fact, an innocent spouse. "Mr. Bauers' tax problems are his – not Mrs. Bauers."

Kate and Skylar looked at each other and smiled. The accountant was dismissed, and Kate called Skylar's mother, Sable, as the next witness. Sable began her testimony by describing the times she visited Skylar when she lived with John. "I saw John about twelve times during the eight year marriage because he was seldom home. The few times I saw him, he was outside, working on his car or boat. I never observed him alone with the children. Skylar and the children came to my house for the holidays, but John only came a few times. He would tell me he didn't like coming to my house because he hated my dogs. He said this in front of the children and made them afraid of the dogs."

She continued, "I know John was never home because Skylar would phone me and complain. If he came home during our call, she would whisper, 'He's home; I have to hang up.' He did not want her talking on the telephone. He had a list of rules he expected her to follow and he had a bad temper. I heard him yelling at her when he caught her on the phone with me. I also saw the bruises on Skylar, on her wrists and marks around her neck."

When asked how John treated Skylar, Sable stated, "John was very condescending to her when I saw them together. He belittled her. I never heard her threaten or swear at him. She walked on eggshells around him."

Kate asked, "Do you know anything about the children's medical care?"

"Oh, yes. I attended the pediatrician visits with Skylar when the children had check-ups. John was never there. He didn't go to the hospital when Joshua had a high fever or when Cary had problems breathing. When Cary had surgery, I went to the hospital, and John didn't even visit him." She segued into Skylar's prenatal visits. "When Skylar was pregnant, John didn't go to any of her obstetrician appointments. Even when she was having contractions for three days, he refused to drive her to the appointment. I was afraid for her to go alone, so I drove her."

She discussed the many outings she had with the children and Skylar. She described the creative birthday parties Skylar would plan, adding, "Skylar is very family oriented and always included extended family members. She is a good mother. She was never inappropriate toward the children or toward John. She stayed at home and never left the house without John or the children. She is very devoted to her children." Her voice wavered, and she wiped a tear.

After a moment, she continued. Her voice was firm as she said, "I knew Skylar wanted a divorce. She was having problems breathing and heart palpitations. She felt John was killing her with cruelty. That's why she wanted a divorce. She didn't want a divorce so she could go out and meet men. That's ridiculous. I never had a conversation with my daughter about getting a hit man. John has always been a liar since the day I met him to his testimony in court. He is a compulsive liar, and I cannot stress that fact enough. If I knew then, what I know now, I would have forfeited anything to keep her away from that man. He is absolutely insane."

Chapter 23

In preparation for Skylar's testimony on December 3, 1996, John assembled an audience. He was seated in front of the courtroom, as close to the witness stand as possible. Maryanne sat by his side. Behind John sat George and Nora Bauers. Bravely, Skylar took the stand.

Maryanne in a loud whisper, commented, "She looks like Mother Teresa."

To begin with a clean slate, Kate addressed John's false accusation regarding his van.

Skylar stated, "I did not key the van and the printing is not mine. This evidence is fabricated, and I would be willing to take a polygraph test." She wanted that fact on record.

Kate began her questioning of Skylar with chronological events beginning with high school, her college education, and the years following until she met John Bauers. She testified to his drug use as well as his side business of selling pot. She provided the names of thirty people whom she witnessed purchasing pot from him. She offered into evidence a picture she had taken of John with a small tray on his lap filled with marijuana.

She stated, "He was preparing to roll a joint. He even did this in front of Joshua. When Joshie was three, he took a piece of paper, rolled it into a cylinder, and pretended to smoke. John just laughed."

To support her testimony, Skylar presented another photograph into evidence. It showed John smoking a joint while seated in his boat. Joshua was seated alongside his father in the boat.

She continued, "On my honeymoon, John refused to take me to

dinner because I wasn't wearing a bra with my sundress. When we got home, he'd check me every day to make sure I was wearing a bra. He forbade me from wearing certain clothes or shoes. Once, he ripped my dress off and tore it to shreds. It was crazy, because I never wore anything inappropriate."

Her testimony continued by describing the joy she felt from her pregnancies and John's displeasure when she announced her first pregnancy with Joshua, his indifference to the difficulty of Skylar's pregnancy with Cary, as well as his demand Skylar have an abortion when she was pregnant with Jillian.

Kate began questioning Skylar about her private moments with John.

She testified, "He wouldn't leave me alone when he wanted sex. Sometimes, it was in the morning and evening. There were days he'd come home in the afternoon, when the children were napping."

Maryanne loudly declared, "Yeah, right. She's a fucking liar."

John smiled broadly as his father patted him on the back, despite Maryanne's comments.

"I think this is a good time to take a short recess," announced Judge Copeland.

As the judge left the bench, Nora stood wooden-faced, and demanded, "George, let's go." She walked out of the courtroom with George trailing behind. John firmly suggested to Maryanne she leave as well. Angrily, she left just as Judge Copeland returned to the bench.

Skylar's testimony resumed with a description of the evening when John disrobed in front of Lori, hoping to engage in his fantasy of a ménage-a-trois. She did not testify about the assaults following the separation.

While preparing for the trial she had sobbed to Kate, "I can't relive them! And I don't want to be subjected to an interrogation. John won't be punished and I'll just be humiliated. I can't do it!"

Instead, Kate focused on John's controlling behavior.

Skylar stated, "John controlled all family finances. He did not allow me to have a bank account, checking account, credit cards, or access to a credit card. He paid all the bills and asked me for receipts for all purchases. I would have to ask him for money when I needed it, and unless I provided some sexual favors, he wouldn't give me grocery money."

Kate questioned, "Did he share anything about his business finances with you?"

"Yes, I knew some things about the business. John would receive cash for some of his jobs. Any time he received a check, he would drive to the bank the check was drawn on, regardless of where it was, in order to cash it so it couldn't be traced back to him."

She testified about the physical abuse. She testified about the time John threw her on the ground and choked her. She described how his eyes were bulging and his face filled with fury unlike anything she had ever seen. "He threw me down on the driveway and was on top of me with his hands around my neck. He was screaming because I kicked the seat of his boat. Afterward, I went into the house and took pictures of what he did."

Kate addressed the court. "We've submitted pictures as evidence to the physical abuse."

Judge Copeland looked at the photographs of Skylar with the prominent bruises from the choking on her neck.

Kate asked Skylar if there were other instances of physical abuse.

Skylar said, "Yes" and she went on to describe the other times of abuse when John would slam her against the wall and scream insulting names in her face or grab her wrists and verbally abuse her. She testified about the time he almost kicked in her car window.

"That happened when you lived in Medfield. You sold the house in 1995. Let's talk about the sale of the house." Kate looked through the evidence file and pulled out a sheet of paper. "This is a copy of the check you received, is that correct?" She handed it to Skylar. The check was made out to John and Skylar Bauers.

Skylar was confused. "I never saw this check." She looked at the copy of the back of the check where it was endorsed. Emphatically, she stated, "That is not my signature."

Judge Copeland asked to see an example of Skylar's signature. Although the check had been signed with her name, Judge Copeland easily determined Skylar did not sign the check.

Kate continued with her questioning. "Tell me about being at home with the children. When Jillian was born, Cary was sixteen months and Joshua was three and a half. You took care of the children alone. John did not take any time off work or make provisions for a nanny or a housekeeper, is that correct?"

Yes, I took care of all of my children," Skylar answered. "John said I could handle it."

"And you did?"

"Oh, yes." Skylar provided a detailed and comprehensive description of her days with her children. She explained how she incorporated her musical background in activities and exposed them to cultural activities as well as time outdoors at parks and playgrounds and day trips. She gave a thorough testimony on what the children liked to eat as well as what they disliked and the meals she cooked for them. She was astute in conveying their medical and dental history in great detail. She related the discipline methods she learned from a book, which was referred to her by one of Cary's teachers.

Skylar had brought in a videotape to show her involvement with the children and the imaginative birthday parties she created. Her voice was heard on the video as she taped the event. The tape did not show John.

"I enjoyed making the parties for my children. Actually, I broke my toe as I was running around decorating, but it all turned out well," Skylar said.

Kate addressed Judge Copeland. "As you saw and heard from this tape, only Skylar's voice was heard, and there was no sign of John." Kate turned back to Skylar. "What happened at Jillian's last birthday party? She was four, is that correct?"

"Yes, she's four. The party was a few days after John left. He never called. He didn't show up. And he never sent Jillian a gift."

Kate focused her next set of questions on John's interest in his personal life. Skylar contributed a great deal of information about his solo trips to Florida, the purchasing of his many vehicles, his wine collection, the pager numbers he would hide, as well as all the stories about women who would approach him during the day.

During another break, Lucas Delmonico, the court officer commented to Skylar, "He's got some issues with control, doesn't he?"

When court resumed, Kate asked Skylar about her twentieth high school reunion. "You attended your twentieth high school reunion with John. What happened that evening?"

She began to describe the evening. "John was in a hurry to get there that evening. I thought it was because he wanted to see Phil."

"Phil who?" asked Kate.

"Phil Lewin," replied Skylar.

"Any relationship to Liz Lewin?" Kate looked toward Liz.

"He's my brother," Liz answered flatly.

"Oh, how interesting." Kate replied flippantly. She paused before she directed her attention back to Skylar. "Then what happened?"

"Phil was supposedly dating Maryanne, and John sat with them all night."

"Wait a minute. Phil dated Maryanne before John dated her?" Kate acted confused.

"No. Phil was *pretending* to date her," Skylar explained.

"Why was Phil pretending to date her?"

Skylar replied, "Because John was dating her."

"Objection!" yelled Liz. "My client didn't start dating Maryanne until after they were separated!"

Kate interjected, "Well, according to the phone records that were presented by Maryanne's ex-husband, Ed Dziwka, they had been dating for over six months."

Judge Copeland looked at John, who sat there expressionless. He addressed Kate. "So, you are saying that Mr. Bauers had a friend who attended Mrs. Bauers' reunion, as, in a sense, a beard, with the woman Mr. Bauers was dating?"

"Exactly, your honor," replied Kate.

"Why?" asked Judge Copeland, looking at Skylar. "Why would he do that?"

"I don't know." answered Skylar softly.

Judge Copeland shook his head. "That's a pretty harsh thing to do. I mean, even if you two weren't getting along, I would say it's excessive."

Liz stood up and loudly interjected, "We'll address this later, Judge!"

Kate's final series of questions focused on Skylar's job search and apartment hunt. She felt it was important to address this because it portrayed Skylar as strong and resourceful by obtaining a job and apartment after being a stay-at-home mom for over eight years. She was proving Skylar as a capable woman and fully competent to take care of her children.

Kate asked Skylar to describe each of her children to the court. It was very emotional for her, as they had been with her constantly for the previous eight and a half years and suddenly they were gone for no reason other than John's desire to punish her. Sadly, this was not an unusual tactic for an abuser, who often uses their children as pawns as retaliation for divorce.

Court was adjourned for the day. Before they walked out, Judge Copeland said, "Mr. Bauers, I am very concerned about the drug sales. That is a felony, and I am considering what to do about it."

John arrogantly replied, "I will bring in every person she named, and they will all testify they did not buy drugs from me."

Liz Lewin began her cross-examination of Skylar on December 6, 1996. Liz asked questions much differently than Kate's orderly inquiry. Liz's questions were random. She would jump from year to year and topic to topic. Trying to answer her jumble of questions was a clever ploy, fashioned that way in order to catch someone who was lying. But since Skylar had not lied, it was just wearing and irritating. To further aggravate Skylar, Liz began throwing in statements she never said.

She said, "Yesterday, you testified..." and would state something outrageous.

Skylar would reply, "I didn't say that," or "I don't remember saying that." Using her former tactic to try to catch a lie was skillful; using the latter tactic was unethical.

John wanted to know everything possible about Jake so he had Liz work that into the trial. But Skylar was sharp and strong as Liz continued her questioning.

"Isn't it true you began dating Jake the night after you threw John out of the house?"

Skylar smartly retorted, "I don't base my life on a calendar of when John left."

Liz asked, "Where does Jake work?"

"I don't think that information is relevant to the reason we are here," she answered.

Judge Copeland was irritated. "Miss Lewin, ask her another question."

Liz asked, "Where does Jake live?"

Skylar looked at Judge Copeland. He addressed Liz. "Miss Lewin, this is inappropriate."

Liz faced Skylar. "Did Jake ever spend the night when the children are in the house?"

"Jake and I do not feel it's appropriate to spend the night together when the children are present," Skylar replied.

Liz continued her questions. "Were you stressed during the marriage?"

"Yes, in the morning until John left the house. And late at night, knowing that John would soon be home and I didn't know what he would do."

Liz jumped on that, twisting Skylar's answer. "So, the children created stress for you."

Skylar sighed in exasperation, "No, I didn't say that... I said, I was stressed until John left the house and before he got home. John was the only one creating the stress for me. I don't feel stressed by my children. I did not feel stress when John wasn't home."

The cross examination went on and on, with Liz asking the same questions over and over a million different ways. She was unable to find any lies in Skylar's testimony. Her cross-examination over, court adjourned for the weekend.

The following Monday, the former marriage counselor for the Bauers took the witness stand. He testified, "I am a marital therapist. I look at how people communicate – primarily how they deal with each other as a part of a couple. I found the Bauers both reactive and vindictive toward each other. Skylar is more verbal, and John is more retaliatory. By that, I mean Skylar wanted to discuss issues. She got frustrated because John needed the control. He would act out and do something, which served as her punishment. Skylar spent a lot of time with the children in the playroom, but John never told me she locked the children in the room."

The next witness for John was neighbor Sally Beaux. She testified, "I lived across the street from Skylar, but we were never friends. She never brought the children outside. She would sit in the room in the back of her house and watch television."

On cross examination, Kate asked, "Isn't that the room the Bauers called the sunroom? And didn't Skylar tell you how hot that room got during the day and the glare from the sun made it impossible to even see the television?" Kate paused. "Sally, how could you even know if Skylar was in that room, unless you came inside the Bauers' back yard?"

Following Sally, former babysitter Connie Taylor was called to the witness stand. Liz asked, "Connie, tell me what happened the night you discovered Jillian's finger was infected."

"When I saw Jillian's finger, I called Skylar but couldn't reach her." Her voice trailed off.

Liz pulled an affidavit from her briefcase that Connie had written in the fall of 1996. She prompted Connie, "You wrote an affidavit in September." She shook the affidavit.

Connie stated, "Can I see that for a second?" She looked at the affidavit. "Wait, *now* I remember what happened. Skylar called me back after ten minutes, and John called me back after one minute. I took Jillian to the hospital and met John there. He arrived with his camera and took pictures of her finger. Skylar didn't get home until one o'clock."

Kate cross-examined her. "Connie, how do you know John Bauers? Hasn't he been a friend of yours for years? And wasn't he the one you used to purchase your marijuana from?"

Connie became flustered and said, "I knew him..."

"I guess you don't remember when you met. Do you remember how Jillian hurt her finger?" Kate asked.

Embarrassed, Connie flushed and said, "I slammed her finger in a door – but it was an accident."

Raising her voice slightly, Kate demanded, "When did you let Skylar know about this?"

"I don't know when I told her. I might have called her the next day."

"But Skylar worked in Newton. She was just on the other side of town. Why wouldn't you have called her immediately? Wouldn't that have been the logical thing to do?" She remained silent. "Connie, let's talk about the night you took Jillian to the hospital. You called Skylar that evening, knowing she was doing the show. Then you called John, who met you at the hospital. Ironically, he showed up with his camera, is that accurate?" Kate's voice rose slightly.

Connie, her voice rising as well, stated, "No. John told me to take the children out for ice cream and then come back to his parents' house so he could take some pictures."

Kate interjected, "Wait a minute, I'm confused. You were babysitting at Skylar's request, at her house, yet you went out for ice cream with John and then back to his parents' house so he could take pictures of Jillian's finger? What time was it?"

"Around eleven," Connie replied.

Kate shook her head. Her voice commanded the courtroom. "So, it's after eleven o'clock and you had three children out, yet you decided it was more appropriate to keep them out instead of bringing them home and putting them to bed!" She paused. "Who was paying you that evening, Connie? Was it Skylar or John Bauers?" She faced Connie, who sat there dumbfounded. Kate showed her one of John's checks. Connie's name was on the check. The date on the check was the same date she had come into court to write her affidavit. "Didn't John pay you to do this?"

Connie looked at John. He shook his head ever so slightly. Connie refused to answer.

"I have no more questions, your honor." Kate told Judge Copeland. Court was adjourned for the day.

Skylar drove home, pleased at how effectively Kate was eliminating the erroneous statements of John's countless witnesses. When she arrived at her cozy apartment, she lit her candles and put her feet up. The telephone rang. It was Maryanne's ex-husband, Ed, who would periodically call Skylar to find out how the trial was going. But today he had his own news.

"Hi, Skylar. I had to go back to court because Maryanne filed a motion to have her child support increased. I never saw anything like this! When the judge denied an increase in my child support, Maryanne threw herself on the floor of the court crying and screaming."

"I would have loved to see that!" Skylar said, laughing.

Ed provided other information. "Maryanne fired her attorney and has a new attorney."

Maryanne's new attorney was Liz Lewin.

Chapter 24

The following day, the trial continued as Liz called Maryanne Szalony Dziwka to the stand. Maryanne flashed a bright smile to Liz and to Judge Copeland. She opened her eyes wide, fluttered her skimpy lashes, and waited for her first question.

Liz began her examination by asking her who took care of the children. Maryanne spoke in a choppy voice, annunciating every word in short, clipped syllables. Liz began to ask a well-rehearsed series of questions regarding the children's care. She shot off the questions in rapid succession, and she answered the questions just as quickly.

To every question, Maryanne would answer, "John." Of the thirty or so questions, Liz asked, Maryanne just kept replying, "John, John, John."

Kate began her cross-examination of Maryanne. "Is there an order from your divorce that states: *No unrelated male shall sleep in your house when your children are present?*" Kate read from a document. "And aren't you in contempt of court because John is living there?"

"The contempt was waived in July," Maryanne stated bluntly.

"How interesting, because I checked and saw it was still in effect." Kate smiled but didn't give her a chance to respond. "Tell me about the night of your high school reunion."

Maryanne began, "My husband did not want to go to the reunion. John was a friend, so he told me his friend Phil could take me."

Kate asked, "Had you ever met Phil Lewin prior to this?"

Maryanne curtly answered, "No, I did not." She began blinking rapidly.

Kate suggested, "So, you chose to go to your high school reunion with a man you did not even know, a blind date, despite the fact you were married to Ed Dziwka?" Maryanne glared at Kate and remained silent. Then, Kate innocently asked, "Isn't it true you were having an affair with a married police officer from Natick while you were married to Ed Dziwka?"

Maryanne exploded. She jumped to her feet in the witness box. "Where do you get your information?!" she screamed. "Who have you been talking to?!" There was uproar in the court.

John immediately dashed to the witness stand. "Maryanne, calm down, calm down."

Skylar and Sable looked at each other, astonished at the pandemonium Maryanne had created.

"She's crazy!" whispered Sable.

They sat and watched as John brought Maryanne a bottle of juice. He gave her a sip as he tried soothing her. It took a full twenty minutes before she would stop screaming.

Kate resumed her inquiry, but she altered her line of questions. She opted to tread lightly, because Maryanne's highly explosive state was now apparent. But Kate had angered her so much, that every answer sounded bitter and abrupt. When Kate concluded her examination, Maryanne defiantly marched out of the courtroom and slammed the door loudly.

Liz continued her collisions on December 19, 1996, by calling Tom Parsons as a witness. Tom had been John's friend since grade school. He was John's roommate during their "cocaine years." One evening, Tom had fallen asleep with a lit candle in his room. The candle fell and began burning the table. The fire spread, and the room filled with smoke. John smelled smoke and dragged Tom to safety. Tom owed John his life and would do anything for him.

Tom lumbered up to the witness stand. He began his testimony by stating, "We have satellite TV and when John and Skylar came to the farm, all she did was watch triple-X movies! John was the one who took care of the kids, not Skylar. John was nurturing." When Tom was dismissed from the witness stand, he purposefully walked to Skylar and said, "Bye, Skylar," before leaving the courtroom. Court was adjourned for the day.

Before court resumed in the morning, Skylar and Kate sat outside the courtroom, waiting for the doors to open. Skylar recognized a tall, statuesque woman with blonde hair walking down the courthouse hall. It was John's former attorney, Zoe Powers, who represented him briefly in 1994. She pointed her out to Kate who looked closely.

"I think I've met her. Wait right here." She got up and greeted her. They walked into another part of the courthouse. When Kate returned, she announced, "She and I had a very interesting conversation. I told her I was here doing your divorce trial. She said she had represented John briefly in 1994. She told me that he is crazy."

The comment from John's former attorney made Skylar feel empowered. If Zoe Powers saw his insanity, maybe Judge Copeland would as well.

The following day provided Kate with the opportunity to judge John's sanity when he took the witness stand. She listened as John began his testimony as a narrative.

"I met Skylar in May of 1985. It was several weeks before I asked her out. She used marijuana, cocaine, and alcohol while we were dating. We became engaged six months after we met. Skylar had this urgency to get married. She didn't allow input from me to plan the wedding. Because of that and her drug use, I broke off the engagement. Skylar was not happy about the breakup. She called me and told me she loved me so much and asked me to have dinner with her. I did, and eventually we became engaged again. I was allowed more input in the wedding. Sable paid for most of the wedding and I paid eleven thousand dollars toward it. Once we were married, Skylar began to show dislike toward my friends. I was used to my friends dropping by whenever they wanted so we could fish, golf, hang out, or work on my car. She didn't want any of my friends coming by anymore. If she didn't like the person, she'd make them feel very uncomfortable. She forbade me from going fishing, skiing, or to the Parsons' farm. We'd argue and Skylar would get physical. She'd use strong language and call me a 'fucking asshole.' She'd go as low and deep like no one I've ever seen in my life. One night, we had an argument when she went into my safe and found pictures of my ex-girlfriend naked. She attacked me verbally and physically so I shut the bedroom door and put a match in the lock so she couldn't unlock the door. She banged on the bedroom door until one-thirty in the morning. At six in the morning, she started banging on the door again. Somehow, she got into the room and was yelling. I got out of there as quickly as I could."

"Who took care of the house?" Liz asked.

"Before Joshua was born, I did the bulk of the housecleaning and laundry. We both cooked. Once Joshua was born, I became an errand boy. I mowed the lawn, did chores, helped out with Joshua's laundry. I did seventy-five percent of the cooking because I like to cook. After we had Cary, Skylar had less time, and the laundry piled up. There were occasions when Skylar would clean. She was concentrating on Cary, and I had to help with Joshua. Whatever was needed, I would do it. Once Jillian was born, things got messier. It became unsanitary. I'd come home between six-thirty and eight-thirty and first let the kids up from being locked in the basement. The room was absolutely destroyed. There was urine in cups and on toys. They'd be locked out of the bathroom. They took the laundry stuff and poured it in the toilet. Skylar was either napping or talking on the phone. She was the one who requested a lock on the basement door. I called the Department of Social Service as an anonymous party and reported I knew a woman who locked the children in the basement. I took the door off the hinges, and Skylar went ballistic. She yelled that the kids would wreck the laundry she was folding. The original intent of the locks was to keep the kids out of the kitchen if the floor had been washed or if water was boiling on the stove. Locks were used as a babysitter. She wanted locks on every door of the house. I would feed the children and put them to bed sixty percent of the time.

When we lived in Newton, it was every single night. When we

moved to Newton, the condition of the house was good but it slowly began to deteriorate. Rugs were soiled and there were markers on the walls. The house was a total disaster. When I came in at the end of the day, I could tell you what they had for breakfast, lunch, and dinner. It was on the counter, floors, and sink. Skylar was on the phone, the computer or watching TV."

"Tell me about the first separation in February 1994," Liz requested. "I thought if I left, Skylar would cool out and she'd appreciate what I did. She would try to hit me and throw things. I don't remember the time frame – maybe a few weeks. I called the house a few days after I left, and she said, 'Fuck you – call your lawyer.' I was very concerned about the kids, so I moved back. She wouldn't let me talk to the kids or see them."

"And the second separation?" Liz prompted

"That was in May of 1994. I was mowing the lawn, and the Medfield police arrived. The children were there. We reconciled in August because I didn't want my children to come from a divorced home. I tried to do whatever she wanted to do. She wanted to move. She didn't like Medfield. After the reconciliation, there were some behavior and money issues. I wasn't paying my taxes in order to achieve the kind of lifestyle we wanted."

Liz asked about their final separation in January of 1996. "What happened that night?"

"I told Skylar I needed her to help out and get a job. She dug her nails into my wrist. She said she was going to stab me. She said she was going to get a knife so I called 911. Joshua was awake and crying and clinging to me. After I left, our neighbor, Jean, would call me when Joshua was there, and I'd sneak over to see him. I was not allowed to speak to the kids. I'd call on the phone, and Skylar would hang up. I tried everything I could."

"After you left, Skylar had a birthday party for Jillian. What happened that day?"

"She wouldn't have let me go to her party. I don't know if I tried to go," John said.

"You didn't try to go, or you did try to go?" Liz gave John a hint.

"No! I mean, I wanted to go. I called the house, and she hung up on me."

Skylar was physically sick every morning during John's testimony. It was stomach-turning for her to have to sit and listen to his revolting slander. Jake insisted on spending the night during that part of the trial. In the morning, he would see her crawl out of bed and literally be curled up on the floor for at least thirty minutes, unable to move.

Jake would talk to her and encourage her to stand up. "Baby, please stand up. You have to keep fighting for the sake of your children." He would help her stand and get into the shower.

The hot water would usually relax her enough to prepare for court. On the drive to Dedham, without fail, her palms would begin to sweat once she passed the Needham exits as the courthouse was minutes away. She would light a cigarette and try to relax in preparation of meeting her tormentors.

John continued his testimony on the witness stand. "Skylar used to take Cary to gymnastics. I went two or three times and videotaped him. When Joshua played Little League, I took him to most games unless he wanted to do something else. Skylar was only there two times. Maryanne came three times because she wanted to see the kids play. Skylar said if I brought Maryanne to a game, she'd pull Joshua out of Little League."

When Liz asked him about Skylar's pregnancies, John stated, "I was surprised at all of her pregnancies, but happy. I never smoked pot while she was in labor with Joshua. I had limited information about the problems when she was pregnant with Cary."

Liz asked, "Did Skylar go out at night?"

John replied, "I had a problem with Skylar going out at night. She'd go out once a week, mainly with Lori. She'd get pretty dolled up if she was going out. She'd wear micro minis, lacy stockings, high heels, and low cut shirts. She'd come home drunk and want sex."

Judge Copeland interjected and asked, with a grin, "Are you complaining?"

John laughed and said, "No."

Liz prompted, "How much was Skylar on the phone?"

"My concerns with her using the telephone were that she couldn't get things done or watch the children. I didn't want her using the phone when I was there because before I got my cell phone, when my pager went off, I had to use the phone to return a call. I wanted to know who she was talking to during the day, but when she found out I was checking the phone bill, she started ripping up the itemized part. I became suspicious, so once, I dug a bill out of the trash and saw she had called an old boyfriend. Strange men would call the house. One time, I answered using a woman's voice." John spoke in falsetto, "Hello?" Lowering his voice, he continued, "I got the guy's name, but I forget it now."

"John, did you stalk Skylar?"

"I didn't stalk Skylar. I didn't send people to spy on her. I just asked a few of my neighbors to let me know what was going on at the house."

That afternoon, a document from the drug testing laboratory was faxed to the courthouse. In January of 1996, attorney Roger Woodman, who had been representing Skylar, had requested a drug test for John Bauers. Liz vehemently refused the test on behalf of her client. In anticipation John would be required to take a drug test when the trial began in November 1996, Liz instructed him to stop smoking marijuana to insure he would test clean. Liz then demanded Skylar be drug tested as well, knowing how unpleasant it would be for her. Judge Copeland ordered that both parties have hair follicle tests, for signs of drugs.

The document with the results of these drug tests for John and Skylar indicated they both showed negative for drug use.

Chapter 25

The anticipation of John undergoing a cross-examination was reassuring as well as a reprieve from anxiety for Skylar. Now Kate was in control, and it was certain she would skillfully expose and eliminate all the deceitful discrepancies in his slanderous testimony.

"Let's get this story about your truck being damaged out of the way before we start," Kate said to John on a cold morning in late December 1996. "Did you confront Skylar regarding the keying incident?"

"No, I did not," John replied.

"You stated Skylar keyed your van, yet you didn't get a restraining order against her. Did anyone witness this?" asked Kate with incredulous affect.

"There were no witnesses. I did request fingerprints, but the police wouldn't do it."

"Well, yes, you did say that, however I made an inquiry to the detective bureau of the Needham police department. The detective told me their policy of obtaining fingerprints." Kate read from her notes, *If a victim of property damage believes they know who the perpetrator is, and they request fingerprinting, we will do a fingerprinting.* Hmm, that's interesting. They wouldn't take fingerprints from your truck. Maybe they were too busy."

John sat stone-faced.

"Well, let's continue. Mr. Bauers, you testified you beat your boys because they took the laundry detergent and poured it in the toilet. Where is the laundry detergent kept?"

"On the shelf in back of the washing machine."

"How did the children get it?" Kate wanted to know.

"I don't know. It's much too high for any child to reach."

"But Mr. Bauers, you also testified that Skylar would lock the children in the basement, and the children would urinate in the playroom because they had no access to the toilet. But, if they had no access to the toilet, how would they be able to pour the detergent in the toilet... which got you angry enough to beat them until they were black and blue?"

John shifted uncomfortably in his seat.

"Objection!" Liz screamed, jumping to her feet. "She's badgering my client. We will address these discrepancies on my re-examination!"

John grinned at Liz and slouched down in a relaxed position.

Kate changed the topic. In answer to her questions regarding the children's schedule, John testified he didn't know if the children napped, didn't know their daily routine, if they attended playgroups with other children, or what Skylar did during the day with the children.

Kate asked John about his involvement with the children. He admitted he never attended a parent/teacher's conference. He didn't recall the name of Joshua's first grade teacher or remember she had testified they'd never met. He didn't remember the name of the director of the preschool where Cary and Jillian attended or that she had testified.

Kate changed topics. "During your separation in 1994, did you seek custody?"

Matter-of-factly, John stated, "No."

Kate asked, "Did you have a girlfriend at that time?"

John began laughing. Still laughing, he answered, "I had *lots* of girlfriends."

Unsmiling, Kate responded, "Lucky you." She paused. "At that time, did you have just *one* girlfriend willing to take you into her house with your three young children?"

John was silent.

Kate dug deeper. "So, in 1994, you were separated from your wife, out of the marital home yet paying a mortgage on that house. Wasn't it easier to convince Skylar to take you back until you could sell the house and lose that financial liability? And isn't that the reason you are seeking custody at this point? You were able to sell the house and you found a woman willing to take you in. To me, it sounds like a calculated plan."

Liz jumped to her feet again. "Objection! My client doesn't have to answer that!"

Innocently, Kate turned to the judge. "No problem, your honor." She looked back at John. "Let's talk about finances. You testified you didn't receive cash as payment for your work."

"That's correct," John stated.

Kate said, "I show you these bank statements." She pulled out his bank statements. "These are for several months, yet there's no activity. What did you do for cash during those months?"

John shifted and smiled, "I don't remember... I guess I used a credit card."

Appearing happy with his response, Kate stated, "Okay, well, here's your credit card bill. There's nothing listed. Can you explain now how you got money for those months?"

John didn't answer.

Kate said, "I guess you don't remember. Let's talk about expenses. You replaced a septic system in Medfield. If your account shows no activity, where did you get the money?"

John began to show some anger. "I took fifty-five hundred dollars out of my Needham account to pay for the expenses. I know I paid them. They didn't work for free."

Kate kept pressing forward, "What about the money from the sale of the Medfield house? Why didn't you use that to pay the temple so your children could stay in preschool?"

John's voice rose, "I wasn't going to take the money out for any reason."

Kate looked puzzled and asked, "But you recently purchased a yellow Oldsmobile 442 convertible, is that correct? The car you had showed Skylar and wanted to purchase?"

John frowned. "No, that's Maryanne's car. She wanted the 442."

"I see," Kate smiled, "So, instead of paying for your children's pre-school, you bought the Oldsmobile 442 for Maryanne."

"No! I didn't purchase that car for her!" John's eyes began to bulge.

"But you did purchase a British Triumph TR6 convertible in 1994, even though you didn't file taxes."

"Yes." John glared at Kate.

"Why?" Kate asked with a puzzled expression.

"Because, it was a steal!" John explained to her excitedly.

Kate questioned John about the kind of communication he used for business and pleasure. Angrily, he testified he would hide any incoming calls from Skylar, hotly stating, "It was my cellphone. It wasn't for her." He testified that all his mail went to a private post office box.

Kate shuffled through her papers. She noticed the more irritated John became, the more contradictory his testimony. She approached him.

"You didn't want your wife having any access to your business dealings. But you must have kept careful records in the privacy of your office. And since you appear so diligent and meticulous in the upkeep of your boat, truck, and car, it would seem to me you would run your business the same way, like keeping some kind of back-up file in the event your computer suddenly, um, crashed...like yours." Kate purposely tried to make it sound as if she didn't believe him for a minute.

Her sarcasm was lost to John, who chuckled. "Well, I guess I should have done that."

Kate completed her cross examination. She turned to Judge Copeland. "I have nothing else at this time, your honor." Court recessed for the weekend.

The children spent almost every weekend with Skylar. She would find inexpensive activities to attend on Saturday. On Saturday night, they would watch a rented movie and eat popcorn while cuddled on the couch together. But Joshua was feeling the tension from John and Maryanne, as Skylar was the nightly topic of conversation. He became very sensitive to any kind of boundaries. One night, when Skylar set a limit with him, eight year old Joshua went to a drawer in the kitchen and got out a knife.

He brought it into the living room and stated, "I want to kill myself." He brought the knife closer to Skylar and said, "Here," handing her the knife. "I want you to kill me."

Skylar calmly said, "Joshie, put the knife back in the drawer." She handed the knife back to him, and he replaced it in the silverware drawer.

"Now come back here and sit with me." She made room for him next to her on the couch and held him close.

After the children had gone to bed, Skylar called Kate and related Joshua's distress. She told her to find a therapist for Joshua. Although Skylar had no health insurance, she was very resourceful and was able to find a therapist who offered a sliding fee scale.

Kate called Liz and related what had happened with Joshua and the knife. She told Liz that Skylar found a therapist for Joshua.

Liz replied, "She's going to make up lies about my client. If you dare present this in court, I will ask for supervised visits, and Skylar will never see those kids again. Joshua had the knife at Skylar's house and threatened suicide at Skylar's house. I can make her look so bad she'll wish she never set eyes on me. Leave it alone, Kate."

Kate couldn't believe that Liz could be so heartless. "Liz, I promise you that Skylar is only looking for someone to help Joshua."

"Kate, you have my answer." Liz refused to let Joshua be seen by a therapist.

Kate tried one last plea. "Liz, don't you care about Joshua Bauers?'

Liz answered, "Kate, I am working for John Bauers, not Joshua Bauers."

Chapter 26

Ann Bradley, author of *Divorce: The Real Truth, The Hidden Danger: Surviving, Deception, Betrayal and Narcissism,* states: *"Often the abuser who sees he is losing control will escalate the methods of control and abuse. The lies will be bolder, and he will backstab and betray with more intensity. He has a fierce need to regain power and control. They have tunnel vision when you have become the designated enemy."*

On December 30th, 1996, Liz orchestrated the most mortifying, as well as illegal, display of John's vengeance. She set up a tape deck and stereo speakers in front of the courtroom.

"Tell me about Skylar's temper," Liz suggested.

John began his testimony. "She had a terrible temper! This one time, I had a little recorder in my pocket, and when she started screaming at me, I pressed the button."

Kate objected. "My client was recorded without permission. That is a criminal offense."

Massachusetts Law, Ch. 272, Part 99 states: *"It is a crime to record any conversation, whether oral or wire, without the consent of all parties in Massachusetts. The penalty for violating the law is a fine of up to $10,000 and a jail sentence of up to five years."*

Liz insisted the tape be played. Skylar found it difficult to breathe. She prayed she wouldn't faint in expectation of humiliation by John. Judge Copeland abused Skylar's civil and personal rights, as well as the judicial system when he gave his consent to play the tape.

The tape began. Although he had previously denied checking the cupboards after Skylar went grocery shopping, there were sounds on the tape of drawers and cabinets being opened and shut. John's voice was heard. "You went shopping yesterday? This doesn't look like one hundred dollars worth of food. Where's the receipt?" His voice became more vociferous.

Skylar answered, soft and calm. "I guess it was thrown out."

There were sounds of rummaging of cans and boxes. "You didn't buy coffee." John's voice had an accusatory tone which bordered on belittlement. "If you didn't buy coffee, I am going to deduct twenty-five dollars from the money I give you."

Skylar, beginning to sound frantic stated, "Look, here's the coffee. I did buy it." The relief in her voice was palpable.

"I am going to have to do the shopping from now on – that way I know where my money is going." John's tone remained condescending. "Since I had to spend time looking for coffee, I am not taking the kids to school today." His voice echoed amid tiled bathroom walls. Incredulously, the sound of urinating was heard followed by the sound of a flushing toilet. He had stopped to relieve himself during the taped confrontation. "You'll have to drive them." There was a mocking tone to his voice as he returned to the kitchen.

Frustration crept into Skylar's voice, "John, you know I am going to the gym! I will miss my class."

"Too bad," John snapped.

The children are heard in the background. Skylar yelled, "Stop jumping on the bed!" Tearfully, she pleaded, "John, please take the kids to school. They are all ready."

John, very calmly, answered, "No, you can take them. You made me late."

"I didn't make you late! You made yourself late, looking for the coffee."

"No, you didn't get coffee so that is why you have to take the kids to school." John's voice was even and quiet.

"John! I *did* get the coffee! Please, take them now!"

When the tape concluded, Judge Copeland said, "It sounds as if Mr. Bauers was purposefully provoking Mrs. Bauers."

Skylar breathed easier, grateful that Judge Copeland saw through John's sham.

In the book, *The Sociopath Next Door, author and psychologist Martha Stout writes: "Sociopaths are infamous for their refusal to acknowledge responsibility. 'Consistent irresponsibility' in the language of the America Psychiatric Association is a cornerstone of the antisocial personality diagnosis."*

Liz continued her cross examination. She showed John the photographs of Skylar with the bruises on her neck. "Did you ever choke your wife?"

John sardonically said, "I didn't choke her. Those marks are hickeys I gave her while we were making love."

Skylar shook her head. She had never received a hickey from John. He never kissed her neck. His method of lovemaking was an assault, and any kind of kissing was a non-event.

Liz insisted there was no choking and attempted to stage her version with a skillfully choreographed demonstration. It concluded with Liz lying on the courtroom floor with careful placement of John's hand on her neck.

Triumphantly, Liz stated, "According to the marks on her neck, she was not choked." Her reenactment lacked the rage and terror of the actual event.

Judge Copeland was amused and told Liz he enjoyed seeing her lying on the floor and asked would she mind demonstrating again. Judge Copeland was clearly entertained at the choreographed display. It was an act. He didn't see a livid John Bauers, his pale eyes bulging and blazing with anger until he caught his wife and slammed her viciously to the ground. He didn't feel the hands of an enraged person tighten around his neck or feel the stones and gravel digging into his scalp. Judge Copeland's review of the performance was he didn't believe the picture of the bruises on Skylar's neck were the result of choking *or* hickeys.

The final witness appeared in court on December 31, 1996. Former babysitter, Maree Labarini came into court in the afternoon. She sat on the witness stand and smoothed her jacket.

"It's so nice to meet you, Judge. I am glad I was able to take time off work. I've always wanted be a witness." She didn't make eye contact with Judge Copeland.

Maree began her testimony by complaining, "Skylar wasn't the one to call me for a job. John used to call me. I don't know why she never called. She appears very normal, but she isn't. In my opinion, children should not be restricted to the playroom – they should have the run of the house. You have to let them do what they want so they can express themselves."

When Liz questioned her about the condition of the Bauers house, Maree didn't remember anything she had written on her affidavit of 1996. But she claimed she remembered, "Skylar's hairdryer was always plugged into an outlet in the bathroom. And she left her hairspray out!" she stated fervently.

When asked if Skylar went out at night, Maree's reply was almost sing-song as she crooned, "When Skylar would return from a night out, she was always happy and smiling and drunk. She drinks too much, and she does drugs! I know this because once I found a package of rolling papers in a drawer. When I showed them to Skylar, she asked me if I could supply her with marijuana." Maree tucked her chin down and folded her arms tightly across her chest.

On cross examination, Kate asked, "Do you have a degree in psychology?"

Maree looked startled. "Um, no I don't."

"Do you take classes in abnormal psychology?"

Maree giggled and smoothed her hair. "No, I don't have time. I have two daughters."

"How nice," replied Kate. "What I would like to know is why you feel you have the knowledge to state 'Skylar Bauers appears normal but isn't' if you have no degree, no training, and you are here under oath."

Maree chewed on her nail. "Um, I dunno. It's just my opinion."

Kate said, "Maree, you testified Skylar didn't unplug her hair dryer. Isn't it true that there was no place to rest a hair dryer if it were plugged into the wall in the Bauers bathroom?"

"I don't remember what the bathroom looked like," Maree grumbled.

"Then how do you remember the hairdryer was plugged in?" Kate asked.

Maree sat silently and nervously smoothed her hair.

"Since you don't remember that, do you remember Skylar coming home drunk?"

"Yes! I do. She would come home all happy and smiling." Maree smoothed her hair.

"And does that mean she was drunk?" questioned Kate.

Judge Copeland interrupted. "I've been seeing Mrs. Bauers in court day after day. I know people who drink, and that woman doesn't drink. Miss Fabiano, I suggest you ask Miss Labarini something else."

"Thank you, your honor." Kate turned back to Maree, who was chewing on her nail. "Maree, you stated Skylar asked if you would supply her with marijuana."

"Yes, after I told her I found the rolling papers." Maree kept her finger in her mouth.

"What was her tone of voice? Was she happy, angry, excited, eager?"

"She was laughing," Maree answered. She began chewing on a lank of her hair.

"Laughing as if she were kidding? As if she was joking with you? Don't you think they may have been John's rolling papers that he left there?"

"Mmm. I dunno. Maybe." Maree began smoothing down her hair again.

"I think we're done, Mrs. Labarini." said Kate, and she turned her back on her.

"It's MISS Labarini!" shouted Maree.

Kate flinched when she heard her shout. Before she could say anything else, Maree stood up, grabbed her coat, and stormed out of the court room, slamming the door behind her.

Maree Labarini was the last witness that day.

New Year's Eve was bitterly cold, but when Skylar arrived home, she found her apartment toasty warm. Jake was there, and he had lit a fire in the fireplace. Although she was sad she wasn't sharing New Years Eve with her children, she found comfort enveloped in Jake's warmth. They shelved their dinner plans and spent the evening cuddled by the fireplace, eating hors d'oeuvres and sipping champagne. It was lovely and peaceful for her to be with a man like Jake who was content to just relax and enjoy her company. As they curled up on the couch, they toasted in the new year with the wish that 1997 would be happier than 1996.

Court resumed on January 2, 1997, beginning with several Natick teachers who testified that John appeared as a responsible father since he had enrolled the children in school the previous September. They offered the information forms parent complete on the first day of school. The cards John filled out showed he had omitted Skylar's name on every form.

The bright spots for Skylar were her times with the children. During their Wednesday night dinners, she would help them with homework. On weekends, she would find interesting events that provided adventures for her children. When the weekend ended, John would pick them up at her Stoneham apartment at seven o'clock on Sunday night. The children would enthusiastically tell their father about their new experiences.

John would interrupt them and sarcastically say, "Sounds like real fun. Didn't you think that was boring?" He would belittle every place Skylar took them and the children would get very quiet and stop talking. Joshua would look out the window. Jillian would pull out a little stuffed animal and hold it to her cheek, and Cary would chew on his shirt.

One Sunday evening, Skylar was surprised to see George and Nora standing with their faces pressed against her large picture window. They were there to pick up the children instead of John, but they didn't ring the doorbell. Skylar walked to the window and pulled down the shades.

Although she could shut Nora and George out of her home, she still had to contact them about the return of her personal belongings.

When Nora answered the phone, Skylar politely asked when she could come by and collect her property.

Nora replied, "We have to wait until after the divorce, so we know what belongs to you and what belongs to Johnny."

"Nothing belongs to *Johnny*. They're *my* family pictures and mementos," Skylar said.

"Well, I will have to talk to Johnny first. He can decide if you can have them." Nora snapped, and hung up the telephone.

John had stripped her of everything, except her desire to remain an involved parent. Part of this responsibility was maintaining the Jewish tradition of attending religious training. She contacted a synagogue in Natick and met with the rabbi. After she explained the situation, he offered scholarships to the Hebrew school for the children. Kate presented the information regarding the children's religious education to Judge Copeland at their next court date. Wanting to appear acquiescent in front of the judge, John and Liz agreed it was a good idea.

Although he had agreed, John felt he had given up some control. He needed to remind Skylar who was boss. He knew a way to upset her would be to cut Jillian's long, beautiful hair.

When Skylar picked up Jillian on Wednesday, her hair was up to her chin.

Jillian got into the car and began crying, "Daddy made me cut my hair. It's all gone! Mommia, I want to have long hair, but Daddy won't let me because he said you want me to have long hair."

Skylar was livid and wanted to cry, but she managed to hold it in so she wouldn't upset Jillian. In an even voice, she told her, "Honey, you look so cute. Your hair will grow back."

John manipulated the boys as well. One evening he called Joshua at Skylar's apartment. She heard Joshua say, "You did?! Cary, Dad got us bunk beds!" He turned to Cary as John's voice reverberated from the phone. "But we're with Mom," he said in a small voice.

Skylar put her ear near the phone and listened to the exaggerated enthusiasm in John's voice, exclaiming, "Joshie, these beds are so cool! If you were here, we could put a blanket on the top and make a fort! Too bad you're not here having fun."

She took the phone away from Joshua and said, "John, that's inappropriate. You are upsetting the boys. I am hanging up now."

John screamed, "You little cunt! If you hang up on me you'll be so fuckin' sorry!"

Hearing the intense fury in his voice, she hung up the phone. Her heart was racing. She took the phone in the bedroom and quietly called the Stoneham police to report John's threat. Then she called Kate and related the incident. Kate reassured her that she did the right thing.

At ease, Skylar hung up the phone. She put in a video and snuggled on the couch with Joshua, Cary, and Jillian. About a half hour later, the children could barely keep their eyes opened, so she tucked them into their beds.

She went back to the living room just as the phone rang. It was Kate.

"Liz just called me. John is in jail in Natick."

The thought of him sitting in a cell pleased her, although that was not her intention. She merely wanted to report the threat. She conveyed this to Kate. No sooner did their brief conversation end, when the phone rang again. It was the Natick police calling to make sure she wasn't frightened and to reassure her that John was in custody. They asked her whether to keep him in jail or not. Skylar replied to the police that all she wanted to do was report a violation of the restraining order that was still in effect. She merely wanted John's threat documented.

Liz was incensed. She called Kate, "Tell Skylar she cannot have the kids this weekend for throwing my client in jail. If she shows up at John's house, she will be arrested."

The two attorneys corresponded, exchanging numerous faxes, yet Liz continued her threats to have Skylar arrested for trespassing if she attempted to see her children.

Kate informed Skylar, "Liz is making a unilateral decision on this. We are going to have to go court. You should use this weekend to do something fun. In the meantime, why don't you send the kids a bunch of balloons?"

Skylar loved the idea and found a service which offered balloon deliveries. She chose a bright, multi-colored bouquet with a little card attached. Skylar simply wrote, *"Dear Joshua, Cary, and Jillian, I love you! Love, Mommy."* She already missed the children unbearably.

On Monday, court reconvened. John vehemently denied threatening Skylar, and widely opened his eyes, his typical affectation when he was lying, as blatant as if he held up a sign.

Judge Copeland read the police report and ordered him to refrain from calling the children when they were with Skylar. He admonished both John and Liz against making unilateral decisions.

At dinner with the children on Wednesday evening, no one mentioned the balloon bouquet, so Skylar finally asked, "Were you surprised by the balloons?"

Cary's blue eyes went wide. "Mom, how do you know about the balloons that came to the house?"

Joshua interjected, "Those balloons were from Dad's friend, Phil Lewin."

"No, honey, I sent them. Didn't you see the card?"

"No. Dad looked at the card and put it in his pocket. Then he said, 'Phil sent you these balloons...I have a great idea. Why don't we let them go up into the sky?'"

Jillian piped up in her little voice, "Daddy let the balloons go up into the sky and I cried."

Chapter 27

The six month trial was nearing its end as the first hints of spring were in the air. It was the second longest trial in Norfolk County, due to the excessive number of witnesses, consisting of mostly personal friends, for the defendant. The disproportionate number of witnesses for the plaintiff were less than half of the defendants, and were primarily objective professionals.

"The plaintiff rests," announced Kate, representing Skylar Bauers.

"The defense rests," repeated Liz, representing John Bauers. Court was adjourned as the lawyers were preparing their closing arguments.

Kate referred to the trial as a lynching. A lynching is the practice whereby a mob takes the law into their own hands in order to injure a person. In a lynching, the issues of the victim are usually secondary, since the mob serves as prosecutor, judge, jury and executioner.

"Liz Lewin and John Bauers were leading a judicial lynch mob," Kate declared.

Skylar was at work when she received a telephone call from Ed Dziwka. He had just returned from court, where Maryanne was found in contempt of court for having violated the order stating no unrelated male sleep in the house when her daughters were there. The judge ordered John to vacate the premises. Skylar gleefully called Kate and informed her of the potential change in the situation.

Kate filed an emergency change of custody in court on May 8, 1997 and presented the motion to Judge Copeland's in his chambers. He read the motion, took off his glasses, and looked at Kate.

"I am not going to change the custody. I know you disagree, but hear me out. I know Liz Lewin, and she is relentless. John Bauers will be right along with her. They will never give up their pursuit of custody. Kate, your client does not have the financial means to continue the fight indefinitely. Do you want to see those children going back and forth? Mr. Bauers will support them if they are with him. He's got the money. He didn't even ask for child support. If they go back to Mrs. Bauers, she will struggle financially just to support them, in addition to her ongoing court costs. In a sense, I am doing your client a favor by saving her years of endless litigation instead of enjoying the time she has with her children. Don't you think it's in your client's best interest just to mother her children instead of dealing with Mr. Bauers and Liz Lewin?"

Kate could see logic in the judge's explanation but she felt awful. She already had a taste of John Bauers and could predict that he was not the kind of man who would take kindly to court ordered child support. Judge Copeland was saving Skylar years of litigation, attorneys' fees, and abuse. Kate picked up her briefcase and went out to meet her client. Skylar was sitting nervously in the hallway, waiting for her. "I'm sorry, Skylar. He's not going to change the custody." She repeated the conversation she had with Judge Copeland in his chambers

She was devastated and she fought back the tears. "It's not fair. How can custody be determined according to finances? It doesn't even seem like it's legal."

Kate comforted her. "They will come back to you on their own. I promise."

They left the courthouse discouraged.

John and Maryanne chose to ignore the contempt of court order and he remained in Maryanne's house. In order to enforce the order, Ed would have to pay his attorney to go back to court and present a contempt order and he simply could not afford to keep going back to court.

The final divorce judgment was written. Judge Copeland had already told Kate that the children would not return to Skylar. She got a liberal visitation schedule and nothing more. John retained physical custody as well as sole legal custody – the ability to make all the decisions for the children when Skylar had been doing so, alone, since their birth. There was too much damage, too many unjust decisions, and too many biased reports written. Ultimately, the verdict was based solely on financial merit, and Skylar lost all her rights to her children.

"This isn't justice!" she fumed to Kate. "This was theatre. This was the judicial Tony awards," she commented wryly. The court was the stage, and the litigants were the actors. John Bauers won for best actor, and Liz Lewin won for best director. While they celebrated their victory, the children were the ones who suffered defeat.

But Skylar won her freedom from an abusive narcissist. Her award was a life where she could make her own rules. She felt she fared better than the children. Although it pained her greatly to know her children were living with an abuser, Skylar maintained control. Although she felt like screaming in frustration, she knew she had to remain strong because one day, she knew, her children would return to her.

After the trial, Skylar began concentrating on healing. She read many self-help books. She went to the gym every day. As she recovered, she began to excel at her job. Jake was moving forward in his career as well. His company transferred him to their Japan location for two years. It was hard for them to lose each other, but now it was time to stand alone.

The children loved being with their mother and clung to her, especially Jillian. They complained about Maryanne and their father. Skylar heeded the words she heard during the parenting class and never spoke ill of John or Maryanne. She offered comfort and love. She knew it was just a matter of time before the children would be able to speak for themselves.

She began to think of the obstacles life had handed her. In spite of the years of abuse, the travesties in court due to malevolent manipulation by John and Liz, the eternal optimist in Skylar told her there was hope. She recognized she had to make decisions resulting from those obstacles. She suddenly understood there came a time when a choice must be made. This was the time to select her future. She felt she had only two clear options. She proclaimed, "My options are to lie down and die or fight for my children and never give up. I choose the latter."

Chapter 28

Relieved that the trial was over, Skylar began to recover with positive thinking, insightful reading and daily visits to the gym. As time went on, she became calm, relaxed, and felt hopeful about her future.

In mid-May 1997, she was pleasantly surprised when she received an impromptu call from a cast member who had performed with her previously. He had a role in a local movie, which was still being cast. He suggested she call if she was interested in performing. He gave her the telephone number of Lance Levine, who was casting the movie. Skylar thought about it and one evening made the spur of the moment call.

"Lance Levine." The person answering the phone had a low, gruff voice.

She introduced herself and told him the reason she was calling.

Lance gave her a brief synopsis about the movie. "It's about a piano player who falls off the wagon. He vanishes and is eventually discovered in Bellevue Hospital. He stops drinking and makes a comeback. It will be filmed in black and white. What experience have you had?"

They talked for hours and discovered many commonalities. They both played the piano. They both grew up in Newton. Divorced, they each were parents to two sons and a daughter.

Lance openly asked her, "Are you dating anyone?"

"I date platonically, only when I feel as if I need a good meal," she joked.

Lance laughed. "After the audition, I'll take you out for dinner – no matter what you look like."

She giggled at his humor. They made plans to meet on Sunday evening.

That weekend, after the children had left, Skylar dressed for her meeting with Lance. She selected tailored black slacks and a blue silk shirt, and slipped on black boots. She brushed her hair and misted herself with a light, floral cologne. She was ready for her interview. She drove to Lance's condominium in Brookline. She entered the gates of a gorgeous complex with European styled buildings, climbed the stone steps, and rang the bell.

Lance answered the door. He was 5'7" tall with a medium build. He had a moustache and a trim beard. His brown hair was held back in an elastic band. The length was undeterminable, as it ended in a tightly coiled curl. In one ear, he wore a tiny diamond stud. The dimly lit room contained a magnificent grand piano and contemporary furniture.

"Hello, I'm Lance," he said. He shook Skylar's hand and invited her to take a seat.

She sat on the couch, and he handed her several pages of dialogue. "You're reading for the part of the singer who was the girlfriend of the piano player."

Before she could glance at the script, the doorbell rang. It was a limousine driver picking them up for dinner. Once inside the beautiful car, he gave the driver the name of their destination, one of the most opulent restaurants in the city. As they entered, Lance was greeted by name. The maître d' brought them to a beautifully set table.

Over dinner, Lance told her his life story. He was born into a privileged family fifty-two years prior, on Christmas Eve. He was a rebellious child, but his family had the means to do whatever was necessary to help their son. He graduated from a prestigious private high school and went on to college to study piano with extremely talented and esteemed musicians. He then enrolled in an Ivy League business and entrepreneur program. Following that, he started and managed several successful companies, financed a popular music group and led a fairly high-profiled life. His successes and eclectic lifestyle had been featured in articles in several prestigious publications. The anomaly in Lance was the fact that he was an alcoholic. But it seemed inconsequential as he told Skylar he stopped drinking. He was older, sophisticated, and educated. He was charming and generous. He shared music with her. It was evident that he was interested in her not merely as a potential actress. She was equally compelled.

Two nights later, they met again so Skylar could recite her lines. Afterward, he took her to a tiny, exotic restaurant. The attraction was magnetic. The driver took them back to the condo, parked the limousine, and left them alone in the car.

Lance murmured, "What's happening?"

Skylar whispered, "I don't know," as he reached over and kissed her. Outside, the rain began to fall.

After that night, they were inseparable. Even compared to Jake, she was not used to being treated so well. Lance wanted to do everything for her. He had her car repaired and gave her his new Lincoln Continental to drive. He sent flowers to her at work and had meals delivered to her apartment. He fell in love with her, which he freely declared as the movie was being filmed.

At the wrap party, Lance announced his plans to marry Skylar. He promised to hire a top attorney and get her children back. She felt he was her soul mate and guardian angel.

Lance was anxious to meet her children. She hadn't introduced her children to anyone since Jake, but Lance was serious and wanted a future with her. One Saturday, he picked the children up in a limousine and brought them to an arcade. The children adored Lance. In turn, he loved to spoil them. He took them traveling all summer, from Cape Cod to the coast of Maine. He made them laugh all the time. The children were having a wonderful time, and Skylar was deliriously happy.

John picked up the children at Lance's condominium one Sunday in August. It was the first time he had been there. As he drove into the gorgeous, lushly landscaped complex and saw the beautiful stone building, it was a thorn in his side. Skylar wasn't destroyed; she was thriving. And for a narcissist and an abuser, this was enough to send him over the edge.

He called her that evening. "Where's Jillian's Snow White sweat-shirt?" he demanded.

She replied cheerily, "I have it. Sorry, I forgot to take it out of the dryer."

He stated flatly, "The kids are missing socks and underwear."

Skylar patiently explained, "I washed their clothes with mine. If I miss something, I can just give it to them next time." John was not going to ruin her mood.

"You don't have to wash their laundry. Just put everything back into their suitcases, and I'll wash it all when they come home," he advised. "It will be easier for you."

"Sure, I can do that. Why don't you put that in writing and I'll be happy to leave the laundry for you?" She wasn't going to get sucked into his scheme.

John was irritated as he realized she had caught on to his plan. "I am NOT putting that in writing!" His anger was palatable.

Skylar forced her smile into her voice. "Well, then I guess I will continue doing their laundry." She was learning to play his game and he didn't like it. She knew if she stopped washing the children's laundry and sent back unwashed clothing, he would bring her into court with his wide-eyed lying look and tell the judge Skylar refused to wash the children's laundry. She had learned how John operated. Since she won that battle, he had to retaliate. When she picked up the children the following Saturday, they brought their suitcases as always. However, when Skylar opened them, she found they were empty.

Lance was utterly in love with Skylar and wanted her to move in with him. In turn, she adored him. He was everything she wanted. He was unselfish and he respected her completely. He was brilliant and talented. They shared the same interests. And he was fun. He made her laugh.

Lance's condo was gorgeous, but it was too small for Skylar's children as well as Lance's teenaged son, Lyle, so they looked for a house to rent. They found a large, brick colonial atop a hill in Brookline beside a small playground. There was a breathtaking view of the Boston skyline. It was quiet and peaceful, yet right in the city. They moved into the house in late August 1997. Skylar had never lived in a house that was so beautiful.

In early September she received her final divorce document. That day, Lance knelt in front of her and slipped a magnificent platinum and diamond engagement ring on her finger.

"Will you spend the rest of your life with me?" he asked.

It was the most romantic moment in Skylar's life. With Lance's love and support, the future appeared rosy and welcoming. There was light at the end of the tunnel. And in time, she was certain, her children would be returned.

They began planning a January wedding when all the children would be home on school vacation. In addition to his fourteen year old son, Lyle, Lance also had two children attending college in Florida. Michael was twenty, and Liliana was eighteen. They returned home for winter break and the wedding. When his children were there with Skylar's children, they made a lively and lovely group. Lance desperately wanted another child with Skylar.

He pleaded with her, "Let's have a baby. It will blend the families." Although Skylar felt she was too old to have another baby, the more she thought about it, the better she liked the idea. She had left her sales job and was working for Lance's company doing the advertising and administration. Her time was very flexible. If she got pregnant, this would be the last child for both of them.

"Let's do it!" Skylar enthusiastically agreed.

As the briefest chill of autumn grazed the days, Lance and Skylar boarded an airplane for a romantic get-away to Florida. They stayed at a luxurious hotel in Bal Harbor. At night, they dined at the finest restaurants. If there was a pianist performing, Lance would ask, "Do you mind if I play something for my fiancée?" and he would sit down and play a beautiful piece for her. During the day, they would sit by the pool and later shop at the upscale boutiques. Skylar's life was almost idyllic.

When they returned from their trip, Lance was occupied with his business deals. Skylar was assisting him as well as finalizing the details of their wedding. She addressed and stamped their wedding invitations, and then she brought them to the post office to be mailed.

They had been home a few weeks when one Sunday evening in November, after the children had left, Skylar felt abnormally tired. She attributed her sudden fatigue to her busy weekend except she suddenly realized she was overdue for her period. When she mentioned it to Lance, he immediately went out and bought a pregnancy test. Although she was only a few days late, the test was positive. Lance kissed Skylar in jubilation. They were going to have a baby.

Wedding plans were kept under wraps as well as the news about the baby. She did not want John to know any details about her life. He was angry enough after seeing her beautiful house so she needed to be very careful. She knew if he found out when she was getting married, he would do something to prevent the children from attending so she managed to make all the wedding plans discretely. She couldn't risk letting the children know, so she pretended she was making preparations for a summer wedding.

During the winter school vacation, the children were scheduled to spend six days with her. In late December, she picked them up. They tumbled into the car with shrieks of joy.

Once they were buckled in their seats, Skylar began driving away and suddenly announced, "The wedding is Sunday!"

They shouted in joy. "We thought you were getting married this summer!"

Skylar replied, "We wanted to surprise you." And she smiled to herself as she silently said...*And John.*

Six days later, she awoke to a beautiful day with sparkling sun combined with the briskness of early January 1998. It was a perfect day for a wedding. Skylar wore a suit in cream colored silk and lace. Lance wore a dark suit. Michael, Lyle, Joshua, and Cary had matching tuxedos. Liliana wore a sleek black cocktail dress, and Jillian wore a white, fluffy taffeta dress. A private ceremony was held in the house. Under the chuppah, the rabbi pronounced Lance and Skylar as husband and wife. Everyone hugged. It was an emotional and euphoric moment because it meant they were officially a family. The sun beamed down on the new family as they got into the limousine and drove to a beautiful hotel in Boston to meet their guests for a celebration brunch.

The room at the hotel was ablaze with red and purple flowers. A sumptuous brunch was served and Liliana played selections by George Gershwin on the piano.

Lance's brother made a toast, proclaiming, "Skylar is a gift from God!" The love in the room was palatable and joyful, celebrating the blending of families and lives and happiness.

Since Skylar and Lance were staying at the hotel that evening, the limousine took all the children back home after the reception. Liliana helped the children change their clothes. After a light dinner, she cut a generous piece of the remaining wedding cake and carefully wrapped it.

"Joshie, this is for you and Cary and Jillian to take home with you."

John picked them up at seven o'clock. Joshua carefully carried the large piece of wedding cake in a bag. Liliana walked the children down the driveway. When she returned back to the house, she turned to her brothers and said, "Their father looked angry!"

When the children got home, Joshua placed the carefully wrapped piece of wedding cake on the table. "Liliana gave us a piece of Mom and Lance's wedding cake," he told John.

John looked at the cake. The children were anxious to enjoy another piece.

John suddenly yelled, "This cake is stale! You're not eating this garbage!" He picked it up, crushed it together with the wrapper, and threw it in the garbage.

"Noooooo!" the children screamed.

"You better stop this noise right now, or I won't let you see your mother again! Now, go to your rooms, and I better not see a fuckin' light on!"

The children scurried out of the kitchen. Terrified, they ran into their dark bedrooms. It had been a long day, so they quickly fell asleep.

Skylar and Lance were able to spend a lovely evening in their hotel suite before flying to their honeymoon destination in the morning. Skylar was happy, but Lance was tense. Although he wasn't drinking, it was a constant desire generating through his body. He had been without alcohol so long but he still had such a desire to drink, he would lie awake at night thinking about that first cold, stinging sip.

On the second day of their honeymoon, Lance announced, "Many doctors advise older men to drink one glass of red wine. They say it's good for your heart."

Skylar frowned and said, "I am just worried about you drinking any alcohol."

"Skylar, it's just one small glass a day. It will be fine."

Lance drove to the local store and returned with a case of red wine. One glass turned into two. He drained glass after glass until he had finished the first bottle. He had accomplished a mere eight months of sobriety.

Upon the return from their honeymoon, his behavior rapidly changed and his drinking escalated. Instead of drinking red wine, he soon switched to vodka. He was never without a glass in his hand, filled with clear liquid and a couple of tiny white onions.

He gruffly admonished Skylar, "Don't look at me like that. I'm drinking water. This is just a glass of water."

"Lance, I am not stupid. No one drinks water with little onions on the bottom. I saw the bottles of vodka you think you're hiding." She walked away, confused and saddened.

He was becoming distant and pulling away from her as he plunged deeper into the bottle.

By February 1998, their relationship rapidly began to deteriorate. Skylar began attending Al-Anon meetings, hoping they would provide an answer for Lance's renewed love of the bottle. Although Al-Anon gave support, she felt it was hopeless when, during a bout of inebriation, she overheard Lance tell a room full of men, "I don't fuck women when they're pregnant. If Skylar wants to get fucked, she better find someone else."

She was mortified. The chapter of her life which had begun so perfectly was dissolving in a pool of vodka.

In Lance's circle of friends was a man named Norman Carson. He was former boxer and still had the appearance of a pugilist. He was short and stocky. He kept his dark hair cut very close to his head. He walked with a little bounce to his step as if he were preparing to spar. He was a former heroin addict and former convict. He had been in jail for the rape of a minor. Norman needed a job so Lance hired him for odd jobs, warning him to keep his sordid past hidden from Skylar.

Although Lance became belligerent and angry when he drank, he still had sober moments where his kindness and concern for Skylar returned. He knew she needed a spacious vehicle for the children and new baby so he made arrangements and ordered a minivan. One cold afternoon in March, he instructed Norman to drive Skylar to a car dealership to pick up the new vehicle.

"Lance is so lucky to have you, Skylar. I'm gonna have a talk with him and tell him to stop drinking," Norman told her as they pulled into the dealership. She smiled at him politely as she got out of the car. Her new white minivan was parked in front of the building. After she got the keys from the dealer, she slid into the soft leather seats and breathed in the new car smell. As she drove away, she turned on the radio, and music emanated from all six speakers. She opened the sunroof just a little to get a tiny bit of the fresh air. It was a top-of-the line vehicle and she felt perfectly luxurious. She was eager to get home and thank Lance for getting her such a beautiful minivan. As she drove, she almost forgot that most of the time, he was inebriated.

Skylar heard Lance screaming as she entered the house. He was pacing the floors, telephone to his ear. She tiptoed upstairs to the bedroom and quietly closed the door. About thirty minutes later, the front door slammed so she went downstairs. No one was home. She made a light dinner and ate in front of the television in the family room. It was almost midnight before she went upstairs and got into bed. She immediately fell asleep.

Skylar was awakened by the crash of the front door being flung open. She looked at the clock; it was four o'clock in the morning. Footsteps shuffled and begin heading up the stairs. She lay there, feigning sleep. Suddenly, she heard a loud thud at the doorway the bedroom. Startled, she sat upright.

"Skylar, come help me," Lance moaned.

She flatly responded, "You're drunk."

"Fuck you!" he screamed. That was the first time he ever raised his voice to her or swore at her. It was not the last.

Although Lance apologized for that night and for other nights thereafter, the apologies became less frequent. He would rage at her daily without provocation. He would tell her if she left him, she wouldn't get a dime. She saw the writing on the wall. They still slept side by side, with Skylar lying at the edge of the bed, awake and planning for the end. She rented a safe deposit box at a bank for her jewelry and any papers she would need when they finally divorced and started to create a little nest egg of money she took from the large wads of cash in Lance's pockets after he would pass out from drinking. She hid the money under a pile of sweaters in her closet. She felt guilty but justified in making provisions to save herself and her baby.

The children saw the change in Lance. They would be playing with blocks or toys, on the floor and when Lance walked in, he would kick the toys and yell, "Clean up this fucking shit!"

Skylar would hotly reply, "Don't talk to my children like that!"

The children began question the reason why Lance was yelling. Skylar gently revealed that his drinking made him angry. Of course, they related the reason of Lance's downward, alcohol-infused spiral to John.

It was just the information John needed. He would utilize Lance's drinking to his advantage to infiltrate Skylar's marriage.

Lance conducted his business from home using a second telephone line. With one hand holding the phone and the other hand holding a glass of vodka, he habitually would pace the floor. Because John didn't want Skylar to know he was communicating with Lance, he began calling him on the private business number. He used his charm to befriend him. Lance loved talking on the phone and was drunk enough to be a very suggestible target for John. What started as polite general conversation became a series of conversations about Skylar.

John began spewing his poisonous vengeance to a very acquiescent and susceptible man under the influence of alcohol. "Skylar's a Jewish-American princess, a real JAP. She wanted someone to support her. She's looking for money. She never loved you. She married you for your money."

This was the mantra Lance would hear from John's daily phone calls. During his screaming drunken rages at Skylar, he would parrot what John had told him. She started to suspect that John was communicating with Lance. She felt helpless knowing she couldn't escape from her abuser. And now John had Lance, a far more compliant victim, in his grasp.

Chapter 29

By April, Skylar was almost six months pregnant. Her respite from Lance's drunken anger was on Friday afternoons, when she would attend Jillian's ballet class. One Friday in April, John called her to ask if she could pick up the children at six o'clock that evening instead of Saturday morning. She replied, "Sure." Since Skylar had no time alone with Jillian, she asked, "Can I take Jillian after her class at five o'clock and pick up the boys at six o'clock?"

"Hmm. Yeah. I guess that could work. Maryanne is supposed to pick up Jillian. I'll try to reach her and let her know," John answered. When Skylar got to the studio, she saw Jillian dancing in the class. Maryanne wasn't there. About ten minutes before the end of class, she walked in. Unsure if John had contacted her, Skylar approached her to ask if she was aware the schedule had been changed,

"Hi, Maryanne," she stated in a quiet voice.

Maryanne stood there and refused to acknowledge Skylar, who was standing at her side.

Skylar wondered what kind of game Maryanne was playing. So she repeated a little louder, "Hel-lo?" in an attempt to get her attention. Maryanne turned to look at Skylar. She began blinking rapidly. Anger burned in Maryanne's small eyes.

Skylar ignored Maryanne's glare and began speaking calmly. "I spoke to John about taking Jillian after dance class..."

Maryanne cut off Skylar's words by waving a finger in her face. She began screaming, "NO, SKYLAR!! NO!! YOU ARE NOT TAKING THAT CHILD!!"

Skylar lowered her voice until it was just above a whisper and said, "Get your finger out of my face."

But Maryanne continued her outburst. "JOHN HAS CUSTODY!! YOU DON'T HAVE CUSTODY OF THAT CHILD!! JOHN HAS CUSTODY!! YOU LOST CUSTODY!!"

Skylar felt her face redden. Bearing the brunt of Maryanne's raging explosion in front of all the women in the dance studio was acutely embarrassing. The receptionist came running to Maryanne when she heard the commotion.

"Mrs. Dziwka, you have to leave the studio. Jillian's mother is here. Please wait outside until class is done." She tried to usher Maryanne out of the studio.

She shrieked, "This is a free country and I can go anywhere I want!"

The director of the school appeared from the back of the studio. "Maryanne, you need to wait outside." She escorted her to the door.

The women in the waiting area offered sympathetic smiles to Skylar, but she felt humiliated. The director returned to the waiting area alone.

"Come with me, Mrs. Bauers." She gently led Skylar to her office. "Look, I have known Maryanne Dziwka since her daughters began dancing here years ago. My advice to you is to stay as far away from her a possible. She's unstable and has a short fuse."

Skylar said, "Thanks, but unfortunately, I know it. I was hoping we could speak civilly, but I guess that won't happen. It just kills me that my children are living with her."

"One day, they'll figure it out. Now go watch Jillian. The class is almost over."

After the class, she helped Jillian change and bought her a small bottle of juice. She saw the door of the studio open and Maryanne entered.

"I'll pick you up at the house in an hour honey. Okay?" Jillian hugged Skylar tightly.

Skylar walked past Maryanne with her head held high and left the school.

The following Friday, Skylar was able to watch Jillian's dance class peacefully as no one else was there. After class, she brought her in the dressing room and again, bought her a small bottle of juice. She heard the outside door of the studio open and heavy footsteps. John whipped the curtain aside. Some of the girls shrieked at his intrusion and covered themselves. John's pale eyes bulged in anger when he saw Skylar. He grabbed the juice bottle from Jillian, who began to whimper.

"This is not your time, bitch! You shouldn't even be here!"

"There is no reason I can't watch my children during their extra-curricular activities! Please don't speak to me that way." Skylar paused and softened her voice. "John, isn't this kind of ridiculous? For the sake of the children, we should speak to each other with respect."

"Why should I respect you?" he sneered.

She looked at him in disbelief. "Because I am the mother of your children."

John emitted a short, bitter laugh. "You're a whore. That's why I divorced you." Jillian began to cry silently and clutched her mother. "Let go of her, Skylar. You are just an observer here. It's not your time. You're not the mother on my time." John grabbed at Jillian.

Skylar gave Jillian a kiss on her cheek and stood up. She turned to leave the dance studio, but before she left, she looked John in the eye and in a low voice stated, "And for the record, I was the one who divorced you." She tossed her head and strutted out of the studio.

Later that month, when Skylar picked the children up from school, Jillian announced, "My Brownie troop is having a mother/daughter party on Friday. Will you go to that with me, Mommia?"

"Of course I will." Skylar was thrilled.

But when she called John that evening to get the address for the party, he said, "You can't go. It's not your day."

"But it's a mother and daughter party."

"Well, for Jillian it will be a daddy and daughter party," John answered smugly.

John's treatment of Joshua and Cary was just as spiteful. On the day of Little League team pictures in May, Joshua walked out of the house barefoot and wearing shorts and a t-shirt.

"Joshie, you have team pictures today," Skylar reminded him. "Go get your sneakers and your uniform."

Cary and Jillian climbed in the car and distributed kisses all over Skylar. She tickled them as Joshua went back into the house. A few moments later, he appeared, still wearing the same shorts and t-shirt.

"Joshie, where's your uniform?"

"Dad put it in the washing machine. He poured liquid soap all over it." Although he would be ten years old in September, Joshua looked as if he were about to cry.

"Hey, pal, its okay. Get a plastic bag and put your uniform in it. We'll go to the laundromat and wash it."

He ran back inside the house and returned with the uniform in a plastic bag. He was barefoot but carried his sneakers.

"Joshie, did you forgot your socks?" Skylar asked.

"Dad won't let me take socks." He replied in tears.

Skylar was exasperated. "That's okay – we'll buy a pair of socks. Come here." Joshua climbed in the front seat, and she hugged her son.

John's anger reached the boiling point later that month at the baseball field. His eyes narrowed in annoyance when he saw Skylar there with her arms around her children and her pregnant belly. Each time she caressed her swollen abdomen, he felt she was doing it purposely, just to taunt him. It is the ultimate slap in the face for a narcissist and abuser see the woman who left him, carrying the baby of another man. For John, it was a mocking reminder. Trying to appease his fury, he had told the children, "Mom's baby isn't going to be your brother or sister." Watching Skylar all day, he was seething with rage so intense, he was ready to explode.

After the game, Joshua began putting his baseball equipment in Skylar's van. John took Cary and Jillian firmly by the hand and whispered he was taking them for ice cream as he led them to his truck. Skylar noticed Cary and Jillian seated in John's truck, so she went to the passenger's window. As she looked in, she saw her Nikon camera that John had taken from the Newton house, on the front seat of his truck.

She picked up the camera and said, "Hey, this is my camera."

John screamed, "Not anymore!" He bolted out of the truck running toward her.

Terrified, Skylar dropped the camera and headed back to her van in an awkward pregnant gait. He easily caught her, grabbed her purse and deliberately snapped off the strap. He backed her against her van.

"Help!" she screamed. She had never fought back before, but now she was fighting for her baby. When Joshua heard her screams, he climbed out of the van. Skylar struggled to free herself. She closed her eyes as she blindly threw a wild, over-handed punch, which caught John on his face. Joshua jumped on his father's back, his arms gripped tightly around his neck, in an attempt to get him away from his mother. He released Skylar and threw Joshua to the ground. A few people were lingering on the field. When they heard Skylar's screams, they started toward her. Seeing them approach, John ran back to his truck and sped off. Joshua got up and ran to his mother. Skylar's heart was pounding and she was hyperventilating.

"My ex-husband just attacked me!" she told the approaching group. Both her arms bore finger marks from John's grip. Someone called the police, and within minutes, an ambulance and police car pulled onto the field. Skylar was put on a stretcher. Her blood pressure had skyrocketed. The EMTs helped Joshua into the ambulance with Skylar, and they drove to the hospital to evaluate the status of the baby.

When they got the hospital, Skylar was attached to a fetal monitor. A young, attractive female police office came into the room. Skylar recited exactly what had happened on the ball field.

The police officer asked, "Can I speak to your son, privately? I need to get his version."

"Sure." Joshua didn't want to leave Skylar. "Go ahead, sweetie. I'll be fine." She smiled at him.

Joshua left the room with the police officer. They returned about ten minutes later. "Okay. I got his story. It's exactly the same as yours. Do you mind if I photograph those marks on your arms?"

After she took pictures of Skylar's arms, she left. The nurse returned and told her the results on the fetal monitor were normal. Fortunately, the baby was fine. Skylar's blood pressure gradually returned to normal. Joshua was still frightened for Skylar, but she reassured him she felt okay. She didn't want to reveal that she was still shaken. As a precaution, they were sent home in a taxi. She could pick up her car the following day.

On Monday morning, a constable appeared at Skylar's front door. He silently served her with the 209A restraining order John had filed. Skylar shook her head at the irony and gall. She was almost eight months pregnant, and he was serving her with a restraining order? Incredulously, John claimed that Skylar attacked him. He provided pictures of himself with red marks on his neck, caused when Joshua jumped on his back and hung from his neck in an attempt to get him away from Skylar.

In the report, he stated "Skylar tried to choke me and kick me in the groin." He also photographed pictures of his pants lying on the ground with perfectly formed footprint marks in the groin area. The footprints could only have been made if the pants were placed on the ground and someone stepped on them while wearing sneakers, not the smooth soled shoes Skylar wore that day. Upset with the twisted facts, inaccuracies and artful fabrications, she had no choice but to wait for the hearing.

The following day, Skylar appeared in court. She no longer had legal representation, as she could not afford to pay Kate for her services. Judge Copeland entered the room. John testified first, relating his version of the events by physically acting it out as if he were on stage.

Lundy Bancroft, considered one of the world's experts on the subject of abusive men, states:

> "Because of the distorted perception that the abuser has of rights
> and responsibilities in the relationship, he considers himself to
> be the victim. Acts of self-defense on the part of the battered
> woman or the children, or efforts they make to stand up for
> their rights, he defines as aggression against him. He is often
> highly skilled at twisting his descriptions of events to create the
> convincing impression that he has been victimized."

In addition to his narcissistic personality disorder and antisocial personality disorder (sociopath), not surprisingly, John's behavior was also concurrent with the diagnosis of a histrionic personality disorder. A histrionic personality as defined by the *Diagnostic and Statistical Manual of Mental Disorders* (DSM IV-R) as a pervasive pattern of excessive emotionality and attention seeking or dramatization beginning by early adulthood.

The merging of three personality disorders is not an uncommon occurrence, according to mental health professionals. John's behavior was the most realistic example of three personality disorders which merged. 1) His dramatic performance in 2) an attempt to cover up the fact he attacked a pregnant woman and 3) his lack of remorse was the most concrete display of someone severely afflicted with histrionic, anti-social and narcissistic personality disorders.

Skylar vehemently disputed his performance and the erroneous evidence he provided. It was mind-boggling that John was attempting to convince the judge she attacked him in her advanced pregnancy.

"The reports and your testimonies are simply versions of he said/she said," ruled Judge Copeland. "I am issuing permanent cross-restraining orders. This means when one parent has the children, the other parent cannot be there, except for milestone events."

Skylar was heartbroken. Judge Copeland's ruling was so undeserving. She could no longer attend Jillian's dance class, however, she was able to attend her dance recital. The morning of the recital, Sable came with her as they went to pick up the children. When John came outside, Skylar asked him for Jillian's costume.

He replied, "You'll get it before the performance. I am concerned if I give it to you, you'll steal it," undaunted of maligning her in the presence of the children.

Sable looked at Skylar with her mouth pursed in distress and shook her head. Skylar shrugged. She focused her attention on the children and tried to engage them in the music on the radio as she drove to the performance center. Once inside, she sat with Jillian and applied her make-up and curled her hair. Minutes prior to the dress rehearsal, Maryanne's daughter, Sara, approached her, threw the costume at her, and spat, "Bitch!" Skylar ignored her. She dressed Jillian and took a few photographs before she went into the rehearsal hall.

She breathed a sigh of relief as she left the building with Sable, Joshua, and Cary. They had two hours until the dance performance.

"Well, that wasn't too bad." Skylar cheerfully stated.

"Wait, the day is not over." Sable logically replied.

After taking the boys for lunch, they returned for the recital. Overcome with sentimental tear, Skylar watched her beautiful daughter dance on stage. At the end of the show, she waited with the proud families as the little dancers, began streaming through the door, in a flurry of colorful costumes. Congratulated by their families, the dancers were posing for pictures in the garden outside. Skylar looked for Jillian in her fluffy white costume. As the last dancers straggled out, she saw Jillian appear wearing her shorts and a t-shirt. Her hair was tangled, and her face streaked with tears.

"Jillian, what's wrong? Where's your costume?" Skylar took her in her arms.

She cried, "Sara made me to take off my costume because you were going to steal it!"

John's vengeance was unstoppable. He found the perfect pawns in his children. It didn't matter they were hurt in his line of fire toward Skylar. The next time she saw Jillian, her daughter tearfully asked, "Why don't you want to talk to me, Mommia?"

"Baby, what are you talking about? I always want to talk to you." Skylar held her close.

"Sara said that you called yesterday when she was polishing my nails but you didn't want to talk to me." Her little lip started quivering.

"Jillian, sweetheart, I *always* want to talk to you. Sara made a mistake." Skylar hugged her daughter and wondered *When is this going to end?*

In early June, Skylar invited Sable for dinner on a Tuesday evening. She planned to telephone the children when she was there, so they could talk to their grandmother. After they ate, Skylar called the house, and John answered.

"Hello?" he drawled. Skylar asked to speak to the children but he told her none of the children were home.

"It's almost eight o'clock. The children aren't home?" Skylar was exasperated.

She rolled her eyes at Sable, who mouthed to her daughter, "What's going on?"

"Sorry." John hung up the phone. Ironically, in court, he had testified the children were in bed by eight o'clock.

Sable suggested, "Why don't you just ask him how long he's going to continue this behavior?" When Skylar hesitated, she said, "I'll listen on the other phone." Skylar agreed and redialed the number. This time, Sable was listening in on the extension.

John answered the phone, knowing it was Skylar from the caller ID. "Yeeess?"

"Can I speak to my children?" she asked again.

"I told you they weren't here," John stated.

Skylar was frustrated at the game he was playing. She paused for a moment then asked, "John, how long are you going to continue to harass me?"

John quickly and easily replied, "For the rest of your life...until you die." His voice was calm and smooth, and his words chilled Skylar.

In disbelief Skylar gasped. She thought, *Did he really say...until I die?* To ensure total certainty of what he told her, Skylar repeated, "For the rest of my life, until I die?"

Matter-of-factly, John replied, "Yup."

Shocked at his terrifyingly candid response, Skylar merely uttered, "Oh," and slowly replaced the telephone receiver in the cradle.

Sable walked into the room and saw Skylar sitting there, staring into space in disbelief. Sable had heard every word but was less shocked than her daughter.

Robin Shaye

"I had his number from day one! He's never going to stop!" Skylar didn't respond. "Skylar, look at me!" Skylar looked up. "You better be very careful. You don't know what he'll do. I told you he was crazy! You need to figure out how to get those kids back."

Skylar found John's words distressing. She presumed he meant to merely shock her. But, the harassment, insults, and inappropriate behavior just continued. Not just from John, but from Maryanne as well. And not just toward Skylar, but toward the children too.

Skylar began to hear about Maryanne's involvement at random moments. One afternoon, she was putting away the laundry as Joshua was sitting on her bed watching television.

During a commercial, he began, "Mom, I walked into Dad's room, and Maryanne was sitting in bed without underpants."

Concerned, Skylar asked, "Did you knock first? Maybe she was getting dressed?"

Joshua looked away from the television and turned toward her. "No, I just walked in, and she was sitting on the bed and wasn't wearing underpants."

Skylar wasn't quite sure what he was trying to convey, so she asked, "Did she have a sheet over her?"

"No, she was just sitting there. Like this." Joshua arranged his legs with the soles of his feet touching.

Skylar couldn't believe what she was seeing. There had to be a mistake. "Like that?! With her legs spread?! What was she doing?"

Joshua replied, "She was watching television." He tilted his head up and looked at the television. "Like this."

Sickened, she asked, "What did she do when you walked in the room? Did she cover herself?"

"No, she just kept watching the TV," he replied.
Skylar was disgusted at the thought of Maryanne exposed and sitting in front of her son.

Maryanne made inappropriate comments as well. Cary related her comment during a visit with Skylar. "Maryanne said, 'Your mother is fat. She's not having a baby'."

Skylar chuckled at the juvenile comment, and told Cary, "Well, in August, if I have a baby, you'll know that Maryanne was wrong, and if I don't, then I guess she'll be right!"

"Maryanne is the fat one!" Joshua interjected. "She couldn't even fit into your skirt!"

"My skirt?" asked Skylar, confused.

"Your black leather skirt. Dad took it from the Newton house, and Maryanne was trying it on, and she broke the zipper," he told her.

The thought of Maryanne trying on her clothes was peculiar, and made Skylar uneasy as she pictured her attempting to squeeze into her skirt. Maryanne had oddly become John's willing accomplice and thought nothing of the damage she was doing to the children.

Skylar didn't realize the depths of Maryanne's offensive actions until one afternoon as she was brushing Jillian's hair when she suddenly asked, "Mommia, what happens if the baby is born blind and deaf?" Jillian was just six years old.

Skylar was shocked at the question and asked her, "Jillian, where did you hear something like that?" It was upsetting and horrifying.

Jillian replied, "Maryanne said it."

John would not relent in creating problems or interfering with Skylar's relationship with the children, so she wasn't really surprised when he refused to let her take them for their scheduled summer visit. He claimed Cary suddenly developed asthma and needed a nebulizer in the event he had trouble breathing. Skylar had no choice but to take John to court. Although there was no documentation as to Cary's condition, Judge Copeland ruled that he would reinstate her visit on the condition she take Cary to the allergist in order to obtain a nebulizer.

Skylar and John waited in the hall of the court as the order was prepared. She turned to him and asked, "Aren't you getting tired of this?"

John answered, "Nope." He enthusiastically added, "I'm havin' a great time! I'm goin' and doin' and I'm havin' a great time!"

She sweetly replied, "I'm terribly impressed."

His eyes narrowed as he sensed her sarcasm but could only glare at her as the court clerk approached them with the judge's order in hand. When she got home, Skylar called the allergist to make an appointment for Cary.

"Cary Bauers? He hasn't been here in a while," exclaimed the nurse who answered the phone. "Let's see…he is actually nine months overdue for his check-up, but we can see him tomorrow."

How could John be so irresponsible about Cary's medical care? thought Skylar.

The following morning she brought him to the allergist. After he was examined, the doctor stated, "Mrs. Bauers, I have to tell you; Cary doesn't have asthma and he doesn't need a nebulizer. I don't know where you could have got that information."

The doctor's comments were chilling. *What was John doing?* She was terrified for her children. But her hands were tied because anytime she tried to address a concern in court, Judge Copeland would say, "Mr. Bauers has legal custody, so it's his decision." Even when she pleaded for the growth hormones the endocrinologist had recommended for Cary, she was met with non-compliance. The court allowed John to ignore critical medical issues. Why? The unfairness was like a knife in her stomach. Her heart ached all the time. She could never be fully happy until her children were with her and she could resume the responsibility of their care.

The three weeks the children spent with her in July were wonderful. With Skylar in the latter stages of her pregnancy, Lance's behavior mellowed. He still drank daily, but he managed to control his anger. With the house in a state of calm, the children were enjoying their time with their mother. Every day, she packed a large cooler with lunch, snacks and drinks and would drive to the lake. She enrolled the children in morning swim classes, which they enjoyed. After lunch, she played with them in the water. When they left the lake, they would stop for ice cream. It was their summer routine, and the children loved it.

One morning, Joshua crawled into Skylar's bed with her. "Mom, I love you," he said as he hugged her.

Skylar hugged him back. "I love you too, Joshie." She kissed his cheek. She loved that her son, although almost ten years old, could still convey this kind of affection.

Joshua whispered. "You're nice. You're much nicer than Dad." As an afterthought, he whispered, "Don't tell him I told you."

The weeks flew by. Skylar always felt sad when John came to pick up the children. On the morning they were leaving, when she saw John's truck, she brought the children outside.

He loudly shouted, "Hi, kids! I was so worried about you!"

Skylar hid her disgust at his comment. She watched as Cary and Jillian climbed into the truck. But Joshua did not get in the truck. He took a firm stance in the driveway.

"I want to stay with Mom until she has the baby," he announced defiantly to his father.

"No!" John shouted. "You're not staying with her! We have plans! Get in the truck!"

"Then let me stay over just for the weekend," Joshua pleaded.

"Get in the truck now!" John glared at Skylar and gritted his teeth. "If you don't get your ass in the truck right now, I won't let you visit your mother again!" he threatened.

Joshua looked at Skylar with tears in his eyes. She hugged him tightly.

"I'm sorry," she whispered into his ear.

He looked up sadly. "I'm sorry too," he whispered as he climbed in the truck.

Before John retuned to the car, he turned around and smirked at Skylar and mouthed, "Bitch."

Skylar shrugged. She wondered if he would ever stop.

But John just couldn't stop. He felt forced into a marriage with Maryanne who had screamed at him a few months earlier, "Skylar is already married, and you haven't married me! It's been three years! If you don't marry me, you can take your kids and get out!"

He knew Maryanne held the reins, and he had no choice. He was living in her house, and his expenses were low. But on the flip side, she was extremely difficult and unpleasant. She would rage about everything. She didn't satisfy any of his needs, mentally, physically, or socially. John did not want to be legally bound to Maryanne.

It was Skylar's doing because she got married and pregnant, he thought. He wanted to punish her and hurt her in any way he could. He knew that taking away an opportunity a mother and daughter would usually share would devastate Skylar. He instructed Maryanne to bring Jillian to get her ears pierced. Maryanne felt important honoring his request and complied without questioning what kind of man kept trying to hurt the mother of his child. She thought nothing about the fact that he was more focused on Skylar than her.

When Jillian returned with tiny earrings in her ears, John ordered Joshua to call his mother and tell her that Maryanne took Jillian to have her ears pierced. Although Skylar hid her despair until she hung up the phone. Lance overheard the news and kindly comforted her sobs.

Her eyes still swollen from the previous night, Skylar woke to a gorgeous day. She got out of bed and walked into the kitchen to get a glass of orange juice. Just as she got to the kitchen, she felt a sudden gush of liquid pouring down her leg. She looked down and realized her water had broken.

Lance came into the kitchen and saw her standing in a puddle. "Looks like today may be the day," she told him. "I guess I'll call the doctor and get ready to go to the hospital."

After she spoke to her doctor, she showered and dressed, and then they drove to the hospital.

Her doctor met them on the obstetrics floor of the hospital. After examining Skylar, he told her, "Yes, indeed, you are going to have your baby today."

The nurse escorted her to the operating room. Skylar was very calm as she was prepared for the c-section. The surgery began and within a short time, the doctor announced the baby's birth was imminent.

He announced, "Here's your baby." Skylar felt some pressure as her baby was born

"Hi, cutie!" the nurse addressed the baby. "It's a girl! Skylar, she's beautiful!"

She heard the baby's little cry and it reminded her of Joshua's first cries. As the doctor finished stitching her, she could barely lie still as she eagerly waited to hold her daughter. Finally, she was raised to a sitting position and the nurse handed the baby to her. She was a beautiful baby, with pink, chubby cheeks, long eyelashes, full lips, and a button nose. She was exquisite. The nurse wheeled Skylar into the recovery room where Lance was waiting. He went to her side and bestowed kisses on her and the baby.

"She's gorgeous. She looks just like you." He kissed her again. "I'll call you later." He turned and left the hospital. Skylar barely noticed as she was so enthralled with her precious new daughter.

They named their new daughter Alissa. The birth of Alissa promoted the realization for Lance and a renewed respect for Skylar, as she was now the mother of his child. He stopped screaming at her and spoke kindly. Even so, his drinking continued. Skylar found bottles hidden under the sinks, behind the stereo, and in the garage. He would fall down drunk in the house or in the street. He could no longer think or function. He lived and breathed for the bottle. Business was at a new low, and he could no longer pay the rent on the house or make payments on Skylar's van. He was barely maintaining.

In October, Skylar was taking her four children out for Sunday brunch with Sable. She saw her mother's car pull into the driveway as Lance was coming out of the shower.

As she put on the children's jackets, she asked him, "Do you want to go, too?"

"No, I can't." He walked to Alissa and kissed her cheek. He approached Skylar and kissed her on the cheek as well. "Bye."

He watched her van pull down the street from the upstairs window. "Lyle! Get up!" he yelled to his son. He quickly dressed. He pulled suitcases out of his closet and packed all his clothes. He went into Lyle's room. "Are you done?" he asked, as Lyle was closing his suitcase.

The sound of a horn blared outside. "Hurry up! The cab is here!" They walked outside to the waiting cab and put their suitcases in the trunk. Lance told Lyle. "I hope you have everything, because we're not coming back!" They both climbed into the cab. As it slowly drove down the street, Lance stared straight ahead. He didn't look back and he hadn't left a note.

When Skylar returned home, she was surprised to see her landlord parked in the driveway. When he saw her, he got out of his car. "Skylar, can I talk to you?" he called, as Sable took the children inside. Skylar waited. "Lance wanted me to tell you he left and won't be returning. I wanted to give you the option of taking over the lease on the house before I put it back on the market. Can you afford the rent?"

Skylar was stunned at the landlord's words. She didn't understand why Lance chose to have him inform her of his intentions. She was confused at his abrupt departure, and puzzled at the way she was informed. The rent was unmanageable and she knew she would have to move.

As she told Sable, the shock faded when she realized that Lance's departure meant a respite from seeing him stumble through the house inebriated. The tension she had been feeling had vanished with him.

"I'll take the children back to Natick." Sable suggested. "You should stay here and call someone to change the locks in this house. You don't know who has keys."

The children kissed Skylar and Alissa and left with Sable. Skylar called a local locksmith who arrived within a half hour and changed the locks on all the doors, garage, and windows.

When the phone rang, she was sure it was Lance. She was surprised to hear Joshua. "Hi, Mom! I told Dad about Lance. He said he already knew he was going to leave you."

She managed to keep her composure. She couldn't ask Joshua how John got his information. Instead, she changed the subject and asked him about his birthday plans. John had promised to make him a birthday party, but Joshua's tenth birthday had already passed.

He said, "Dad said he's too busy." He started crying.

Damn John, she thought. *How could he do this?* "Hey, pal, I can make a party for you and your friends. How does pizza and make-your-own sundaes sound?" she suggested.

Joshua stopped crying. "Really? That sounds awesome! I love you, Mom."

Skylar began to make plans for the party. She wrote out the invitations, but John refused to provide her with a copy of the addresses of Joshua's friends. So, she distributed them by hand at the school. She managed to pull everything together in time for his party. She served homemade pizzas and baked a chocolate birthday cake, using her car-shaped baking pan. She offered a variety of ice cream with an assortment of toppings.

The boy's from Joshua's class began to arrive. He has also invited Jed, his neighbor from Newton. Jed was accompanied by his mother Jean, who greeted Skylar warmly.

"I appreciate you inviting, Jed," she said, as they entered the house. The boys went into the living room. Jean suddenly grabbed Skylar's hand. "Look, I feel awful about everything that happened and that I even got sucked into going to court that day. I need to tell you something," she paused briefly, then continued. "John used to talk to me at the bus stop every day. He would say, 'My wife is a bitch and you shouldn't trust her. She's unstable.' When I told him I thought you were nice, he said, 'Our neighbors in Medfield and Needham thought so too until they learned Skylar is crazy'."

"I don't understand. It's odd because once we were all friends." In her gut, she knew that John had instigated problems with her neighbors, but hearing it out loud was outrageous.

"That was before he told your neighbors in Medfield you made fun of her kid and called one woman fat. He said he didn't like you hanging out with your friends when he had to work." Jean confessed.

"Oh, my God! I knew he had to be involved in this!" She firmly declared.

Jean continued, "And he told your friend in Needham you called her a Nazi and was glad when she miscarried her Nazi baby."

"Oh, my God! That's disgusting!" Skylar realized how many friendships had been destroyed because of John's lies. It was unfathomable he could be so convincing.

"He didn't want you having any allies. Why do you think your babysitters went to court for him?" Jean asked. "John is very believable. You are lucky to be away from him."

The more Skylar learned about his deeds, the more certain she was that divorcing him was the smartest thing she ever did. She was convinced John was evil.

Fortunately, his malevolence hadn't destroyed her children's love for her, which was clearly evident later that evening when Jillian handed Skylar a note, written in bright pink crayon letter, "Mommy, I want to see you Monday, Tuesday, Wednesday, Thursday, Friday, Saturday and Sunday. I love you! xxx, Jillian."

Her words touched Skylar's heart. "I'm working on it, honey." she told Jillian.

Chapter 30

Skylar convinced the landlord to allow her to stay in the house until December 1. She decided the easiest option was to move into Sable's house. She would bring her bedroom set, Alissa's crib, and their clothing. The rest of the furnishings from the nine-room house were going into storage. She began the arduous task of packing. She was able to focus her full attention on her pending move as she was housebound. Her van had been repossessed when Lance stopped making payments.

One evening, the phone rang. "Hey, Skylar, it's Norm." Norman Carson, the former convict and close friend to Lance, was on the phone. "I just wanted to know how you were doing. I can't believe he's being such a jerk." He asked where she was moving and if she planned on getting a job. He was friendly and comforting. He began calling her often, always encouraging her to keep her spirits up. At that moment in her life, she needed as many supporting people as possible.

On a chilly evening in mid-November, Lance rang the doorbell of the house they once shared. "I brought over a car for you." She looked past Lance and saw an old white, Cadillac Sedan de Ville parked in the driveway. He handed her the keys as he walked in.

"Great," said Skylar. Alissa was in her arms, and Lance bent down to kiss her head.

"Is this my kid?" Lance looked intently at Alissa's face.
Skylar let out a short laugh. "Are you serious?"

"I need to know. Is this my fucking kid?" He had been drinking and began to get angry. "My doctor said I was unable to father a kid. And John said you can't be trusted."

"Really," Skylar responded, more a statement than a question.

"I want a paternity test," Lance demanded.

"Fine. But let's bring it in front of a judge. I'll agree to it." Skylar said honestly.

"I don't want to go in front of a judge. It's too embarrassing." He handed her a business card. "Here, I already scheduled the test for Monday. That's the name and the address of the office. Alissa will have to be tested too. Meet me there at ten o'clock." He reached for the handle of the door, "You better be there." He opened the door and walked out.

Skylar carried Alissa to the loveseat in the living room. As she nursed her, she thought about this new issue. She had been desperately trying to figure out how to summon him to court for child support, but her attempts to get his address had been fruitless. Now she knew where he would be on Monday morning and she could serve him there. He would never suspect it.

On Friday morning, she drove into the Middlesex Probate court in Cambridge. She asked the clerk at the desk for the forms needed to file for child support. She carefully filled out the information sheet, inserting Sable's address instead of her current residence. Although she hadn't moved to Ashland yet, it was a wise decision. If she admitted she was still living in Brookline, she would have to file in Norfolk County, the same court she had been in with John. Sable's address was in Middlesex County so Skylar would be anonymous there.

When the court date was scheduled, she took the summons and left the court, silently congratulating herself on strategically completing that part of her plan. As soon as she got home, she found the name of a constable in the telephone book and made arrangements to have Lance served at the site of the paternity test.

On Monday morning, Skylar's nerves were jumping. She put Alissa in her car seat, drove into Boston, and parked the car. She entered the building with Alissa in her arms and they rode the elevator to the fifth floor. As the elevator door opened, the constable was standing there.

"All set," he whispered to Skylar as she exited the elevator and he entered. She gave a sigh of relief. Although elated, she put a bland expression on her face as she walked into the waiting area. She saw Lance and sat beside him.

"You know, you didn't have to do that." he whispered.

Skylar replied, "Yes, I did, because it will protect you, and it will protect me."

When the nurse called their names, Lance was brought to one room and Skylar and Alissa were ushered to another room. The technician took blood from Skylar's arm and scraped the inside of Alissa's mouth for cells. She was told she would have the results within thirty days. The ordeal was over, so she took Alissa and went home.

The next night, Lance called Skylar. He angrily screamed, "You lied! You lied on the forms you filled out in court! You lied about your address! You don't live in Ashland! You live in Brookline! You filed this in the wrong court! This needs to be filed in Norfolk County probate!" Lance was so angry that Skylar could feel his rage through the phone.

"Really," she drawled, "and where did you get this information?"

"John told me!" Lance sounded triumphant.

"Maybe it's time you stop taking his calls." suggested Skylar.

"I will get the landlord to testify that you are living there!" He yelled.

She laughed. "The landlord isn't going to testify for you."

At that, Lance's garbled words of frustrated anger had reached such a decibel that she hung up the phone.

About an hour later, Skylar's phone rang. It was Norman and he was laughing.

"Boy, is he pissed off! What did you do?"

"I didn't do anything," Skylar said.

"He says you filed in the wrong court." Norman informed her.

"He can say what he wants," she replied.

"Well, I have to tell you something. Your ex-husband told him to file for custody of the baby. He said he was going to show him how to do it," Norman told her.

Skylar began to feel sick to her stomach "Well, that will never happen." she stated with more conviction than she felt. "I need to go."

She was shaking as she hung up the phone. She was terrified and her stomach was in knots. She could never endure another custody trial.

If it came to that, she was going to take her baby and run. There was no way in hell she was going to suffer through that battle again. She went to bed emotionally drained.

It was a cold December day and a light snow was falling. Skylar was moving. The movers would first take her to Sables house and then onto the storage facility. It was a long and exhausting day which lasted past dinner time. She paid the movers with the money from her secret cache in her closet. Although moving in with her mother seemed like a step backwards, Skylar was able to take it as an opportunity to get her life back on track. She applied for welfare and food stamps to tide her over until she found a job.

Norman continued to call her in Ashland. He asked questions about her job search and asked if she was dating. He told her everything Lance was doing. However, Skylar didn't reveal much about her situation because she knew he would repeat it to Lance.

She hired an attorney to accompany her into court the middle of January 1999. She stood quietly facing the judge, her hands folded. She was better versed in the legal system than the last time. She did not look at Lance and did not react to anything he said. When asked a question, she answered the judge in a soft voice, drenched with sincerity.

"Your honor, Mr. Levine began drinking in the morning, and continued all day. He stopped paying the rent on the house and left me and my daughter. He stopped paying for my van, and it was repossessed. All I would like is enough child support and restitution so I can make a life for my daughter."

A few days later, she read the judge's decision and was elated that Lance was ordered to pay a generous amount of child support. His motion for custody was not allowed.

By February 1999, Skylar had obtained a sales position which provided her with the flexibility to work from home. In a very short time, she was excelling at her job, and she was financially solvent. She joined a gym. She was spending quality time with Joshua, Cary, Jillian, and Alissa taking them to statewide, family events. In late March, she was asked to play the piano accompaniment for the children's Hebrew school Mother's Day event in May. Life was good. She was happily moving forward and hoped she would soon move to her own apartment.

In April, she was summoned to court for allegedly filing a fraudulent report against John. The Department of Social Services had received a complaint indicating John had made inappropriate comments to his stepdaughter, Sara Dziwka, regarding the size of her chest. Although the report was pointing a finger at John, he addressed the problem by stating the complaint had come from Skylar.

"What is this?" she asked Liz after reading the DSS report in court.

"You should know – you filed it," John interjected.

"Like *hell* I filed this! I don't care what you do with Sara. Don't think you're pinning this on me!" Skylar turned. She was shaking. John had fabricated evidence when his car was keyed, when he attacked her at the baseball field, and he was doing it again.

Judge Copeland read the report. Skylar emphatically testified she did not file the report. The judge asked Liz if she had anyone there from the DSS to determine if Skylar had filed the report. Liz admitted she didn't.

Judge Copeland stated, "I am not blaming Skylar Bauers for this report. Court is adjourned." He stood up and left the courtroom.

Ironically, the following Wednesday, when Skylar picked the children up from school, Joshua asked, "Do you think Jillian's going to have big tits when she grows up?"

Shocked, Skylar admonished, "Joshie, you should not talk like that!"

"Dad does," Joshua replied.

"Well, he shouldn't talk like that in front of you."

"It wasn't in front of me. It was in front of Sara," Joshua explained.

"Sara Dziwka? But she's only fifteen years old. Where was Maryanne during this?"

"She was shopping." Joshua paused. "Dad always talks like that to Sara."

"Well, what exactly did he say?" Skylar hesitatingly asked.

Robin Shaye

"He said, 'those are some huge tits, Sara.' And then he made a sucking noise." Joshua said, demonstrating the noise.

"Oh, my God!" Skylar gasped. "He's disgusting." Obviously someone was aware of John's behavior and had filed the DSS report. Blaming Skylar was John's best defense.

The springtime days were warm and lovely. On Wednesday afternoons, the boys attended Hebrew school. Skylar enrolled Jillian in a dance class at a local studio where she wouldn't have to contend with Maryanne. Jillian loved her class and was excitedly anticipating the dance recital in June. Skylar finally felt like a Mom again. From school to Hebrew school to dance and Little League, she was involved in all of the children's activities. The few extra hours on Wednesday in addition to the weekends gave her the opportunity to firmly instill her position in her children's lives. It was a very peaceful time for her.

But her tranquility was short lived. In late April, John summoned her to court because she was late in delivering the children following a Little League game.

John yelled, "I am going to stop your mother from seeing you if she can't adhere to the schedule!" The boys cried, protesting that it wasn't Skylar's fault and pleaded with John. Nevertheless, he filed the contempt motion.

Skylar wanted to avoid another frivolous court appearance. She decided to call John and suggest he call the team coach who could confirm the reason the game ran late. But when she tried to call John, she learned that his number had been changed to an unpublished number. So, Skylar filed a counter-motion in order to get her children's phone number.

She attended the hearing in the probate court. The lateness was handled with an admonishment from the judge. Then, Skylar presented her counter-motion to the judge.

"Your honor, Mr. Bauers changed the telephone number at his house. I can no longer reach my children."

John arrogantly stated, "When she calls, she harasses anyone who answers the phone."

"That's not true!" Skylar cried. "Maryanne's daughters usually answer the phone and I am always polite. They're just kids! I would never say anything rude to them!"

"Yes, she does! We can't even answer the phone anymore!" John firmly stated.

"Your honor, this man is lying. He is trying to prevent me from calling my children."

"Well, what if the children call you? We can make a schedule where they can call you," the judge suggested.

"That sounds like a good idea," John smugly agreed.

Although Skylar found it grossly unfair and unjust, the order was written that the children would call Skylar on Tuesday and Thursday evenings at seven-thirty.

Although this new wrinkle was upsetting to her, it devastated Joshua. He complained, "My friends can't call me because I don't even know my own phone number!"

Skylar had just picked the children up from school. It was an exceptionally warm day in May and they were going to have a picnic lunch at a local park.

"Why not?" she asked Joshua, who was seated beside her.

"Dad won't give it to me. He said I would give it to you. Mom, can't you do something? Can't you go to court about this? He's telling us he's going to pull us out of Hebrew school! He can't do that! The rabbi just gave me my bar mitzvah date!" Joshua put his head in his hands.

"I like my Sunday school!" piped Jillian from the back seat.

"Daddy's mean!" pouted Cary.

Skylar calmly answered, "Your dad is very angry at me. I'm sure he didn't mean it."

John was hurting the children, yet Skylar felt compelled to make excuses for him. She couldn't bear seeing her children's pain. She pulled her car into the driveway of the park.

We're here!" she announced, trying to sound cheerful.

"What's the judge's name?" Joshua suddenly asked. "I am writing him a note." He pulled a notebook out of his backpack. "Mom, tell me the judge's name."

"It's Copeland," Skylar said, as she unbuckled Cary and Jillian from their car seats. They pranced around the car as Skylar opened the trunk of the car. She took out Alissa's stroller, unbuckled her from her car seat and placed her in the stroller.

"I want to push her!" shouted Cary.

"Me, too!" yelled Jillian.

"Cary can push her there, and Jillian will push her back. We'll take turns. And Mommy will carry the picnic cooler." She got the cooler out of the trunk. Joshua remained in the front seat, furiously writing in his notebook.

"C'mon, pal," Skylar said to him.

"Okay, I'm done." Joshua carefully tore the page out of the notebook. He folded the paper in half and stuck it in the visor of the car. He got out of the car, and Skylar closed the door.

"Let's make this a fun picnic," she suggested, handing Joshua a blanket. She didn't mention the note left in her car.

The day turned out to be lovely. It wasn't until later, after she dropped the children off at John's house that she remembered Joshua's letter. She reached up and pulled it from the visor and read:

Dear Judge Copeland, My dad is changing my Hebrew school. I want to stay at Temple Israel where all my friends are. I don't want to leave this temple. I already have a bar mitzvah date set. I am asking you to write down secretly everything my dad says and give it to my Mom so I can write if it is the truth.

From Joshua Bauers.

P.S. Don't tell my dad.

P.P.S. Dad won't tell us the phone number. He also won't tell Mom. She doesn't call every five minutes and harass my Dad or Maryanne. My friends can't call me. It is not fair to me!

Skylar thought Joshua's letter was a tragic indication of what happens when the court fails a child. She sadly put his letter in a file in case she needed it in the future.

On the morning of Mother's Day, Skylar picked up the children and brought them to the temple. The room was adorned with fragrant flowers. She sat at the piano as the choir of children and adults filed in. The day became a joyous celebration of music and singing to honor the mothers and grandmothers. She felt as if she was right back when she used to play the piano during Shabbat celebrations at children's pre-school. The performance went wonderfully well. Prior to leaving, she filled out the re-enrollment forms for Hebrew school the following year.

A week later, she received a summons of contempt in the mail. Although in 1996, John had agreed that the children could attend Hebrew school, he was taking her to court for enrolling the children for their third year. Traditionally, Jewish children attend Hebrew school until they become a bar/bat mitzvah at the age of thirteen; therefore, she was not guilty of contempt.

In mid-May, Judge Arlina Roteman was hearing the contempt motion. Judge Roteman was known for her unjust decisions and occasionally falling asleep on the bench. Skylar took the opportunity to bring Joshua's letter which stated, 'I want to stay at Temple Israel where all my friends are. I don't want to leave this temple', into the court room.

Judge Roteman read it, frowned and declared, "I find that this letter was dictated to your son by you!" She squinted down at Skylar.

"No! Joshua wrote it! I wasn't even with him when he wrote it!" Skylar intensely stated. "I don't even know why we are here. John agreed to the children attending Hebrew school. Why don't you look at the order from Judge Copeland?"

John suddenly stood up, interrupting Skylar. With his eyes as wide open as possible, he dramatically stated to Judge Roteman, "I never gave permission for the children to go to Hebrew school. They have to go Sunday, Monday, Tuesday, Wednesday, Thursday, Friday and Saturday!" emphasizing each day rhythmically, like the beat of a drum.

When he concluded his percussive testimony, Skylar timidly asked, "Excuse me, can I say something?"

Judge Roteman answered with a harsh retort, "No! You may not say anything! You clearly don't understand what legal custody means! Supervised visits!" The order was punitive and absurd. She also ordered Skylar to schedule a meeting with the court psychologist.

The next week, Skylar went to the court clinic. She talked to the psychologist and related the facts of the unjust decisions by the judges, the unethical behavior of Liz Lewin and Julie Ginsler and John's continuous abuse.

The psychologist stated, "You got a raw deal. Here's what we'll do. We'll schedule one meeting with your children and then end the supervision." Unfortunately, the psychologist was leaving for her summer vacation, so she was unable to schedule a visit until mid-August.

Skylar didn't want to be kept from her children for months. She was supposed to play the piano for Joshua's elementary school graduation. She would miss Jillian's dance recital too. She wondered if John was even taking Jillian to her recital rehearsals. She called the dance school to ask her instructor, "Has John been bringing Jillian to class?"

"He brought her here once," the dance instructor reported. "He walked in and announced, 'Skylar won't be here anymore. I'm in charge now.' Then he sat on the opposite side of the room from the other parents with an angry face. Jillian hasn't returned to class. I've called and left messages but he doesn't return my calls. Do you think he'll bring her to the recital?"

"I don't know," Skylar sighed. "Keep her costume, just in case she shows up. I'm sorry."

"Why are you sorry? It's not your fault. I hate to say it, but this is child abuse. Jillian loved my classes. She was so excited about the recital. This is child abuse!"

Skylar thanked her for being so supportive and sadly, hung up the phone.

Two days later, she was shocked to receive a criminal complaint requesting she appear at Boston Municipal Court on a charge of larceny. Lance was claiming she stole his telephone calling card. She could not believe what was happening to her life. She was a good, decent, law abiding citizen, and suddenly she was slapped with an unfounded criminal complaint.

Sable answered the phone when Norman called that afternoon. He already knew about the complaint. He told Sable, "Lance was drunk and talking to John on the phone. He was already pissed off about the phone bill. I'm telling ya, I know that John talked Lance into filing the complaint. But I talked to Lance, and he told me if he can talk to Skylar, face to face, he'll drop the charges. I can bring her to him tonight."

Sable believed him. "Maybe if you just meet with Lance, he'll drop the charges," Sable told Skylar, handing her the phone. "Just talk to Norman."

Skylar was apprehensive about Norman's motives, but she reluctantly took the phone.

"Skylar, ya gotta get rid of this criminal complaint. Otherwise, you'll never be able to see your kids." Norman sounded sincere. "I can meet you in Natick and take you to him."

It seemed to make sense to meet with Lance instead of facing another court date.

"Fine, I will meet you in the parking lot of the Natick Mall near Filenes," she agreed, albeit skeptically.

That evening, she drove to the mall and she saw Norman standing next to his car, smoking a cigarette, waiting for her.

"Hi, stranger!" he greeted her. "Look at you!" He admired Skylar as she got out of her car.

She waved her hand and wrinkled her nose as she opened the passenger door and got into Norman's car. Once in the car, he offered her a cigarette and she gratefully took one. She began to feel a little more comfortable as he started driving toward Boston. Once in Brighton, he pulled the car into a parking lot.

"Let's go have a drink. There's a pay phone in there. I'll call Lance." They went into the bar and sat at a small wooden table. Norman sauntered to the back area to use the phone.

When he returned he said, "He said he's just going to an AA meeting. He'll be out in an hour. Let's get a drink."

He ordered a beer and Skylar ordered a diet Coke. He told her, "Lance is crazy. If I had someone like you, I'd never treat them this way."

Skylar smiled. She was nervous. In the past, Norman was working for Lance, but this time seemed more social than business. She just wanted to get through the evening.

Norman said, "You know that you are going to be my wife." He smiled.

Skylar giggled and said, "I am NEVER getting married again."

She continued to deflect Norman's come-ons, which grew bolder with each beer he drank.

After an hour, Norman said, "I know where to find him." They left the bar and drove through Boston. He kept glancing at Skylar, who stared straight ahead. They didn't find Lance.

Finally, she said, "It's getting late. Just drive me back to my car."

He complied and drove her back to the mall. She already had her keys in her left hand, her right hand on the door handle, as they neared her car.

"I really like being with you," Norman said, "Can we do this again?"

"Why don't we just keep this a nice memory?" Skylar replied as she quickly left his vehicle.

Once she was safe in her car, she breathed a sigh of relief. When she got home, she told Sable it was a fruitless endeavor.

She warned, "Don't tell Norman I am home if he calls. He's creepy."

Chapter 31

As the humidity of summer crawled by sluggishly, Norman continued to call. Skylar avoided him by insisting Sable answer the phone and tell him she wasn't home. He persisted.

"Sable, it's very important that I speak to her."

Sable whispered to Skylar, "He sounds sincere. Why don't you just find out what he wants?" Finally, Skylar agreed to take his call.

"It's about fuckin' time you get on the phone!" Norman yelled.

Skylar was surprised at Norman's fervent demand. She asked, "What do you want?"

"I want you to come with me tonight. I know where he is." He sounded as if he was trying to be a little too convincing.

Skylar sighed. She explained, "Look, I didn't take any phone card. The whole thing is ridiculous, so I know it will end at the hearing." She didn't believe Norman, and this time she was not going to be talked into meeting him.

Matter-of-factly, he stated, "I don't know…he's really angry."

"I don't know why he's so angry," she said.

"He wants the baby to live with his brother," he said, hoping to convince Skylar.

"Well, that's never happening," she firmly replied.

Norman cajoled, "Please meet me tonight. Please. I just want to look at you."

"Stop, Norm." Skylar held her ground. She didn't like the direction he was heading.

Norman gave a small, harsh, laugh of disbelief. "You think you're too good for me. You really are a bitch." His voice took on a caustic tone.

Skylar, trying to soften the conversation, answered, "I told you I don't want to get involved with anyone."

"When was the last time you had a good fuck?" he brazenly asked. She hung up the phone and related the conversation to Sable and stressed, "*Do not* make me talk to him again!"

At the end of July, she drove to the municipal court in Boston. Outside each courtroom hung a list of that day's hearings. She looked at every list but didn't see her name so she walked to the clerk's office and asked about her hearing, giving her name to the man behind the desk.

He found a file with her name on the top. "Oh, that was dismissed." Skylar's relief turned to dread when the clerk noticed a police report in her file with *Lance Levine and John Bauers* at the top of the page. "Here's something else," the clerk said, picking up the report.

Skylar's terror increased as she read the report which stated both Lance and John went to a police station together and pressed criminal charges against her for allegedly trying to hire a hit man to kill them. The court date was set for August 2. She burst into tears.

"Does this mean anyone can make up something and you issue a criminal complaint?"

"Look, all we do is take the complaint. I can make you a copy of this, but you'll be getting it in the mail." The clerk made a copy of the report and handed it to Skylar.

This is absurd, she thought. She noticed the police station listed in the report was located across the street from the courthouse. She decided to walk there in the hopes she could speak to the detective who took the information. She left the courthouse and crossed the street to the police station. The detectives' offices were on the second floor. She was greeted by a pleasant looking African-American woman. Skylar showed her the report and asked her if she had any recollection of that day.

"Oh yes, I remember when *they* came in." She rolled her eyes. "One of them was drunk and smelled of alcohol. The other one acted as if he were in charge. But I had to take the complaint. That's my job. I am not supposed to determine what's true or false."

"What can I do about this report? It's a total lie," Skylar asked.

The officer replied, "Well, honey, I don't doubt you after what I saw. Unfortunately, it's out of my hands right now. You'll just have to go to court and get them to dismiss it there." She handed Skylar her card and said, "If you need me to testify, let me know."

When she got home, she showed Sable the report.

"John and Lance did this together? They're crazy! You better find an attorney. You can't go against them alone," Sable said, looking concerned.

Skylar began searching for criminal attorneys in the telephone book. Seeing the word criminal was beyond her scope of belief. Trying to find one for herself was incomprehensible. She wanted a lawyer who could dismiss the allegations and then file charges against John and Lance for false accusations. She began making calls. By the end of the afternoon, it was apparent that she would be unable to find an attorney who would take less than five thousand dollars. Skylar simply didn't have the money. She was going to have to fight the battle alone.

On the morning of Monday, August 2, 1999, Skylar arrived at the magistrate's office alone. She immediately saw Lance and John, sitting side by side on the bench in the hall. She was horrified so she waited around the corner. After a short wait, they were all called into the small office. The magistrate asked Lance to explain what happened.

He stated, "This person came to me. He told me she went to him and said she wanted him to kill me and her ex-husband. She was going to pay him with sex or fifty-thousand dollars. He had been incarcerated before and lived with us for a while. His name is Norman Carson."

Skylar sat bolt upright and gasped at hearing Norman's name.

The magistrate turned to Skylar. "Do you know Norman Carson?"

Disgusted, Skylar replied, "I know him. He never lived with us. He did some work in our house, but I never asked him to kill anyone. That's insane."

The magistrate turned to John, who pompously stated, "This guy called me and told me she wanted me killed. I already filed a report with the Natick police department."

Skylar was stunned when the magistrate said, "I think there is enough evidence to go to trial. However, since Mr. Levine's name is the first one on the police report, he is considered the victim. If Mr. Bauers wants to file his own complaint, he can certainly do so."

Skylar stood aghast. Her entire body was numb. "But I didn't do anything!" she protested, her voice breaking.

"That's for the judge to decide," declared the magistrate. He picked up his papers and walked toward the door. Lance walked out of the room, but John stood there smirking.

"What happens now?" Skylar directed her question to the magistrate.

"You'll get a notice for an arraignment. You'll be assigned a public defender if you can't afford an attorney." The magistrate walked out of the room and continued down the hall.

John paused at the door, waiting for Skylar to pass. As she exited the room, in a low voice, he muttered, "Until you die."

Skylar put her chin up and walked away, determined not to let him see her panic. She left the courthouse, somehow found her car and drove home as if in a fog. Only when she got home, picked up Alissa, and felt her curls against her cheek did she feel she would be able to gather her strength for the battle ahead.

Eleven days after the magistrate hearing was Skylar's birthday. An old friend from high school was taking her out for dinner. It was a perfect diversion. Rob Sails was muscular and a little taller than Skylar. Although his hair was receding, it didn't detract from his handsome face. The minute they began talking, she was reminded why she had liked him in high school. Rob was funny, adorable, and made her laugh. The sparks flew. But as Skylar enjoyed the evening, in the back of her mind, she was counting the days until she would see her children again.

On Saturday morning, she walked outside to get the mail and found a letter from the probate court. It was an ex-parte motion. Ex-parte means "without the other party." It was marked "Allowed" in a bold faced type. The date written on the motion was Skylar's birthday.

The motion stated:

Allegations into whether or not the Defendant, Skylar Levine attempted to hire several men to kill the Plaintiff, John Bauers, and her current husband, Lance Levine. The Plaintiff alleges that a criminal complaint has been issued against the Defendant for threatening to kill her husband, Lance Levine, and that there is an nvestigation into whether or not the Defendant also tried to have the same individuals kill the Plaintiff."

Skylar read in disbelief. John went into court *on her birthday* to stop her from seeing the children, based on yet another lie. This signed affidavit was untrue on three factual points.

1. The only hit man that was named was Norman Carson, not *several men.*

2. The alleged victim on record was *just* Lance Levine, *not John Bauers.*

3. There was no investigation. *John had the option to file his own complaint*

According to the *Massachusetts Rules of Professional Conduct for Transactions With Persons Other Than Clients*, attorney Liz Lewin was guilty of blatantly ignoring Rule 4.1, *Truthfulness In Statements To Others*, which stated: *In the course of representing a client, a lawyer shall not knowingly: (a) make a false statement of material fact or law to a third person.* Liz had signed the motion, *under the pains and penalties of perjury*, despite three false statements in her motion. She boldly presented it to a third person: the judge.

The ex-parte hearing was eleven days after the magistrate hearing. There was time to serve Skylar, but Liz filed ex-parte to prevent Skylar from defending herself in court. It was unethical, as well as a cold and calculated move, because John instructed Liz to go to court on a specific date: Skylar's birthday.

Filing an ex-parte motion is a typical ploy for an abuser. In approximately 2001, a web-site was created on the Internet for father's involved in custody battles. They claim to show men how to "fight dirty" in court. The language is coarse. One part of the site featured an article entitled, *Let's Ex-Parte the Bitch.* The following is a direct quote from the site:

> *"Ex-Parte is lawyer Latin for ambush or blindside. Normally, in a judicial proceeding, the adversarial parties must inform each other of what they are doing -- unless one files an ex-parte motion. To break it down into its parts, "X" is the diminutive of excretion as in "excretion out of luck." "Parte," pronounced par-tay means "to party," as in we're going to partay after you get eX-creted upon."*

On the day of the arraignment, Skylar was assigned to a court appointed attorney who was fresh out of law school. She was cute and flirty and seemed to know everyone in the court. She would greet each new client proclaiming, "I'm gonna fight like hell for you!"

Public Defenders working in the courts make one hundred dollars per case. The clients are usually destitute as well as guilty of drug possession, violating parole or prostitution. The attorneys want to get them in and out of the system as quickly as possible.

Skylar conferred with the young female attorney, Veronica Black. She told Veronica she wanted to fight the charge with a vengeance. There was a crime committed but Skylar was the victim, not the perpetrator. She was eager to turn the tables on the ones who made the false accusation and press charges for criminal harassment.

"We need to get through this trial before you can make any complaints against your ex-husbands," Veronica advised her.

John filed a criminal complaint in November 1999, *three months after* his sworn ex-parte motion. Veronica represented Skylar at the magistrate hearing. She informed the magistrate that John had appeared in court on Skylar's birthday to stop her visits with her children, and not because of any threat to his life. John, wide-eyed, professed not to know it was her birthday the day the motion was filed. The magistrate didn't believe him, and dismissed his complaint.

"At least you won't be facing two men," Veronica told Skylar. "I want you to sit their quietly during the trial. You don't have to testify because they have the burden of proof."

Skylar argued, "But I have nothing to hide. I want to testify."

"It's risky putting you on the stand," Veronica replied.

"Why is it risky? I haven't done anything. I never asked Norman to kill anyone. They need to be punished for filing false charges! The jury will be able to tell who is lying."

"You're not having a jury trial. You're having a bench trial." Veronica declared, "You are going to waive your rights to a jury trial. You're going to agree to a bench trial, which will be just with the judge. I know the judge and he's good. You don't need a jury trial."

Uneasily, Skylar said, "Well, if you're sure… but I want to be able to bring in witnesses."

"I am your attorney and you'll do as I say! They have the burden of proof!" Veronica screamed. "You don't have to do anything or bring anyone in! You're just going to sit there with your mouth shut!"

Skylar flinched at her outburst. Dubious, she reluctantly agreed. Alissa was first and foremost in her thoughts. She didn't know what would happen to her if she was found guilty. She knew a jail sentence was a possibility. Nauseated at the thought, she quietly accepted Veronica's plan of defense.

Veronica's plan was not in Skylar's best interest at all. Working as a new attorney and public defender was a training experience. She wanted to get through as many cases as possible, learn about the system, and learn how to try a case. She needed the practice. To a fledgling attorney, the process was important, not the verdict.

It was a desolate winter without her children. Skylar spend most weekends with Alissa at Rob's house. Alissa played with his children, and Skylar would cook dinners. Rob and Skylar became very close. He was a tremendous source of comfort as they waited for her trial.

The trial was scheduled for April 2000. The day was cold but sunny as Rob drove Skylar to Boston. She shivered as they walked through the halls leading to the courtroom. She cringed as she saw John and Lance, casually dressed in jeans, seated in the rear of the courtroom.

Veronica called her to the table in the front of the courtroom. "Nice suit," she commented when she saw Skylar's beige suit and ivory blouse. "They look like derelicts." Veronica nodded to the rear of the courtroom.

Skylar smiled nervously as she sat down. Rob sat on the bench behind her.

As the trial began, Skylar felt as if she were watching in a class at a law school. The judge kept coaching the two inexperienced attorneys on how to form their questions and what to ask next. He prompted and reminded as they prepared to question the first witness.

Norman Carson was brought into court from South Bay Correctional Facility to testify. He was back in prison for violating his parole. He walked into court wearing an orange jumpsuit, the badge of an inmate.

Norman answered questions by saying, "I heard *things*. She told me *things*." He didn't embellish on what he heard or what was said. He repeated, "Skylar wanted Lance to disappear." The vernacular he was using was more in line with someone who was associated with organized crime, not a mother who lived in the suburbs.

Lance was called to testify. He stood up and rapidly made his way to the witness stand.

He testified, "I am so frightened. I am afraid to go outside. I'm afraid Skylar is going to be in the bushes in a combat stance." He raised his arms as if holding a gun. His testimony did not contain any reference to the original complaint of a hit man hired to kill him. Instead, he put the gun in Skylar's hand.

Following Lance, John Bauers was called to testify. He strutted to the witness stand. His demeanor was arrogant, and there was no fear in his voice. "I received a call from Norman. He said that my ex-wife had talked to him about killing me. He was trying to protect me from *her*."

The judge asked, "Did you ever meet Mr. Carson prior to that telephone call?"

John chuckled, "No...but he introduced himself when he called."

The judge looked at Veronica. "Now, you need to object. He never met the man, so he doesn't know for sure that he was the one who called."

"Objection, your honor!" shouted Veronica. "The court has no way of knowing who made the call to Mr. Bauers."

"Sustained." said the judge. He paused and looked at Veronica.

"I move that we strike his testimony from the record!" Veronica declared.

"Very good," said the judge, smiling. He turned to John. "Mr. Bauers, you are dismissed."

"Oh! I am?" chuckled John. "Okay, then." He stood up and walked back to his seat.

"I think we should break for lunch," stated the judge. "Everyone return at two o'clock."

Rob approached Veronica. "It went well, didn't it?" he asked.

"I guess we'll see. I have some paperwork to do. Why don't you two go have lunch?"

Rob put his arm around Skylar and they left the courthouse and went to a nearby deli. During lunch, he made her laugh by doing imitations of Norman, Lance, and John. "Babe, this is a slam dunk. There is no way the judge is going to find you guilty. Did you hear them? They sounded like a bunch of idiots! When this is over, you can make plans to start seeing your kids."

Skylar was convinced that his impression of the trial was accurate. She returned to the courtroom smiling, certain the judge was going to announce she was not guilty.

At two o'clock, the judge entered the courtroom. "I am ready to render a verdict."

Veronica poked Skylar. "Stand up!' she whispered. She timidly rose to her feet.

"After careful deliberation of the evidence, in the case of the State of Massachusetts versus Skylar Levine, I find the defendant," the judge paused, "guilty of the crime of threats."

Skylar caught her breath. Rob sat back in his seat, stunned.

"Before I pass sentence, is there anything you'd like to say on your behalf, Mrs. Levine?"

"Yes," whispered Skylar. Shakily, she stated, "The only reason we are here is because of my ex-husbands' custody issues. This is only about custody. I never tried to hire a hit man. I did nothing wrong, and I am completely innocent," her voice breaking as she finished.

"Very well. I impose a six-month suspended sentence and five years probation." The judge stood up and left the courtroom.

Skylar was devastated. Her head was buzzing, and her heart was palpitating in fear. She nodded when asked if she wanted to request an appeal. The paper was placed in front of her, and she blindly scribbled her name on the form. Due to a backlog in the courts, she was told the appeal wouldn't be scheduled until the following year.

In the car on the way home, she tearfully told Rob, "I can't wait another year to see my children! It's already been almost a year!"

He replied, "If I didn't see it with my own eyes, I wouldn't have believed it. That judge is a fool. You didn't do a thing. Even if I thought you may have done something, after listening to those morons in court, I would have found you not guilty."

Five days later, she had recovered somewhat from the initial shock of the verdict and went to the probate court to file a motion requesting visits with her children. The guilty finding was with Lance, not her children. A hearing was scheduled for the first week of May 2000.

On that day of the hearing, she faced Judge Roteman. Expressionless, the judge read the motions and listened to the discrepancies in the case. In a bored tone, Judge Roteman announced she would take it under advisement. The decision arrived in the mail the next day. It was an order from the Judge which stated she was not allowing any of Skylar's motions at that time.

There was nothing she could do until her appeal. The unfairness was like a knife in her gut. It was unfathomable that two men would have such anger toward her. Skylar didn't know what she did to hurt them so badly. She only knew she would not go down without a fight.

She focused toward utilizing other methods to bring attention to her case. Motions at the probate level were futile, so she wrote a comprehensive appeal to the Chief Justice of the State Supreme Judicial Court. She received a response informing her that appeals needed to be filed by an attorney. She refused to be discouraged, so she forged a campaign to bring attention to the travesties occurring in probate court. She created tri-fold brochures revealing the corrupt inconsistencies of her case. She mailed them to every radio station, television station, and newspaper, both local and statewide, and Canada. She contacted renowned attorneys, politicians, and families of other abused victims. She received a few responses and met with journalists, but no one was willing to publicize her case. She attended political events, rallies, collected signatures, and talked to mayors, governors, senators and political pundits. Skylar couldn't just sit by idly waiting for her appeal. Her continuous quest for justice was keeping her strong and healthy as it promoted hope. She would never give up.

Chapter 32

In mid-May of 2000, with Rob's help, Skylar and Alissa moved into a project-based building in Cambridge. It was a large, institutional-like space on the twentieth floor with a fantastic view of the city. She retrieved her furniture from storage and moved it into her apartment. She hung pictures of the children on all the walls and made the bland apartment look homey. She kept the lights on in the kitchen and bathroom to keep the roaches away. The mice didn't stay away, but she didn't see them too often, as her place was scrupulously clean.

Logistically, she couldn't have asked for a better situation. Her new job and Alissa's daycare were all within walking distance of her apartment. Her salary as assistant director at a computer training facility allowed her to begin to build a savings account. She was saving money so she could hire an attorney in order to go to court and fight for her children.

Skylar felt compelled to find a therapist during that time. The effects of the years of abuse had been traumatic and she welcomed the support. She found a therapist who was an expert in the field of domestic abuse and borderline personality disorder. The therapist evaluated her and felt she was a survivor who had handled much abuse but was still mentally healthy. Skylar was suffering from post-traumatic stress, but she was functioning on a high level. After hearing her description of events leading up to the present, the therapist felt John presented as a narcissistic sociopath with histrionic personality disorder as well as antisocial personality disorder. He was an abuser and a batterer. Although her evaluation of John was based on hearsay, she found that Skylar's depiction of her life with John never deviated and the chronicles of abuse never changed. Supporting Skylar's description was John's own testimony during the custody trial, which was a clear indication of the validity of the therapist's assessment.

Skylar enjoyed living in Cambridge. From her apartment windows, she could see the leaves change to autumn colors and the snow filled clouds of the approaching harsh New England winter. As 2001 began, Skylar prayed for a happier year. She enjoyed her job. Her weekends were for Alissa and activities, which sometimes included Rob and his children. Some evenings, when the children were asleep, she would show Rob the video tapes she had of Joshua, Cary, and Jillian. He would comfort her sobs of anguish. Although she tried to be strong, sometimes the unfairness of being denied her children because of a false accusation was unbearable. As the winter months passed, the seasonal changes brought a renewed hope that her April 2001 appeal would reverse the guilty verdict.

On the day of her appeal, Skylar nervously sat in court with the appeal lawyer assigned to her case. His argument was flawless and amazing. She left court that day in high spirited optimism. As the wait for a verdict began, she was positive she would be vindicated.

At the same time, Sable filed a motion utilizing her grandparent's rights to see the children. When John stopped Skylar's visits, he also refused to let the children see Sable. He was livid when Sable brought him to court. He heatedly objected to reuniting her with her grandchildren. Despite his outburst, the judge granted the motion under the conditions the visits were supervised by a therapist.

Her visits with her grandchildren began the spring of 2001. Although they were quiet when they first met with Sable, they began speaking freely after a few visits. Joshua excitedly informed her he was going to become a bar mitzvah in September of 2001, by a rabbi who ran a small school in Framingham.

"My father said our mother can't go," Joshua told her. "He said we can't see her because she did something really bad. He showed me the papers from court."

Sable asked, "Do you think your mother would do something really bad?"

"That's what our father said," announced Joshua.

"I want to see my mother," interjected Cary.

But Jillian remained quiet. When Sable asked her a question, she would whisper her answers. Sable felt her responses were robotic, and expressed her concern to the therapist.

"Why is she like that? She barely talks. When she does talk, it's like a little whisper. She never did this before." Sable wiped away her tears.

"You told me that the step mother is volatile?"

"Oh, my God, yes! I heard her scream in court, and sometimes when I've been to her house with Skylar to pick up the children. She's screamed at Skylar many times. The director of the dance studio told her that Maryanne has a short fuse. And the children would tell her that Maryanne yelled at them and at John often," Sable related.

"Well, that's your answer, I'm afraid. You see, when a child is put into a situation with an adult who is verbally abusive or prone to quick-tempered explosions, the child counteracts that behavior. Since Jillian was so young, she found a way to cope by communicating in ways contrary to her step mother. It will probably to take years of therapy to overcome this." She paused. "I think I'll call John and see if I can find out what is going on in that house."

When the therapist questioned John, he became extremely defensive.

"I am in charge, and I am doing what I think is right. Sable is acting as Skylar's agent and providing her information about the kids. I'm the custodial parent, and I don't want Skylar or Sable to know anything about the kids. In fact, I think the kids have had their last appointment." He hung up the phone.

Sable and Skylar were upset when John stopped the visits, but they weren't surprised at his reaction. Predictably, when things got too hot for John, he would pull back defensively.

Although the visits had ceased, Sable had learned some details about

Joshua's Bar Mitzvah. On Skylar's day off, she made preparations in the hopes her efforts would allow her to share this important milestone with her son. With the information from Sable, she easily discovered the facility where Joshua was probably taking lessons. She drove to the makeshift school and parked her car. When she entered the building, she found his instructor.

"So you're Joshua's mother. I'm Yaakov." He shook her hand.

Yaakov wasn't an ordained rabbi nor was he Jewish. He was a teacher who found a fascination with Judaism and opened a small school. He seemed very pleased to meet Skylar.

"Your son is a very good student," he told her.

"Thank you," she said. "I am hoping I will be able to hear him read from the Torah."

"That would be wonderful, except it's up to his father," Yaakov replied.

Skylar smiled. "Actually, it's up to the court. And I have a document, which they've updated for me, that states both parents can attend milestone events." She showed him the court order, bearing a September 2001 date she had just picked up from the Norfolk courthouse.

"There is nothing that I would like more, and I know that Joshua would agree with me. However, I have to let you know that John planned to have bodyguards there in case you make an appearance," Yaakov informed her. "He has no qualms in making a scene. He'll have you thrown out. Is that how you want your son to remember his bar mitzvah?"

"No, of course not," she quietly answered.

"Listen, let me talk to John. We can meet for lunch to discuss the options, perhaps on Wednesday? I can go wherever you are." She agreed to meet with Yaakov at a small restaurant across the street from her office.

On Wednesday, Skylar sat across the table from Yaakov in the restaurant. "I'm sorry. John is adamant you do not attend," he told her.

Skylar was heartbroken. "How about my mother? And Alissa, his little sister?"

"I can ask him. In the meantime, would you like to write something? I can read it to Joshua during the ceremony, if John will allow it." They made plans to speak the next night.

When Yaakov called her on Thursday night, he told her, "Here's John's offer. Your mother can go, but your daughter cannot. Did you write something for Joshua? John will have to approve it first. And he offered to give you a videotape of the ceremony."

Two and a half weeks prior to Joshua's Bar Mitzvah, the United States was attacked by terrorists who hijacked and crashed four American passenger planes, killing thousands of people. It made people realize the importance of their own families, knowing they could be eliminated as randomly as all the innocent victims on September 11, 2001. Although the tragedy was fresh on everyone's minds, John heartlessly refused for Skylar to be present at her son's Bar Mitzvah.

Sable bravely attended alone. As she warily walked through the doors, two burly men blocked her way and demanded her invitation. Yaakov ran to them and assured them she was an invited guest and escorted her to a seat. As she waited for the service to begin, Jillian saw Sable. She ran to her and hugged her. Jillian sat at her side and tucked her small hand into Sable's hand. She remained with her grandmother throughout the entire ceremony.

During the bar mitzvah service, Yaakov told Joshua, "I had lunch with your mother the other day." Joshua walked to the back wall, turned his back to the guests, and burst into tears.

John interrupted the ceremony and went to Joshua. He tried to console him quietly. Ten minutes later, Joshua had regained his composure.

"Your mom wrote something for me to read to you today. Would you like to hear it?" Yaakov asked. Joshua nodded and Yaakov began to read.

Skylar's message began with a request that everyone celebrating with Joshua say a prayer for the victims of the recent terrorist attack. She wrote: *"Sometimes life hands us things we don't understand, things that are unfair and things that make us sad."* She wrote it in the hopes that Joshua would interpret her absence as something unfair as well. Skylar copied the well-known text, *Footprints*, about having faith in God during difficult times. It was a piece which always gave her comfort and hope and she wanted Joshua to feel that as well.

After the bar mitzvah ceremony, a luncheon was served in the adjoining room. Ungraciously, John did not include Sable in the celebration so she stood up and left.

Skylar tried to move on from the heartbreaking exclusion at this milestone in her son's life. The fall chill was in the air, and in no time, the winter snow was on the ground heralding in 2002. She had a casual contact with her parole officer, who was unconcerned about her sporadic visits. She continued therapy for post traumatic stress. The only communications from Lance were his monthly support checks. Alissa was an adorable toddler who attended preschool while she was at work. They spent their weekends in Newton with Rob and his children.

Yaakov kept in touch with Skylar to find out the progress of her appeal. He provided a status update on the children. During one of these telephone conversations, Skylar asked, "When am I going to get the videotape of Joshua's Bar Mitzvah?" Yaakov had been avoiding that topic.

"I'm sorry, Skylar, but John said you cannot have a copy of the videotape."

"But that was the deal. I complied, and now he's withholding the tape? Did he tell you why?" Skylar was angry and upset. She *knew* she never could make an honest deal with John.

Yaakov replied, "John said your mother held Jillian hostage during the bar mitzvah."

"What?! Hostage? He's crazy! My mother told me that Jillian sat with her. She didn't force her to stay there! What kind of crap is that?" Skylar was livid at his explanation.

"I know you're upset and disappointed. But you have to learn how to play his game."

Skylar said, "I can't play his game. I am an honest person. He's a liar."

"I know." Yaakov sighed.

Skylar thought of Jillian's tenth birthday, which had just passed. The bleakness of winter was fading as spring arrived and the one year anniversary since Skylar's appeal. She didn't feel the seasons change. She was functioning, but it felt as if she was surrounded by a cloud of grief. The summer brought Alissa's fourth birthday and a month later, Skylar thought of Cary as he turned twelve years old and Joshua, who was now fourteen. She had missed so many years.

The wait for the results of her appeal was interminable. In late October of 2002, Skylar received the long awaited call from her appeal attorney. This time, her screams were from utter delight. The official document was brief and simply stated:

In the case no. 12-A-3456, Commonwealth vs. Skylar Levine,
it is ordered that the following entry be made in the docket: Judgment
reversed. Finding set aside. Judgment for the Defendant.

It was May 1999 when Judge Roteman first ordered supervised visits because Skylar had enrolled the children in their third year of Hebrew school. She had not seen her children for almost three and a half years.

The criminal charge was dismissed and her probation ended. She wanted to file a motion to reinstate her visits with her children, but she felt she would need good legal representation. She needed an attorney who knew about domestic abuse cases. Her therapist provided her with a referral. She knew an attorney who specialized in representing women who were victims of domestic abuse. Skylar contacted attorney Saul Zion. She met with him for several hours, reviewing the history of her abusive relationship with John. Saul agreed to take her case at a reduced rate. He filed a motion to reinstate her visitation with her children. A hearing was scheduled for the middle of January 2003.

For the first time, the onset of the arctic winter air didn't bother Skylar. She was bathed in the glow of anticipating a reunion with her children. It was an especially sweet beginning of 2003 when Rob presented Skylar with a diamond ring and asked her to marry him as they rang in the new year. She agreed to wear his ring and take things slowly. Her first priority was seeing her children. She wanted to find a safer environment for them, hoping they would be visiting soon. She looked in Newton and found a pretty apartment five minutes from Rob's tiny house.

Two weeks later, Rob accompanied Skylar and her attorney, Saul Zion, to the probate court. As they approached the steps, she saw John standing in front of the courthouse. His eyes narrowed when he saw her accompanied by an attorney and a man who had his arm around her waist. He was incensed when he noticed the diamond ring on her left hand.

Upon checking in, they were directed to meet with a family worker prior to going in front of the judge. John and Skylar sat in the office of Lucas Delmonico. Lucas was the court officer who had been there during their custody trial. He was the officer who had commented, "Boy, is he controlling!" to Skylar during the trial. Since the last time she had been in court, Lucas had been taking college classes in order to be promoted to a family worker position. He still expressed compassion toward her. He felt she should absolutely see her children and suggested, "Since it's been a while, you should see the children in a supervised setting, just to get reacquainted, at least the first time. This is what the judge usually orders in cases like this."

Skylar was totally agreeable. John was not.

"I don't agree with that at all! I don't think she should see those kids! She walks in her with her fiancé and thinks she's gonna start seein' those kids? I don't think it's a good idea! I wanna go in front of the judge!"

"John, this has gone on long enough. It's time for Skylar to be reunited with her children." Lucas was firm. "That is going to be my recommendation to the judge."

The judge that day was circuit court judge Meryl Miller. She was a very attractive brunette who traveled from courthouse to courthouse.

She was the only judge who routinely sent men to jail for non-payment of child support. She was tough. When Skylar stood in front of her, she shockingly told her, "I don't know if you should ever see your children."

John smirked. "Too bad," he whispered to Skylar.

Saul told Judge Miller, "My client has done nothing wrong. She was fraudulently charged in a made-up case, and her children have been without a mother for years."

Judge Miller said, "Before I make a decision for visitation, I am appointing a guardian ad litem to evaluate the situation. You will receive the information in the mail."

Although it was a step in the right direction, Skylar was dismayed when she received the court documents. Judge Miller had assigned Julie Ginsler as the guardian ad litem.

Skylar had toughened up considerably over the years. She told Saul, "I am not using that woman. She's biased and unethical. Judge Copeland found her entire GAL report biased and filled with contradictions! I might as well take my money and set it on fire."

"But if you don't use her, you won't see your children," Saul pleaded with her.

"And if I use her, I *still* won't see them, and I'll be out thousands of dollars. She wants a five thousand dollar retainer, for crissakes, Saul!" She adamantly refused to contact Julie. It was a waiting game.

When Julie did not receive a check, she took it upon herself to go to court and asked to be removed from the case. In Skylar's opinion, it was the only time she did something right.

"Saul told me since Julie removed herself from the case, the judge would assign another GAL at the status hearing next week," Skylar told Rob as they cuddled on the couch one evening in March 2003. Her phone rang. "Hello?"

"Hi Skylar, it's Yaakov. I have a message from John for you."

"A message from John?" She sat on guard.

"Yes, he wants to speak to Rob."

Warily, she wondered, *Why does he want to speak to Rob?* She handed Rob the phone. "Here. Talk to Yaakov."

"Hi Yaakov, it's Rob." He leaned in so Skylar could hear what Yaakov was saying.

"John wants to talk to you, just to get to know you. If Skylar plans to see the children and you are in her life, he wants to get to know you." Skylar was shaking her head fervidly. She couldn't believe what he was hearing.

Rob spoke into the receiver, "So, if I talk to John, he'll let her see her children, right?" He paused for a few seconds and then continued, "Well, then I don't see any point in talking to him. But thanks for the call." Rob hung up the phone.

By then, Skylar was pacing the floor. "Oh, my God! He always does this! Why does he need to know about my life?" she wailed.

"Hey - you know he's crazy, and I know he's crazy. Someday, your kids will figure it out as well. Things are moving forward for you. It will happen. Come and sit with me."

Skylar sat down, and he wrapped his arms around her. She felt safe.

Rob attended the status hearing to support Skylar. His ex-wife, Trish, planned to meet him there as well, in order to transfer their divorce file to Norfolk probate from New Hampshire.

Skylar and Trish knew each other from high school. They had a very cordial relationship, even occasionally having coffee together. After Trish completed her business, she walked into the courtroom to give Rob their new docket number. John's eyes narrowed as he saw her talking to Rob and Skylar. He whispered something to Liz and nodded toward Trish.

The Bauers case was called. Saul, Skylar, John, and Liz walked up to Judge Randi Kleinman, who was on the bench that day. She asked for financial statements from both parties. These statements, periodically updated, revealed each parties income and expenses. Incredulously, Skylar read John's financial statement. He claimed he worked for a company called *"SuperKey"* and made a salary of twenty-five thousand dollars a year. She knew he wasn't working for anyone else as she kept abreast of his advertising for Security Safe, with his name still prominently displayed in the telephone directory. Disregarding the financial form as a legal document, John filled in the name of a false company. At the bottom of the form was a line requiring signatures to attest the information given was truthful under the pains and penalties of perjury. Despite that, both John and his attorney, Liz Lewin signed the form on that line.

Judge Kleinman barely glanced at the financial forms. Instead, she ordered that both Skylar and John undergo a comprehensive psychological examination. Liz screamed her objection, but Judge Kleinman was insistent on both parties being tested.

"Objection denied, I am ordering that both parties undergo psychological evaluations."

Liz shrieked, "My client doesn't need testing. Only Skylar should be tested!"

Judge Kleinman replied, "Miss Lewin, I am ordering both parties be tested, because I would like to know about both parents of the Bauers children."

"But John has custody!" Liz protested.

"Just because Mr. Bauers has custody doesn't mean he's psychologically sound. Both parties will be tested." She looked at the other documents. "Now, I see you are in need of a guardian ad litem, so I am going to assign Nancy Greenbaum. After her report, visits can commence at the visitation center. I am going to rule the costs associated with the supervised visits are the mother's responsibility. The fee will be about fifty dollars per visit." She looked at Skylar questioningly.

She nodded, and said, "of course." She was happy to comply.

She was elated as they left the courtroom. "I have a new GAL! I told you it would work!" She whispered gleefully to Saul. As they reached the door, John and Liz exited first. They stopped, and held the door opened for Saul, Skylar, and Rob.

As Trish began to leave the courtroom, John touched her arm. "I saw you talking to Rob and Skylar in the courtroom. How do you know them?" he asked her.

She was a little confused he had stopped her. "I'm Rob's ex-wife."

John smiled broadly. "Well, I'm Skylar's ex-husband. Can you come over here? I have a lot of information to show you about the woman who is spending time with your children." He pulled her into a small alcove.

Liz was waiting with a broad, wolfish grin on her face. "Let me give you my card, in case you need an attorney," she told Trish, pushing a business card into her hand.

"I think you'll be interested in this," John said as he opened a folder. Skylar, Rob, and Saul had walked toward the main staircase. Skylar couldn't believe her eyes when she turned around and saw Trish standing with John and Liz. John was showing Trish a document inside an opened folder.

"Trish! What are you doing?" she yelled.

Liz looked at Skylar and sneered, "Mind your own business!"

Skylar was furious. "This is my business! Trish, why are you talking to him?"

Liz placed her hand on Trish's arm. "You have my card. If you need any legal advice, call me. I can bring her into court to keep her away from your children, if you want."

John interjected, "Take my card." He handed her his business card, where the words Security Safe were printed in bold letters. "Call me. I can help if you have any issues with Skylar being around your children or your ex-husband."

Trish was stunned as she turned and walked down the hall toward Skylar and Rob. She slipped the business cards in her pocket.

Skylar screamed, "Trish! What the hell is wrong with you? Why are you talking to him? You know what he did to me! He always tries to get involved with the people in my life! I can't believe you are that fucking stupid!" She was livid. A court officer approached the group and asked them to take it outside.

Skylar left. Rob looked at Trish and just shook his head. Trish stood there, baffled. As she slowly walked toward the courthouse exit, she began to cry, feeling as if she was the one who did something wrong. When she reached the heavy courthouse door, she pushed it open.

Standing on the steps waiting for her were Liz and John. They approached her.

"Are you okay?" John asked, sounding concerned. "Remember, I have a whole folder of information about Skylar. Call me. I'd be happy to share it with you." He paused. "Why don't you give me your number so I can call you too?" He took a pen from behind his ear.

Trish was confused and upset. "No, I'll call you if I need to."

"C'mon. It'll be okay. I want to call you later and make sure you're all right." He paused, placing his pen on the top of the folder he carried. Trish, uncertain and confused, reluctantly recited her telephone number for him.

"Thanks. I'll be in touch." He flashed a quick smile and then walked away with Liz.

Rob saw them as he drove past the courthouse. Skylar had calmed down, but Rob was incensed Trish had stopped to speak to John.

"It's not her fault, Rob. John is a master manipulator."

She truly liked Trish who was a genuinely nice person that wouldn't hurt a fly. Skylar realized the catalyst of her outburst was caused by John, who was still trying to infiltrate her inner circle of acquaintances. Trish was a vulnerable person and an easy target for him.

Rob's cell phone rang. It was Trish asking to speak to Skylar. He handed her his phone.

"Skylar, I'm sorry, I'm sorry." She sobbed. "He just stopped me." "I understand," said Skylar, soothingly. "And I'm sorry I yelled at you. It is not your fault. John is a manipulator. He can't let go. He will forever be angry I divorced him."

That afternoon, Skylar called the GAL's office and arranged a meeting in early June. Saul accompanied her to the meeting. She wanted to make sure the GAL was accurate in documenting the facts of their conversation, unlike the slanted report Julie Ginsler had submitted. Nancy Greenbaum appeared sympathetic as she listened to her story.

"I need to review this, and then speak with John to assess his information as well. Following that, I'd like to visit your apartment. What if we schedule a visit in mid-August?"

It was a lovely day in August 2003 when Nancy rang the doorbell to Skylar's apartment. As she entered, she saw an apartment which was lovely, sunny, and immaculate, with a crisp blue and white décor. There were cookies baking in the oven, and the smell of the melting chocolate chips permeated the apartment. Skylar invited her to sit on her pastel striped couch in the living room. As they talked, Alissa rested her curly head on her mother's lap.

Nancy acknowledged Alissa's interaction with Skylar and commented, "Someone loves her mommy."

The visit seemed to go very well, but so did her visits with Julie Ginsler. Skylar nervously awaited the final report. She still had to undergo the psychological testing prior to starting her visits so she searched for a clinician. She found someone near the visitation center who accepted medical insurance. Skylar scheduled the tests for early September.

Psychological tests, according to Raymond Lloyd Richmond, Ph.D., author of *A Guide to Psychology and Its Practice*, were administered because it was easier to obtain information from a test instead of a clinical interview. End results were considered more scientifically consistent with standardized tests. The answers were more conclusive to subconscious thought. Furthermore, psychological tests provided clues to any personality disorder, such as the narcissistic personality disorder, borderline personality disorder, histrionic personality disorder, and antisocial personality disorder.

Skylar's results were consistent with a victim who had endured years of abuse. There was a recommendation to continue therapy, if needed. The report did not show her to have any psychological illnesses or personality disorders. John refused to be evaluated.

Nancy Greenbaum wrote her report and submitted it to the court. To her delight, Nancy supported Skylar beginning visits with her children at the supervision center in Brockton.

The final step prior to scheduling a visit was an intake interview at the visitation center. This was routine in order to review the history of each visitation case. Skylar met with the director and related the history of her marriage to John, the control, the abuse, and the reason she was facing supervised visits. She talked about Lance, how their relationship fell apart once he began drinking, and how John began contacting him when he was inebriated. It was very draining reliving the unpleasantness, but it needed to be told.

When her intake interview was completed, the director sat back in her chair and said, "You can begin your visits as soon as there is an opening in the schedule." Skylar practically jumped out of her chair with joy. "Also, I am going to waive the fee for your visits. It's clear you are a victim of domestic abuse, so there will be no cost to you for using our center."

She was thankful to find empathy conveyed because of what she endured. Someone finally believed the horror of her ordeal. Her reunion with her children was forthcoming.

Alissa started her kindergarten in September of 2003. When she was in school, Skylar went to Rob's house to use his washer and dryer. She made a pot of coffee as she waited. Suddenly, there was a knock at the door. Trish had come by to pick up a check Rob had left. Skylar offered her a cup of coffee. Both women sat on the living room couch with their cups.

"Any news about seeing the kids?" Trish asked.

"Not yet. I am hoping it's soon, though."

"I have to tell you something. John keeps calling me. He wants me to talk to the GAL. I can't even answer my phone." Trish frowned.

Skylar gave a ladylike snort. "It's his form of stalking. He wants to infiltrate every aspect of my life. He was angry when Jake ignored him. He got Lance to speak with him only after he started drinking. He already tried to contact Rob. He's crazy, and he's a liar. The last time we were in court, he lied on his financial statement. He said he's working for SuperKey and making only twenty-five thousand dollars a year." She paused to sip her coffee.

"Wait a minute!" Trish sat upright. "That was the day he stopped me and gave me his business card. I still have it here." She pulled out her wallet, opened the zippered compartment, and took out a business card. "Here it is. You can keep the card – I don't need it."

Skylar looked at the card Trish had handed her. Minutes after John had submitted a sworn statement in court claiming he worked for a company called SuperKey, he boldly handed out a glossy, two-sided business card. Printed on the front was:

SECURITY SAFE SERVICE
The Best in Locks, Hardware, Safety & Security
For a FREE estimate or showroom appointment
call JOHN BAUERS

On the back side of the card was a colored photograph of a lovely furnished room. Aligning the walls were glass showcases filled with expensive hardware.

Skylar shook her head. "Thanks for the card." She thought for a minute. "Trish, why don't you talk to the GAL? Just talk to her. Let's just tie up all the loose ends. Then he won't bother you anymore and he'll have no one else to harass. And, he won't be able to do anything else to me."

Skylar spoke sanguinely. But she didn't realize the vital intensity of John's anger. She didn't know as she calmly sipped her coffee, that John was calculating his next plan. He was going to ensure she would never see the children.

Chapter 33

John was enraged after he spoke to guardian ad litem, Nancy Greenbaum, when she told him, "I've recommended Skylar begin her visits with the children." Furiously, he hung up the phone and angrily punched in another number.

"I told you what to tell the GAL! How fuckin' difficult was that?"

"I'm sorry, John. I agreed to speak to Nancy, and I did. In my opinion, Skylar is a good mother to Alissa, and my kids like her too," Trish smoothly replied.

He slammed down the phone as a hot, red haze of anger blinded him excruciatingly. The agonizing pain of defeat tore through his head, and he cried out as a white hot rage gripped his viscera and he sank to the floor. After several minutes, the intensity of the pain lessened and he was able to breathe calmly. He stood up and sat at his desk. He began to review a plan which had been hovering in the back of his mind. He went over every detail in his mind. *It could work,* he thought. He picked up the telephone and called a number.

Maryanne's mother Helga, answered the phone.

"Jak idzie ono, Matka," he said, greeting her in her native Polish. "Yes, Maryanne and I will be there for dinner tomorrow, but I'm wondering if you are busy now. I need to talk to someone. Matka, I am so afraid for Skylar to see my kids! Someone needs to know how dangerous she is!" John's voice dripped feigned sincerity as he asked, "Can I come by to talk?"

Replacing the receiver, he smiled. Smugly he thought, *She's never gonna see those kids.*

Weeks later, on a warm autumn evening in 2003, Skylar received a telephone call from Saul, who flatly stated, "Well, they've halted your visits."

"What!?" Skylar was flabbergasted. "What are you saying?"

"It appears some threatening notes were left at the home of Maryanne's mother, Helga Szalony, in Newton. They've gone to the police, and John is saying you wrote the notes."

She was outraged. "That asshole!" she cried. "This is not the first time he's tried to frame me for something. This is NOT going to happen again!" She hung up the phone.

Maryanne's mother Helga Szalony was a widow who lived in Newton with her sister, Dita Hedwig, who had never married. Both sisters had traveled to the United States from Poland as adults. Helga was a quiet, plain woman. Skylar had met her once at Jillian's ballet class. She had never met Dita.

Assuming a proactive position, Skylar called the Newton police department. She asked to speak to the detective who was handling the case regarding notes left at a home of Mrs. Helga Szalony. She was connected to Detective Thomas.

In a cordial tone, she began, "Hello, my name is Skylar Levine, and I am calling about the notes left at the Szalony residence."

Detective Thomas replied. "Skylar! I'm glad you called. I was going to call you. I'd like to talk with you. Can you come to the Newton Police station tomorrow, around nine?"

"That's fine," Skylar agreed.

Detective Thomas surprised her with his next statement. "Your ex-husband feels your fiancé Rob has a part in this as well. According to his work schedule, your ex-husband feels that he could have been the one dropping the notes."

How well he planned this, thought Skylar.

"How would he know Rob's work schedule?"

"Well, he didn't tell me that..." He paused. "Do you think Rob will talk to us?"

"I am certain that will not be a problem," she stated. "I'll tell him to call you, and I will see you at nine tomorrow." After she hung up the phone, she dialed Trish's number.

When Trish answered the phone, she said, "John already called. He told me about the notes. He said someone who looks like Rob was seen leaving the notes and I should be concerned and that both you and Rob are dangerous." She paused. "Let's meet for coffee tomorrow at the Bagel Place at eleven. I'll call John on my cell phone, and you can listen in."

After Skylar hung up with Trish, she immediately called Rob. "Saul called to tell me my visits are halted because of threatening notes left at Maryanne's mother's house." She repeated the conversations she had with Detective Thomas and Trish.

"He said John knew my schedule? Isn't that kind of odd?" Rob sounded surprised. "I mean, think about it. This house isn't one you'd happen to drive by. This neighborhood is pretty secluded, and I am at the end of the road. He must have been watching the house."

"Rob, I *told* you that John will stop at nothing. He has a pattern of stalking me and a history of making up stuff to harass me. He'll never stop." She felt helpless. She remembered his promise of years earlier, to harass her for the rest of her life...until she died. And she was still dodging his bullets.

Rob could hear the desolation in her voice. "Babe, it'll be okay. You're innocent. I'm innocent. Be strong. I can be at the police station around ten-thirty. Don't forget to call me when you are done so I'll know you're okay." He hung up the phone.

Skylar drove to the Newton police department the following morning after bringing Alissa to her kindergarten class. She was brought into a small interrogation room and read her Miranda rights which she impatiently waived.

She immediately asked, "Can I see the notes?"

Detective Thomas produced the notes, wrapped in plastic and a photograph of the car with block letters on the roof. Then he asked her for a handwriting sample.

Skylar gestured to her purse and said, "Help yourself." She read the notes and commented, "It seems like the writer does not have English as their first language."

The first note was in an envelope addressed as: *To My Love, My Ex*

The contents were confusing, as the note read: *I will take my kids, Out of sometime, This and kill them and me. Someone will do it for me. Love your Ex Wife*

The second note was in an envelope, which was simply addressed: *To My Ex.*

The contents of the second notes had a definite foreign flavor, as it read: *The letter that I send to your Mother-in-law, I am very sorry to do that. You do understand that I want to see only Joshua not the other ones. I want to have Joshua live with me and my daughter. I only want him. Love, Ex*

Before leaving, Skylar complied with the police's request and was fingerprinted.

She was unaware of the series of incident reports that had already been filed with the Newton police department in the fall of 2003. The first incident report had been filed September 28. The type of offense was listed as *Destruction of property over two-hundred fifty dollars, Malicious.* The report stated that both Helga Szalony and Dita Hedwig heard a loud banging noise from the back door. They found a note written on the door in black marker which stated: *You will be killed on Thursday night.*

Another incident report was filed on September 30. The offense was listed as *Motor vehicle, malicious damage to.* John Bauers made the complaint at the police headquarters in Newton. He reported a message written in black marker - *I want to see my kids or everyone will die* - was written on the roof of his old Pontiac Grand Am, which was parked at the home of his mother-in-law, Helga Szalony. John accused his ex-wife, Skylar Levine of writing the message.

A third report was filed on October 2 where Dita provided a description of a man who was dropping off an envelope in the back of the house. She claimed to see this man at four-fifteen AM, holding a flashlight. He ran off when he saw her, but she was able to give an accurate, detailed description of a *stocky, white male, balding.* In the report,

John Bauers suggested that Skylar's boyfriend Rob fit the description.

Unfortunately, Skylar was not privy to the reports or the last comment, which alone was telling, because neither Dita nor Helga had ever set eyes on Rob. But John had.

Following her interrogation by the detective, Skylar got into her car and drove to the Bagel Place. Trish was already sitting there with a cup of coffee.

"How'd it go?" Trish asked.

"I'm innocent, so I guess it went well." Skylar shrugged.

"Let's just see what John says when I call him." Trish began dialing John's number. "Voice mail," she informed Skylar. She left a message. "John, it's Trish. Call me." She hung up the phone. "He's not there, but he'll call me right back," she said sounding confident. Before she could take her first sip of coffee, Trish's phone rang. She looked at it. "It's him." She answered the phone and motioned to Skylar to move closer so she could listen in as well.

"Well, I have some news," John began. "Skylar and Joshua have been communicating all along. It was their idea to leave the notes. Joshua hates Maryanne, and Maryanne hates Joshua. He wants to live with Skylar." Skylar raised an eyebrow after hearing John reveal that piece of information. "Oh, and your ex-husband is involved as well."

"Well, I haven't talked to Rob or Skylar," said Trish.

"Skylar's unstable, so just keep me posted if you learn anything," he replied cheerily.

"Okay." Trish closed her cell phone and turned to Skylar. "Wow! He's nuts! Who knows how this will all play out, but if you need me to go to court and testify about this, I will."

In the morning, Detective Thomas called Skylar. "Maryanne's aunt, Dita Hedwig, provided a handwriting sample. It matched the writing on all the notes. It looks like you and Rob are exonerated."

Why on earth did Maryanne's aunt write these notes? Skylar wondered. The concluding police report documented three additional notes found at the Szalony house on October 3 at five forty-five AM, October 4 at midnight and midday on October 6. A fourth note was found on October 7, six o'clock AM. However, the report stated there was no evidence pointing to an outside party as writer of the notes, so they began looking in the home, specifically to Dita. When the police suggested that polygraph tests were going to be administered, Dita appeared very nervous. After seeing a sample of her handwriting, they were quite certain she was the responsible party.

At two o'clock in the afternoon of October 9, John received a phone call from Detective Thomas. "We brought the handwriting samples to a handwriting expert. Dita's writing matches the notes. We are going to inform her this afternoon."

At four o'clock, Detective Thomas and a police officer went to the house in Newton but John intercepted them at the door of the house. "Dita admitted responsibility to us, but she's way too upset to speak. Can you come back tomorrow?" The officers left the house.

One hour later, there was a 911 emergency call requesting an ambulance at the Szalony residence. Dita was found semi-conscious from an apparent overdose and she was taken to the hospital.

The following day, John contacted Detective Thomas. "Dita is still at the hospital in the psychiatric unit. She admitted to me she wrote the notes to make it appear as though Skylar was a bad person, intending to do serious harm to others. She thought it would help the custody case to show that Skylar was a dangerous person."

Neither Detective Thomas nor any member of the Newton police force had ever questioned Dita directly.

Detective Thomas related the story to Skylar, who replied, "*John* told you this. I bet if you talked directly to Dita, you'd find that John was the mastermind and manipulated her into writing these notes." But when a police investigation is concluded, it remained closed. Again, John had beaten the system and the police, but he didn't beat her.

Skylar documented everything John had done which constituted criminal harassment, beginning with the keying of his own vehicle in May of 1996. She came up with *fourteen* separate acts which she thought could be constituted as criminal harassment.

Chapter 265: Section 43A. Criminal harassment; punishment

(a) Whoever willfully and maliciously engages in a knowing pattern of conduct or series of acts over a period of time directed at a specific person...and shall be punished by imprisonment in a house of correction for not more than two and one-half years or by a fine of not more than $1,000 or by both such fine and imprisonment.

Rob had a friend who was a top criminal attorney in Boston. He suggested, "Why don't you just talk to him? This guy needs to be stopped."

Skylar agreed. She brought the list to the attorney, who read it with interest.

"Absolutely! These instances would be undeniably constituted as criminal harassment. I would say this is worthy of the two and one-half years incarceration. However," he cautioned her, "if he manages to beat the charge, his retaliation could be dangerous."

Skylar simply couldn't bear to go through another trial, especially if there was no guarantee John would stop the harassment she had endured for years. Her only focus was on her children. The visitation center had scheduled a visit with her children the moment she had been absolved of the situation with the notes.

The day of the visit was in mid-October 2003. Skylar arrived at the visitation center with a myriad of feelings: nervous, anxious and happy. When the children finally entered the room, Skylar began crying. It had been almost four and a half years since she had last seen them. They were no longer young children. Joshua was fifteen years old. He was handsome, albeit slightly chubby. Cary was thirteen and small. His blonde hair had darkened, but his eyes were still bright blue. Jillian was almost twelve and lovely. Her hair was long again. She was taller than Cary and very slim.

Skylar asked, "Can I have a hug?" Cary and Jillian hugged Skylar. Joshua hung back for a moment, and then tightly hugged his mother.

They sat at a large table and Jillian held Skylar's hand. They related how excited they were when they learned of their reunion with their mother. They talked about school, asked about Alissa, and shared snow skiing stories. It was a bittersweet reunion as Skylar was reminded of the years she had lost for no reason of her own.

At subsequent visits, the children began warming up. Alissa was allowed to visit as well. Skylar would bring homemade dinners to the center. The staff at the Visitation Center would announce, "Here's the perfect mom," when she would appear bearing delicious meals. There were never problems with the visits. The staff allowed her to have full access to the facility instead of being escorted like the other visitors. They did not understand why she had supervised visits. Originally scheduled for a brief reintroduction, the visits lasted for over a year. To get unsupervised visits, Skylar knew she would have to take a more aggressive approach. She got copies of the visitation notes taken at each visit as supporting evidence. Because there was no reason for supervised visits, all her reports contained only the dates of the visit and a clean white sheet. There was no documentation of inappropriate behaviors.

Because the case had dragged on, it had become a financial hardship for Skylar and she could no longer afford to retain her attorney. Bravely, she went back to court in October of 2004 without representation, but she was armed with her perfect reports and a supportive letter from her therapist. She submitted a motion to Judge Kleinman requesting unsupervised visits.

At the hearing, Liz loudly objected and screamed that she wanted yet *another* psychological evaluation and *another* guardian ad litem.

Skylar was fed up. She stood up and said, "Your Honor, I have been abused by this man and by Liz Lewin manipulating this court. I love my children, and I have done nothing wrong. I had an evaluation which stated I have no psychological issues despite all the abuse I have endured. Mr. Bauers won't submit to a psychological evaluation. I suspect he's afraid of the results. I also have a letter from my former therapist which states I was seen due to post-traumatic stress disorder due to the years of abuse from John." She offered the letter.

"I'm not allowing that to be admitted," muttered Liz.

Skylar shook her head and boldly continued to address the judge.

"Fine, then I will let you know that in this letter, my former therapist says I do not need therapy. I refuse to accept more abuse. I will not be evaluated again, and I am not talking to another guardian ad litem."

Judge Kleinman stopped her. "Wait." She then addressed Liz. "Miss Lewin, I am going to allow four hours of unsupervised visits with the children. We can review this in three months. Also, there are to be no changes in the schedule without prior approval from me."

Skylar was ecstatic. She had stood up in court without an attorney. On her own, she fearlessly faced her abuser. She told the judge what she would accept and what was unacceptable. And amazingly, the judge had listened to her!

It was a joy being able to see the children and go wherever they wanted. Skylar planned activities and events. The visits were going well, and the bonds were being renewed. All her efforts were devoted to her children. As a result, she began to drift away from Rob. She realized she wasn't ready to make a commitment to anyone else. She needed to only focus on her family. She began looking for an apartment in Natick so she would be closer to the children.

In early December 2004, Joshua told her, "Liz said she could go into court and change our schedule so we can go skiing with our dad on the weekend."

"Sweetie, if you want to go skiing, I understand. But the judge wants your father and I to go into court at the same time so she'll know we both agree," Skylar explained.

However, Liz insisted Skylar was not needed in court. But she didn't trust Liz and knew that making an agreement with Liz was like making a bargain with the devil. Any deal made outside of court was Liz's ploy. Skylar imagined if she stopped seeing the children on the weekends, Liz would bring her to court on contempt. She could picture Liz screaming, "She doesn't want to see the kids on weekends!" Skylar felt stuck between a rock and a hard place, but then again, so was Liz Lewin. The question was, who would break first?

Liz made the first move. She surprised Skylar one evening in

January 2005 with a telephone call. She said, "The kids are going skiing and are not going to see you this weekend."

Skylar replied, "You cannot make that unilateral decision. That's a direct contempt of a court order." She had learned a lot since her first experience in the legal system.

Liz meanly answered, "They won't like to miss a weekend skiing. They'll blame you. But frankly, I'd rather see you fighting with your children." She tried to frighten Skylar with her comment, but she read her wrong. That was just what Skylar was waiting for, because it enabled her to file a contempt of court motion for non-compliance with a court order.

On the day of the hearing, Liz approached Skylar in the empty courtroom and asked, "What are you doing?" referring to the contempt motion Skylar had filed.

Skylar simply stated, "You gave me no choice. You told me yourself you'd rather see me fighting with my children."

Liz looked her directly in the eye. "No, I didn't," she impudently responded.

Showing no fear, Skylar looked straight back at Liz and innocently asked, "Are you on medication?"

Liz turned and walked away.

When the parties were assembled in front of Judge Kleinman, she addressed Skylar. "Mrs. Levine, why are we here today?"

Skylar stated, "We are seeking a change in the schedule so the children can ski on weekends. I am complying with your order that all changes be brought into court."

Judge Kleinman thanked her for adhering to her court order. "I will allow the change in the schedule so the children can ski, but after ski season, it will revert back so the children can spend weekends with their mother. I will set up a review date for November 2005."

The months flew by. Before long, it was a week before Thanksgiving. Skylar went to court for the review. She sat in the empty courtroom, waiting.

"Hi." She looked up to see John standing there. "So, I guess it's going well." He said and sat down near Skylar.

"Of course it's going well," she replied. "There was never any reason for any of this."

"Well, that's in the past," said John, dismissing the years of harassment, abuse, and punishment with a few brief words. "I think it's time we forgive and forget. You can see the kids whenever you want. That's what we are bringing into court today."

Skylar was consumed by emotions. She was stunned, wary, suspicious, pleased, and relieved all at once. She was also speechless. *Can this really be over?* she thought.

When Judge Kleinman was on the bench, she called their case.

Liz stood up. "Your honor, we don't want to have to come back to court. We want to let Skylar see the children whenever she wants. We want to drop the entire case. John will agree to vacate the restraining order against Skylar if she vacates the one she has against him." Liz finished and looked at Skylar. "It makes sense to vacate the restraining order, that way you can go to the house and pick the kids up. You'll be able to go to the same events together."

Seeing Skylar's hesitation, Judge Kleinman reassured her, "If you vacate the restraining order, you can always file another one."

Skylar didn't want to ever go back to court so she agreed to vacate the restraining order.

Judge Kleinman stated, "We will close this case." She asked everyone to wait until the documents to vacate the restraining orders were prepared for their signatures.

As they waited, John approached Skylar. "Well, this is good. This is good." She nodded. He continued talking. "Skylar, can we be friends? Can we just forgive and forget and start from this point on? It will be good for the kids to see we can get along."

She could not believe what he asked. "I don't think I can ever forget everything you did to me. And how do you expect me to forgive you?"

"I'm just asking if we can move on from today," he said, emphasizing with his hand.

Skylar sighed. She would never forget, and she could never forgive, but she put her feelings aside for the sake of the children and said, "I will agree to move on from today."

The court clerk brought the papers out to sign. John and Skylar signed their respective documents.

"Well, that's it," John stated. "Skylar, have a Happy Thanksgiving." He offered his hand to her.

She uncomfortably extended her hand. John barely gripped her fingertips, and the handshake was awkward. She removed her hand and said, "Bye," And then walked out of the courthouse for what she hoped was the last time.

As she approached her car in the parking lot, she heard a ringing sound coming from her cell phone she had left in the car, indicating she had a message. She picked up phone to retrieve the message on her voicemail. She heard the excited message from her friend Lindsay.

"Skylar, you have to call me right away! Boy, do I have some gossip for you!"

She smiled. As a hairstylist, Lindsay was privy to all the gossip in town. She wondered what new tidbit she wanted to share.

Skylar called her. "Hey, it's me."

"Oh, my God! You will never believe what I found out! John is leaving Maryanne. He has another girlfriend. She lives in Natick with her kids."

"What?!" Skylar was confused. "I just saw him in court. How do you know all this?"

"This woman came in to get her hair done. She's married to Maryanne's brother. She started telling me about her sister-in-law's husband who went home one night and said, 'I guess it's time for me to move on.' She started telling me Maryanne was devastated and stopped eating and cries all the time. I didn't put two and two together until she mentioned the names."

"Did you tell her you were my friend?" asked Skylar.

"Well, I was going to mention it and tell her that John was not a nice person, but then my boyfriend walked in. She was done, so she paid and left."

"I'm glad you didn't say anything," said Skylar. "I don't want John knowing that I heard about his situation. Don't say anything if she comes back in."

Lindsay laughed. "She's not coming back in. She thinks I'm too expensive!"

Skylar laughed too. "Thanks for the information, but I'm not really surprised." After she hung up the phone, she thought, *A leopard really doesn't change its spots.* She knew there had to have been a reason for his change of heart regarding her visits with the children. He didn't want the court to know he was leaving Maryanne. He wanted the court to still believe he was a responsible man in a stable home.

Skylar began spending as much time with the children as possible. She learned they had not been for physicals in years. They hadn't been to the dentist. She set up doctors' visits as well as the dental visits. When the children's teeth were examined, Cary had seven cavities and Jillian was badly in need of braces. When Skylar took her to the orthodontist she learned Jillian had severe and complicated issues that needed to be addressed immediately by an oral surgeon. Skylar managed to rectify almost everything that had been neglected for years.

She also began to tie up the loose ends her life. She and Lance began to move toward finalizing their divorce. At a pre-trial hearing in early 2006, Lance approached her.

Skylar, will you talk to me? I just want to apologize for everything I did. I am really sorry, and I hope you can forgive me."

"Lance, I only want to know one thing. Whose idea was it about the hit man?"

"John had the original idea, and Norman was willing to come on board for a price." Lance explained, "I was drunk. I was drinking all the time and John was relentless. He told me if you were convicted, I would never have to pay child support. He said he would show me how to get custody of Alissa. He told me how easy it was and how I could punish you by taking Alissa. I never wanted to do that to you. Never. That was not my plan. I kept hoping I could stop it, but he kept badgering me. He called me night and day. After the trial, Norman was controlling the rest of my life. If I tried to stop drinking, he would appear with a bottle of vodka. He took everything I had and then wanted more. One day, I just walked out. I left everything with Norman. I had to lay low. That's why I haven't seen Alissa. Please forgive me."

Skylar nodded. "I kind of figured John had a lot to do with it. He's tried to set me up over and over. This has been going on for years."

"Just stay away from that guy. He's bad news. How's Alissa?"

"Well, actually, I have something." Skylar dug into her purse and produced some photographs of Alissa. She handed them to Lance.

He studied them. "I knew she'd be beautiful. She looks just like you. Maybe someday I could see her. When I'm ready, I mean." He looked sad. He had aged. He was grey and bloated from the alcohol. The earring in his ear was missing and his ponytail was gone. The sparkle he used to have in his eye had died, leaving his gaze dull and vacant. Skylar felt sad, as she remembered the vibrant man he once was and how many gifts he had been given that he disregarded.

At the final divorce hearing in April 2006, Skylar requested sole physical and sole legal custody of Alissa. Lance immediately signed the document. They were in front of the judge for minutes and she granted their divorce.

During the hearing, Lance cried and apologized again. He told her, "You know I still care about you."

Skylar simply said, "I know."

After the divorce, Lance moved to Florida, but he kept in contact with Skylar with telephone calls every two weeks. Although sporadic, he maintained Alissa's child support. Like Jillian, she had complicated orthodontic problems and Lance paid his portion to begin her treatment. During his frequent calls to Skylar, he often expressed his desire to talk to Alissa, but he wasn't quite ready to face questions posed by his seven and a half year old daughter. For Lance, they would be the hardest questions he would ever have to answer.

Chapter 34

Days after the divorce, Skylar had moved into a large apartment in Natick. Alissa was in private school, so she remained in the same school. Skylar hoped that living in the same town would promote a closer bond with all of her children. Once she was settled, it was simple to see that the move was a good decision. The apartment had three spacious bedrooms, so all the children could sleep there. It was a perfect place for everyone to gather with its high ceilings, tall windows, brightly colored walls and close proximity to Natick Center.

One Saturday night, Skylar suddenly found she was alone. All of the children were involved in their own activities. Joshua was seventeen and out with friends. Cary was fifteen and with his friends as well. Jillian was fourteen and spending the evening with her best friend. Even Alissa was at a second grade slumber party.

I should go out, she thought. Although the idea of relaxing in front of the television was appealing, she chose to make the effort and go out for the evening. She made a few calls and was able to make impromptu plans to go out dancing with several friends. She showered and got ready, putting on black slacks and a lacy blouse. She picked up her purse and keys and left her apartment.

Standing at the bar in the nightclub, she noticed a man watching her. He raised a drink to her, and she smiled. The bartender approached and placed Skylar's drink in front of her on the bar. She juggled her purse and jacket and paid the bartender.

She turned to her friend, "I'm going to put my jacket in the coat room. I'll be right back." She walked quickly to the coat room.

As she put her coat check in her purse, she heard a man's voice ask, "You're not leaving, are you?" She turned around and saw the man who had saluted her with his drink standing there. "Let me buy you a drink," he suggested.

"I left one on the bar," she gestured in that direction.

"Let me buy you another one. I don't want you getting away from me," he smiled.

Skylar allowed him to guide her to a small table and ordered a drink for her. He told her his name was Antonio. He was dark and handsome and very Italian. He was raised by traditional Italian parents and had a close family. The conversation flowed. He was six years older. When he mentioned he was divorced and had four children, they laughed over the coincidence. He was on the same page as Skylar, looking for a peaceful relationship.

"Can I take you out for dinner?" Antonio asked. She agreed.

They began dating in April and were deeply in love by June. Antonio adored Skylar and would call her every day as soon as he returned home from his sales job. In July, he took her to meet his family.

He told her. "I love you so much. I want to meet your children."

One afternoon, she arranged a time for the children to meet Antonio at her apartment.

When he left, Joshua said, "I like him. He's smart."

Cary stated, "He's a good guy."

"He's funny," giggled Jillian.

And Alissa declared, "You should marry him, Mom!"

The children told John about Antonio. When Skylar moved to Natick, John remained very cordial to her, approaching her at town events and chatting politely. He would call her to discuss the children. At a fall fair in Natick Center, he pleasantly greeted Skylar and Antonio, offering a friendly handshake to Antonio. It was almost as if he had moved on.

Almost.

Antonio knew he wanted to marry Skylar. They spent hours talking about their future. Although he worked in Rhode Island, he chose to purchase a house with Skylar in Natick so she could remain in the same town as her children. He just wanted to make her happy.

On a cold December day, Jillian and Alissa cuddled up in front of the fireplace in their new house and watched a movie. Antonio announced he was taking Skylar for a drive. They drove to the ocean and walked out on the rocks. The day was sunny but windy and the ocean was dark with plentiful whitecaps. By the fierce ocean, he got down on one knee and formally asked her to marry him. He presented her with an exquisite platinum and flawless diamond engagement ring.

Upon returning home, Skylar's girls jumped for joy and admired her ring.

"Oh, Mom, it's so beautiful!" exclaimed Jillian. She hugged Skylar and Antonio.

Once John learned that Skylar was engaged, his friendly demeanor began to cool and he was less communicative. She would catch him looking at her with an angry scowl on his face. He became even colder the day they dropped the children off in their new Mercedes. John's face changed when he saw the car, and he didn't even greet Antonio as he usually did. It felt like a kick in his guy when John saw Skylar seated in the luxurious car. He glared at them and stared at the car with venomous fury in his eyes.

John bore a similar facial expression in 1988 as he sat on the beach at the lake and watched the competition ski boats speed pass. His envy consumed him that day so acutely that he refused to talk. He *had* to have a ski boat. He was *nothing*, until he had his own boat.

Expert on narcissism, Sam Vaknin states that, *"The narcissistic personality disordered individuals are full of negative emotions, with hatred and pathological envy. They are constantly seething with rage and jealousy."*

But for John, it was more than envy of a car. It isn't odd for a man to feel jealous when he sees a former love with someone else. A gamut of emotions can be dredged up; insecurity, sadness or anger. These feelings usually fade in time as the man moves on. But with a malignant sociopath, those emotions remain raw. For John, seeing Skylar flourishing, particularly incensed him even though it was a decade after their divorce.

The beginning of 2007 was spent on planning their June wedding. On the day of the nuptials, the purple hued rays of the setting sun made a stunning background. The music played, *some people wait a lifetime, for a moment like this,* as Skylar walked down the aisle in a cream colored beaded gown, escorted by Joshua. At eighteen, her son towered over her, but their resemblance was undeniable. Antonio watched Skylar approach with tears of happiness in his eyes. The wedding was beautiful and full of love especially since all the children participated in the ceremony. As they were pronounced husband and wife, the music sounded Mozart's *"Eine Kleine Natchmusik"* in triumphant joy.

The party after the wedding ceremony was perfect. An appetizing array of food was served and the music was energetic. The lively festivities were enhanced with the arrival of Joshua's high school friends whom he invited to join the celebration. The vivacious group of teenagers brought the merriment up a few more notches and kept the dance floor lively.

At the end of the evening, Skylar and Antonio drove away to an elegant hotel where they had reserved a suite for their wedding night. It was the perfect start to their life together. In the morning, they went out for brunch and then returned home to open their wedding gifts.

When they arrived home, they saw the dining room table strewn with envelopes and several boxes.

"Let's open the boxes first," suggested Skylar. The boxes were elegantly wrapped except for one, which was wrapped in wrinkled gold paper. She opened that box first. Inside, wrapped in tissue paper, she found a small, white, plastic shovel, and a note written on a post-it. The note read: *Skylar, I know it's not GOLD but YOU get the idea!!!* Skylar recognized John's block printing on the note. She remembered how he had called her a gold digger for marrying Lance, and now he was calling her a gold digger for marrying Antonio. He had promised to harass her for the rest of her life....until she died. He never forgot his promise.

Although John was determined to forever hold onto his anger, Skylar's relationship with Lance continued to be very amicable. Despite his recent move to Florida, he kept in touch with friendly phone calls. He cared deeply for her and wanted the best for her. Skylar was concerned about him, so she did not tell him she had married Antonio. He was fragile and she didn't want him to feel another man had become a father figure to Alissa. Lance always asked about Alissa and wanted to see her when he returned to Boston. Most of his conversations were about their daughter and how he hoped he could prepare himself to speak with her on the telephone.

He finally felt ready to talk to Alissa on the Jewish New Year in September 2007. Skylar had made a holiday dinner for the children, so they were all there. Lance called and Skylar handed Alissa the telephone.

"Hello?" said Alissa in her sweet nine-year-old voice.

"Is this Alissa?" Lance asked.

"Yes."

"Alissa, my name is Lance, and I am your father."

"Oh." Although she knew who Lance was, it was a little overwhelming for her, and she didn't know what to say.

"I am sorry I haven't seen you in all these years. I've been sick. But I want to see you soon."

"That's okay. When can I see you?" asked Alissa

"As soon as I can come to Boston. I am living in Florida. Do you know where that is?"

"Yes. I was there at Disney. Do you live there?" Alissa held the phone with wide eyes, thinking about Lance living in the same place as Disney!

"Not right there," Lance chuckled, "but not too far away. You're a very smart girl, just like your mother and just like me."

"Yes, Mom told me you were really smart."

"Did she tell you that I play the piano? Has she taught you how to play piano?"

"Yes, but we don't have a real piano yet, just a keyboard," stated Alissa.

"We'll have to do something about that. I really am looking forward to seeing you."

"Me too. Bye." Alissa handed the phone to Skylar.

Lance asked to speak to Joshua, Cary and Jillian. As they spoke to Lance, Skylar asked Alissa what she was thinking about.

"My father lives in the same place as Disney!" she declared.

Jillian, still giggling after speaking to Lance, handed Skylar the phone.

"You know, I really miss them. And Alissa sounds adorable. I can't wait to see her. Skylar, you are a great mother. I wish things could have been different. You know I still care about you," Lance told her sincerely.

"I know," she said.

In late October 2007, Lance called Skylar. His speak was slurred as he told her, "You know, I am playing the piano all the time. I play until all hours in the morning. Do you know what that is like, to be playing all night long? All the way until the morning."

Delicately, Skylar asked, "Are you okay?"

"Why shouldn't I be okay?" A hint of anger came into his voice, a clear indicator to her that he had been drinking.

"I meant you sound kind of tired." She skillfully deflected his drunken anger.

"Didn't you hear me say I had been playing piano all night? I am just so tired." He paused. "Can you send me a picture of Alissa? Norman took all my pictures and my wallet too. I had to walk out of the place and leave everything just to get away from him." Lance was silent.

"Lance? Are you there?"

"Yes, I am still here. Well, I'm so tired from playing piano all night. Maybe I will try to sleep for a little. Can I call you later? I mean, not today. Another day, I will call you."

A strong premonition made her feel she needed to say something warm to Lance. From her heart, before she hung up, Skylar softly said, "You take care of yourself, okay?" She didn't know why she told him that but she felt the need. She suddenly felt very sad.

Lance usually called at least every other week. In November, she realized she hadn't spoken to him for over two weeks. She assumed he would call any day. When the phone rang on November 11th, Skylar was shaken to hear Lance's daughter, Liliana crying. "My father died."

"Oh, no!" cried Skylar.

Her former husband was found on the floor of his tiny hotel room, dead from an accidental overdose. Skylar cried for Alissa, who would never meet her father, and she cried for Lance, remembering the talented, funny, and brilliant person he had presented to her when she first met him. She knew he was now at peace.

The following day, she happened to see John at the grocery store. She approached him and told him Lance had died.

He responded, "Oh, yeah?" as if he was told something benign. His blue eyes were like ice and his face was expressionless. His reaction chilled her to the bone. That was when it hit her with absolute clarity: John was sick. He was an unfeeling machine and it terrified her. She then had no doubt that he was capable of anything. Frightened, she abruptly left market, vowing to cut all contact with him.

But Lance's death prompted deep emotions within his children. Michael, Liliana, and Lyle were hit with the realization that a piece of their father remained in their youngest sister, Alissa. When Lance and Skylar had separated, his children were afraid to maintain their relationship, as their father was spinning rapidly out of control, faster than they had ever experienced. They became his caretaker, solely focusing on him and taking care not to discuss anything which would cause him to increase his alcohol consumption, especially his baby daughter, who he did not see. With Lance at peace, his children immediately sought to meet their sister and embrace her into the family. They arranged to send his piano to Alissa. They lavished their affection on her and renewed their relationships with Joshua, Cary, and Jillian.

Skylar sat with Antonio in front of the fireplace, one chilly evening in late November. She was the recipient of so much love from all the children and her new husband. As George Herbert, an English clergyman and metaphysical poet wrote: *Living well is the best revenge.* Skylar was indeed living well, as she had attained true love, happiness, and peace. Her heart was warmed, not just by the fire and Antonio's arms around her. "I think I have finally found peace," she murmured to him. "I feel so safe." The love she felt was an impenetrable shield against John. He would never harm her again. His vow to harass her, until she died, was nothing but a narcissist's empty promise.

Afterword

Skylar's happiness angered John relentlessly. He was enraged when she remarried.

How could she be happy? Women love me! he thought. It was the ultimate in humiliation within John's narcissistic soul for people to know the mother of his children had rejected him and happily moved on. Seething, he went on a campaign to smear her name and began telling everyone who may have ever known Skylar that she was an unfit mother.

The absence of John was inconsequential to Skylar. However, Maryanne was devastated when he left her and refused to accept it. "I will never divorce your father!" she declared and maintained her grasp, like a drowning person, holding onto the Bauers children as if they were the life raft that would bring John back. She never outgrew her solitary and friendless existence of her childhood, so she willfully remained a prominent figure in their lives.

Dr. Linda Martinez-Lewi, author of the book *Freeing Yourself from the Narcissist in Your Life*, states: *"Leaving a spouse in a state of psychological chaos is of no consequence to them. They have no shame or regret."*

Maryanne shamelessly relished any bit of attention from John, and yielded to his wishes. She declared, "We are husband and wife but live in different places," as justification for her compliance. She couldn't accept that he used her as his pliable pawn. Her lack of self-esteem allowed her to remain the willing victim of his manipulation. Realizing the depth of Maryanne's devotion, John knew she would still serve as a useful accomplice to hurt Skylar.

"I want you to plan a Sweet Sixteen party for Jillian. I'll pay for it. You figure out the details," he told Maryanne one afternoon in November 2007. "Skylar will be pissed off if she thinks you're makin' a party."

That evening, he told Jillian, "I talked to Maryanne, and she wants to make a Sweet Sixteen party for you. Isn't that nice of her?"
Jillian squealed with delight. "Oh, thanks so much! I have to call Mom and tell her!"

"Hold on. What are you thinking, Jillian? You cannot invite your mother to your party. I am paying for it. Maryanne is going to be there, and I don't want any drama."

She protested, "But Dad, Mom doesn't fight with Maryanne. I want her at my party."

John retorted, "Jillian, you heard me. If you invite her, I will cancel the party!"

She called Skylar from the privacy of her room and sadly whispered, "My Dad told Maryanne to plan a Sweet Sixteen party, but he said I can't invite you." Jillian held back a sob.

"Oh, honey. I'll call him and see what I can do." Skylar's heart ached for her daughter.

Skylar tried one last time to reason with John. She telephoned him and asked, "John, what is going on? Why are you telling Jillian I can't go to her party?"

"Skylar, you *could* go, if you just admitted you still want me." Skylar gasped loudly in disbelief of what she was hearing. "You don't love Antonio 'cuz you never got over me."

She was flabbergasted. "John, you're crazy." She didn't know what else to say.

"No one else wanted to leave me! Maryanne still loves me very much. Jennifer still calls me. I have a girlfriend and could have lots more!" His voice rose to a hysterical shout. "I think *you're the one* who's crazy Skylar. You'll never get over me! Never! You bitch! You fuckin'…"

But Skylar had hung up the phone. She needed her life free of

John. She would miss Jillian's Sweet Sixteen party just the way she missed Joshua's bar mitzvah. Jillian and Cary never had a bat or bar mitzvah because John ignored all religious education and milestones after Joshua's bar mitzvah. Skylar was heartbroken anticipating future events she was certain to miss. John's anger toward her was boundless, narrow in scope, without merit and without reason.

Antonio comforted her, "There's something wrong with John." He put his arms around her and she rested her head on his shoulder. "Listen, my sister can watch Alissa on the night of the party. I'll take you out for dinner to get your mind off it."

On the night of Jillian's party, they drove to a quaint restaurant in Sturbridge. They sat in front of a stone fireplace and enjoyed a lovely meal.

"Honey, you have to realize John is doing this to hurt you. Your kids will come around, but it may not be for a while. I never did anything like this to my ex. I even paid her mortgage so my kids could stay in the house. It was hard for me, but this is what a man does, Skylar. He takes care of his children."

She knew he was right. He treated Alissa as if she were his own daughter. Skylar felt blessed.

John refused to be denied. After creating a sizable crack in Skylar's bond with Jillian, he began chipping away at her relationship with Joshua. As the first born, Joshua had a special connection with his mother, from their strong physical resemblance to their shared sense of humor. Since childhood, Joshua admitted Skylar was his only dependable parent. To destroy his commitment to his mother, John methodically forged a campaign to generate profound reservations about Skylar.

"I can't believe you still talk to your mother after she hired a hit man to kill me. You don't know how close it was, Josh!" he dramatically told his son, his blue eyes widely opened.

He mocked Joshua, "This is you, Josh... ...Mama, Mama," John would say, imitating a baby's cry. "Only losers spend time with their mothers." It hurt Joshua, who was always a gentle soul, kind, and well liked. John announced, "I'm gonna make you a man!" Because Joshua was in the school band and didn't have a girlfriend, John would ridicule, "My son is gay!"

He taunted Joshua, telling him, "She doesn't care about you. She loves Alissa more. She sends her to private school and camp when she should be paying for your college!" He took every opportunity to point out Skylar's devotion to Alissa while denying her firstborn. Joshua was heartbroken at the perceived loss of his mother's affection and began to avoid her. John drove the wedge deeper by giving Maryanne cash for Joshua.

"Just say it's from you." he told Maryanne.

Joshua began to turn to Maryanne instead of his mother. He ignored Skylar's calls and disregarded Alissa, cutting them both from his life.

In June 2007, the magazine *Psychology Today* featured an article, *House Divided* by Mark Teich, which discussed how divorced parents use their children's affections as pawns. The article questioned whether or not the parent-child bonds could ever be restored. Richard Warshak, University of Texas psychologist and author of *Divorce Poison: Protecting the Parent-Child Bond from a Vindictive Ex*, explained that the child rejects the parent seemingly overnight. Oddly, it's the emotionally healthier parent who usually gets rejected. That parent realizes it does not benefit the child to lose the other parent. In contrast, the alienating parent craves revenge against the ex, and then uses the child to punish the other parent. Warshak states: *"It's a form of abuse. Both the parent and child are victims. In pathological or irrational alienation, the parent has done nothing to deserve that level of hatred or rejection from the child."* The tactics used by the alienating parent were: limiting the time a child can spend with the other parent, making false accusations (especially in court), and saying negative things about the other parent.

It was easier for John to convince Joshua than his younger son. Cary had been a challenging child, having been diagnosed with attention deficit hyperactivity disorder. Skylar had the patience to address his issues, but John simply disregarded his son. The assistance Cary was receiving stopped following the false criminal charges against Skylar in 1999. As a result, the likelihood of Cary graduating from high school was slim. It wasn't until the Bauers court case was closed that Skylar was able to schedule a conference with the school administrative team. Cary expressed to Skylar, his desire to graduate from high school and confided that he wanted to move away from John.

Skylar encouraged him, "You know what to do. Go to class and do the homework. If you need extra help, I'll hire tutors. I'll do whatever you need."

Skylar attended the frequent conferences at the high school to discuss Cary's graduation status. In April of 2009, his guidance counselor pulled her aside and said, "I'm very concerned John never appears at these meetings. He doesn't return my phone calls. Do you know why?"

Skylar felt she needed to set the record straight. She replied, "I wasn't going to say anything, but you are wasting your time calling John. He only cares about himself."

"He's a narcissist," the guidance counselor bluntly stated. "I could tell that just from talking to him and from what Cary told me."

Finally! Someone who can see the real John Bauers! thought Skylar. "I will do whatever I can to help Cary graduate," she firmly replied.

"I know we can depend on you. It'll be hard, and it may not happen for Cary this year."

She maintained continuous contact with the guidance counselor, teachers and vice principal. Four days before the graduation, the vice principal told her, "Cary is graduating. He will be walking on Sunday." Skylar burst into happy tears.

She saw Cary graduate in June 2009. He hugged her after the ceremony and promised to meet her for lunch. That was the last time she saw or spoke to him. He subsequently cut all communication with her. She couldn't understand why until she saw a copy of the 2009 high school yearbook at the library. Beside Cary's picture, he had expressed his thanks to his father for helping him graduate.

"But I helped him graduate! John wasn't even there!" she sobbed to Antonio. "I can't even find Cary! He doesn't return my calls. And Joshie doesn't talk to me either!"

Antonio comforted her. "You know John is controlling them. Honey, I know it hurts, and I know you love them. Someday, they will realize it."

But John was unable to totally destroy the bond Jillian had with her mother. She remained in contact with Skylar, asking her for advice and consulting her about her college plans. From a beautiful little girl, she grew into a stunning teenager who spends most of her time with her boyfriend.

One quiet evening in late fall of 2009, Antonio was watching television after dinner while sipping a small glass of beer. Skylar was in the kitchen with the water running.

Antonio shouted something to Skylar that sounded like, "The cops are here."

Oh no, thought Skylar. *What did John set me up for now?* She shut off the water and dried her hands, then walked into the living room. "The cops are here?" she asked him.

"I didn't say that. I said, 'I dropped my beer.' Can you get me a paper towel?" He had a little puddle of beer on his lap.

"Ohhh," laughed Skylar and turned to get a paper towel for Antonio. She realized how she was on guard, waiting, always waiting and always anticipating John's next move.

&

Since 1985, Skylar had endured John's escalating abuse. The pain remains raw, especially after John's taunting of Joshua resulted in the pregnancy of a young girl after a brief relationship. Skylar hopes Joshua will remember who to select as his role model in helping to raise his son. Skylar bears no guilt from her past, although still suffers from symptoms of post traumatic stress disorder, sleepless nights, and periodic sadness.

Antonio has been her rock. He stands by her to provide a comforting embrace, support, and encouragement. "You have Alissa, and one day you'll have them all. Someday, your children will figure it out and return to you."

Her home radiates warmth and happiness. Alissa is thriving in every way due to Skylar's nurturing. Skylar prays daily for Joshua to resume their relationship and for Cary to outgrow his rebellion and turn to her for future guidance. She believes one day Jillian will realize nothing can compare to a mother's love and distance herself from Maryanne.

Skylar's arms and heart will remain open for her children, to embrace them into her life which is a reflection of light, clarity, honesty, and unselfish love. She knows her story may not end until John's promise is fulfilled, *to harass her for the rest of her life...until she dies*, but until there is some ending, she wants these chapters of her life shared in the hopes it will help other victims of abuse.

The façade John created for himself is a tragic parody. Dr. Linda Martinez-Lewi sums up the life of the narcissistic sociopath in one startling sentence: *"Ultimately, in the depth of his unconscious, he knows he is an empty fraud."*

Reference: For additional information, please visit these websites:

Robin Shaye
"...Until You Die": The Narcissist's Promise
www.robinshaye.com

Lundy Bancroft
http://www.lundybancroft.com/

Battered Mother's Custody Conference
http://www.batteredmotherscustodyconference.org/

Steve Becker
http://www.powercommunicating.com/

Ann Bradley
http://www.narcissisticabuse.com/

Pamela Kulbarch Crisis Intervention Contributor
http://www.officer.com/article/10248968/the-malignant-narcissist

Dr. Linda Martinez-Lewi
http://www.thenarcissistinyourlife.com/

Ilan Shrira
http://www.psych.ufl.edu/~shrira/

Sam Vaknin
Malignant Self Love – Narcissism Revisited
http://samvak.tripod.com

The Wellesley Center for Women
http://www.wcwonline.org/

Other References:

American Psychiatric Association Diagnostic and Statistical Manual **Diagnostic and Statistical Manual of Mental Disorders DSM-IV-TR** Fourth Edition (Text Revision) (ISBN 0890420254/ 9780890420256)

Martha Stout, PhD
The Sociopath Next Door: The Ruthless Versus the Rest of Us
First published in the USA by Broadway Books, February 2005
• ISBN-10: 076791581X   • ISBN-13: 9780767915816

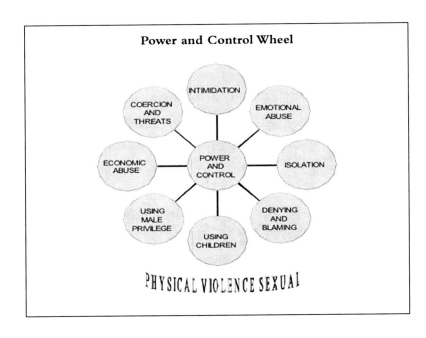

Power and Control Wheel

INTIMIDATION

EMOTIONAL ABUSE

COERCION AND THREATS

POWER AND CONTROL

ISOLATION

ECONOMIC ABUSE

USING MALE PRIVILEGE

DENYING AND BLAMING

USING CHILDREN

PHYSICAL VIOLENCE SEXUAL

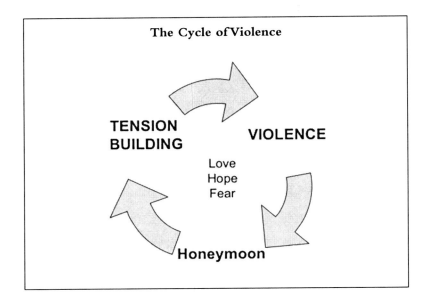

The Cycle of Violence

TENSION BUILDING

VIOLENCE

Love
Hope
Fear

Honeymoon

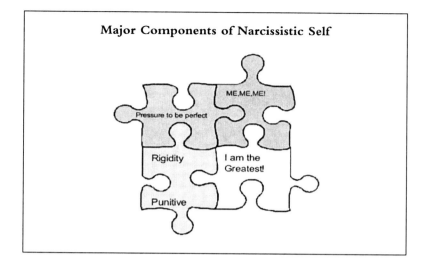

Major Components of Narcissistic Self

ME,ME,ME!

Pressure to be perfect

Rigidity

I am the Greatest!

Punitive

Narcissistic Personality Disorder (NPD), is a personality disorder defined by the *Diagnostic and Statistical Manual of Mental Disorders* (DSM IV-R) as a pervasive pattern of grandiosity, need for admiration, and lack of empathy, beginning by early adulthood and present in a variety of contexts, as indicated by five (or more) of the following:

1. Grand sense of self importance

2. Preoccupied with fantasies of unlimited success, power, brilliance, beauty, or ideal love

3. Believes he/she is special and can only be understood by, or should associate with, other special or high-status people

4. Requires excessive admiration

5. Sense of entitlement; expects special treatment

6. Interpersonally manipulative or takes advantage of others to achieve his/her own ends

7. Lacks empathy

8. Is often envious of others or believes that others are envious of him/her

9. Shows arrogant, haughty, patronizing, or contemptuous behaviors or attitudes

Antisocial Personality Disorder (ASPD or APD) is defined by the *American Psychiatric Association's Diagnostic and Statistical Manual* as a pervasive pattern of disregard or violation of the rights of others beginning by early adulthood and present in a variety of contexts, as indicated by three (or more) of the following:

1. Failure to conform to social norms with respect to lawful behaviors
2. Deceitfulness, repeatedly lying, or conning others for personal profit or pleasure
3. Impulsivity or failure to plan ahead
4. Irritability and aggressiveness, as indicated by repeated physical fights or assaults
5. Reckless disregard for safety of self or others
6. Consistent irresponsibility, repeated failure to sustain consistent work behavior or honor financial obligations
7. Lack of remorse; indifference to or rationalizing having hurt, mistreated, or stolen from another

★People having ASPD are sometimes referred to as sociopaths and psychopaths

Histrionic Personality Disorder (HPD) is a personality disorder defined by the *Diagnostic and Statistical Manual of Mental Disorders* (DSM IV-R) as a pervasive pattern of excessive emotionality and attention seeking, beginning by early adulthood and present in a variety of contexts, as indicated by five (or more) of the following:

1. Is uncomfortable in situations in which he or she is not the center of attention
2. Interaction with others is often characterized by inappropriate sexually seductive or provocative behavior
3. Displays rapidly shifting and shallow expression of emotions

4. Consistently uses physical appearance to draw attention to self
5. Has a style of speech that is excessively impressionistic and lacking in detail
6. Shows self-dramatization, theatricality, and exaggerated expression of emotion
7. Is suggestible, i.e., easily influenced by others or circumstances
8. Considers relationships to be more intimate than they actually are
9. Compulsiveness

CPSIA information can be obtained
at www.ICGtesting.com
Printed in the USA
FFOW02n1318270418
46400986-48161FF